The Pubs of Pembroke, Pembroke Dock, Tenby & South Pembrokeshire

The Pubs of Pembroke, Pembroke Dock, Tenby & South Pembrokeshire

by

Keith Johnson

Logaston Press

LOGASTON PRESS
Little Logaston Woonton Almeley
Herefordshire HR3 6QH

First published by Logaston Press 2003
Copyright © Keith Johnson 2003

ISBN 1 904396 07 0

Set in Times New Roman by Logaston Press
and printed in Great Britain by
Bell & Bain Ltd, Glasgow

Contents

Acknowledgments   vii

Chapter One   Hotels, Inns & Beer-houses.   1
Chapter Two   The Angle Peninsula.   15
Chapter Three   Monkton & Orange Gardens.   29
Chapter Four   Pembroke East.   39
Chapter Five   Pembroke West & The Green.   53
Chapter Six   Pembroke Dock: Front St. & King St.   83
Chapter Seven   Pembroke Dock: Queen St., Commercial Row,   97
                       Brewery St., Wellington St., & Clarence St.
Chapter Eight   Pembroke Dock: Pembroke St., Market St.,   111
                       Princes St. & Melville St.
Chapter Nine   Pembroke Dock: Pennar, Bufferland, Prospect   127
                       Place & Llanreath.
Chapter Ten   Pembroke Dock: Bush St., Park St., Meyrick St.,   139
                       Lewis St., Laws St., Dimond St.
                       & Apley Terrace.
Chapter Eleven   Pembroke Dock: Water St., Llanion, Waterloo &   159
                       Pembroke Ferry.
Chapter Twelve   Eastwards from Pembroke: Cosheston, Lamphey,   171
                       Freshwater East, Jameston, Manorbier, St.
                       Florence, Lydstep, Penally & The Ridgeway.
Chapter Thirteen   Tenby: High St., Tudor Square, St. Julian St. &   191
                       The Harbour
Chapter Fourteen   Tenby: Upper & Lower Frog St., St. George's St.,   215
                       St. Mary's St. & Cresswell St.
Chapter Fifteen   Tenby: Outside the Walls.   229

Bibliography   237
Index   241

The landlord he looks very big
With his tri-corn hat and his powdered wig,
Methinks he looks both fair and fat -
But he can thank you and I for that.
O good ale, thou art my darling,
And my joy both night and morning.
                    (Traditional folk song.)

Acknowledgments

Any historian attempting to write a book on south Pembrokeshire pubs based on primary source material would end up with rather a thin volume. While the various census returns contain a certain amount of information, few records were kept of licensed premises between the Beerhouse Act of 1830 and the Licensing Act of 1872. Unfortunately the records of alehouse keepers in the early 1800s appear to have been lost for the boroughs of Pembroke, Tenby and Haverfordwest (although they survive for the rest of the county).

Fortunately I am not a 'proper' historian, so I haven't felt obliged to restrict my researches to original documentation. Instead, what you have in this book is a mish-mash of material cobbled together at first-, second- and sometimes tenth-hand, from old newspapers, trade directories, estate papers, guide books and travel journals, together with information learned by word of mouth and jotted down on the back of beer-mats.

Other amateur historians have been down this road before. Mr. A.G.O.Mathias in Pembroke; Harry Reynolds and James Meyrick Owen in Pembroke Dock; Anthony Thomas and Arthur Stubbs in Tenby have all published material on the 'lost' pubs of their respective towns, and nearly all felt obliged to fill in the gaps in their knowledge with a certain amount of educated guesswork — and cheerful fabrication.

And, of course, there's nothing wrong with that. A published work about pubs shouldn't be 'dry' in any sense, and a few tall tales all add to the flavour of the finished brew. Having said which, there does need to be an accurate framework of dates, names and addresses on which to build the story of each pub. Striking a balance between the two aspects can be tricky; there is always a danger of having too many landlords' names and dates cluttering up the text. (Beachcomber's famously boring 'List of Huntingdonshire Cabmen' springs to mind ...).

On the other hand, a remarkable number of people seem to be researching their family trees these days — and most of them appear to have had a great-great-grandfather who once ran a pub in Pembrokeshire. So, partly for their benefit, the names and dates of numerous licensees are included with each pub reference — although the list is far from exhaustive.

When this book was in the planning stage, much discussion took place as to where to set the boundaries. The coastline determined most of the parameters, but a line had to be drawn somewhere. In the end it was decided to take in the towns of Pembroke, Pembroke Dock and Tenby, together with all the parishes in the Castlemartin Hundred licensing area — a very long pub crawl, starting in Angle and finishing at the Three Bells on the outskirts of Tenby. Future books are planned in the next few years to cover the pubs of the rest of the county — a social history of Pembrokeshire as seen through the bottom of a beer glass.

My thanks go to Sybil Edwards who first suggested I write this book and also to Ron Shoesmith and Andy Johnson of Logaston Press for their guidance and encouragement.

Very many people have provided information for this book and it would be impossible to list every one; my thanks go to them all. In particular I would like to thank the following for their special contributions: Mrs. Nancy Phillips, Pembroke; Mr. Robert Scourfield, Cresswell Quay; Mrs. Kay Scourfield, Carew; Mr. Albie Smosarski, Tenby; Mr. Stan Bittle, Pembroke Dock; Mr. John Neil, Pembroke; Mr. Owen Vaughan, Pembroke; Mr. John Lyons, Templeton; Mrs. Pam Stringer, Angle and Mr. Peter Brown, Tenby. Also special thanks to the staff of the following: The County Library, Haverfordwest; the County Records Office, Haverfordwest; Tenby Museum and Art Gallery; Tenby Library; Carmarthen Library and the Wilson Museum in Narberth.

I also owe a great debt of gratitude to the late Mr. John Hogg of Pembroke who kindly allowed me free access to his research material on 'lost' Pembroke and Pembroke Dock.

The illustrations in this book are taken from a variety of sources and I am grateful to all the people who kindly loaned items for copying. Except where indicated in the captions, the illustrations come from my own collection or from those of Andy Johnson and Ron Shoesmith.

Thanks are also due to Katy Shoesmith who produced the three maps, and to Roger Barrett for his considerable help with the index.

CHAPTER ONE

Hotels, Inns & Beer-houses
LEGISLATION & SUNDAY CLOSING

Pembrokeshire people have always enjoyed a drink. As far back as the 6th century, St. David himself — a confirmed teetotaller and mortifier of the flesh — was forced to issue the following edict to his fellow monks:

> Those who get drunk through ignorance must do penance 15 days; if through negligence, 40 days; if through contempt, three quarntains.

(a 'quarntain', from which we get the word 'quarantine', being a period of 40 days).

Ironically, perhaps, it was the shrine of St. David which brought many thousands of pilgrims flocking to the county in the Middle Ages, resulting in numerous hostelries being opened up along the pilgrim ways. But the concept of the inn can be traced back to a period long before the Age of the Saints. It is thought that the Romans introduced the idea to Britain, setting up *tavernae* along their network of roads, where travellers could rest and perhaps enjoy alcoholic refreshment. This was predominantly wine, which the Romans imported from other parts of their empire for the benefit of their legions in Britain, although it is thought that they also brewed a kind of beer from cereals. This idea caught on, and by Saxon times there were houses in every village where the men would gather to hold petty courts and to quaff ale out of drinking horns, the real fore-runner of the modern pub.

The earliest ale-houses in Pembrokeshire would probably have been fairly primitive affairs, thatched wooden huts where the inhabitants owned a cauldron capable of boiling up a brew of sweet ale. None of these would have been 'full-time' pubs; they would simply have rustled up a brew when there was a demand, perhaps for a feast day. By the 6th century these ale-houses had become slightly more sophisticated, to the extent of offering a choice of alcoholic beverages. Mead, made from fermented honey, was a well-established favourite of the Celtic people; one early Welsh law specified that a cask of mead should be nine palms high and wide enough to serve as a bathtub for the king and one of his court! And in Wales there were two types of ale — *cwrwf*, which was an everyday kind of ale, and the highly-flavoured (and more expensive) *bragawd* which was spiced up with cinnamon, ginger and cloves.

By AD 745, ale-houses were so widespread and had gained such a low reputation, that the Archbishop of York had to issue a Canon: 'That no priest go to eat or drink in taverns'. Indeed, there were so many inns by the time of King Edgar (959-975) that he tried to limit them to one per village.

The arrival of the Normans in Pembrokeshire and the creation of castle towns such as Pembroke, Tenby, Haverfordwest and Newport meant the establishment of permanent ale-houses in the county. These were often found alongside the market square and close to the church — the historic link between the monasteries and the brewing industry being a strong one. Outside the protection of the towns there were fewer ale-houses, especially in the disputed countryside. These were sometimes known as 'hedge ale-houses' because, with their thatched roof and low walls made out of 'clom' (mud or clay strengthened with straw), they were barely distinguishable from the surrounding vegetation. But as time went by and St. David's began to gain a reputation as a shrine of international importance, so rather more substantial wayside inns were opened to provide hospitality for the pilgrims and later for travelling merchants.

A 14th-century inn.

Moves to regulate the pub trade began at an early date. The Magna Carta included a decree designed to standardise the measurements of wine, ale and corn throughout the land, while in 1266 the Assize of Bread and Ale recognised that these items were the necessities of life and sensibly linked their retail price to the current price of grain. Breaking the Assize of Ale became an offence which was to keep the manorial courts busy for centuries to come. In 1606, for example, Caria Tanner, a resident of Newport, Pembrokeshire, 'broke the Assize of Ale, selling small measures in illegal measures, therefore she is in mercy 12d'.

The widespread introduction of hops in the 15th century meant that ale slowly began to give way to a new, bitter drink called beer. Despite

2

considerable opposition to this 'pernicious weed' — it was even prohibited for a while — the hop proved very popular with brewers and eventually with drinkers, beer having a sharper flavour and better 'keeping' qualities than the traditional ale. There seems to be no record of large scale hop-growing in Pembrokeshire, although hops were grown in the Carew area at one time (as the name Hop Gardens testifies) while the name Hopshill at Saundersfoot might indicate another area where the vines were cultivated successfully.

As the number of common ale-houses increased, so did the number of regulations controlling them. It was Henry VII, a son of Pembrokeshire, who introduced Acts in 1495 and 1504 giving local Justices the power to suppress ale-houses which were badly run or which were responsible for keeping men from their all-important archery practice. A further Act in 1553 made a legal distinction between the different kinds of hostelry; ale-houses sold only ale and beer, taverns were restricted to towns and cities and sold only wine (though later they sold beer as well), while inns also offered accommodation. Most of these places would have brewed their own beer, although in the smaller houses, where the part-time ale-house keeper had a trade which occupied most of his day, it was the practice to buy beer from better-equipped inns and later from full-time brewers.

A 16th-century brewer.

Although both Tenby and Haverfordwest were notable wine-importing centres at one time, it seems unlikely that there were too many taverns in Pembrokeshire that offered only wine — ale and beer were the order of the day for the Welsh lower classes. However a complaint made to the Star Chamber in 1602 stated that an Irish priest who visited Pembroke was 'a comon haunter of alhouses and wintaverns', so there must have been wine bars in the town 400 years ago. Even so, most of the wine that the merchants shipped into the county was destined for the castles and manor houses of the gentry; according to the bards who sang his praises Tomas ap Phylip of Picton Castle once took delivery of a shipment of 20 tuns of wine — about 5,000 gallons.

Despite this impressive statistic, the Elizabethan historian George Owen thought that heavy drinking was rare in Pembrokeshire. However he did

3

concede that an influx of Irish settlers into the county in the days of Henry VIII had given the locals a taste for whiskey. As Owen explained:

> Those Irish people here do use their country trade in making of *Aqua Vitae* in great abundance which they carry to be sold abroad the country on horseback and otherwise, so that weekly you may be sure to have *Aqua Vitae* to be sold at your door, and by means thereof it is grown to be an usual drink in most men's houses instead of wine.

By the beginning of the 17th century, there were plenty of licensed ale-houses in Pembrokeshire, and more than a few unlicensed ones as well. In 1606, the Court Leet and View of Frankpledge in Newport dealt with the case of a tailor named Richard ap Ievan and ten others who 'kept taverns in their houses and sold ale without licence', whilst in 1615, Hugh Johnes of Llanychaer and Thomas Price of St. Dogmael's were separately presented at the Great Sessions for 'keeping without a licence a common tippling house and for selling ale and beer'. What was unusual about the this case is that as well as running an illicit shebeen, Price was better known as the Rev. Thomas Price, vicar of St. Dogmael's!

In the towns, the inns and ale-houses tended to cluster around market squares and harbours where there was always a lively trade. Quay Street in Haverfordwest and the area around Tenby Quay would have had their share of rough and ready 'sailortown' pot-houses, while the pubs on Fishguard Square, Narberth Square and the East End of Pembroke came alive on market days and fair days. Out in the countryside, wherever there was hard work to be done, ale-houses — legal and otherwise — sprang up to provide refreshment for the labouring man. Bread, cheese and 'table beer', as opposed to strong ale, sustained the quarryman and labourer, ploughman and collier throughout the long working day.

Many smaller country ale-houses had names designed to encourage the passer-by to enter, some of which live on in the name of Pembrokeshire localities. There were several ale-houses called 'Step Inn', as well as a 'Venture Inn' (now Venterin) near Lampeter Velfrey, the 'Stop-and-Call' at Goodwick and the 'Step Aside' near Kilgetty. It is also likely that Cold Inn near East Williamston was once 'Call Inn', a rather more inviting name. With the Cleddau River carving its way through the heart of the county there were numerous ferry crossings, and all of these had an ale-house on at least one side of the river, usually run by the ferry-man and his wife.

In the towns, inns of a more substantial nature had been established, perhaps following the dissolution of the monasteries when pilgrims could no longer seek shelter in abbeys and other religious houses. The sadly-demolished Swan in Haverfordwest was said to date from the 16th century,

A mid-18th-century brewhouse.

while there are references to both the King's Arms in Pembroke and to the King's Arms in Tenby in 1617. These inns offered reasonable accommodation for travellers, stabling for their horses, and a ready meal, but the golden age of the inn — the era of the stage-coach — had yet to arrive, and they were far from the bustling establishments they were to become.

The 18th century saw a further development with the arrival of purpose-built public houses. Where ale-houses were basically cottages with a room in which refreshments could be enjoyed, the public houses might have several rooms to cater for the different classes of drinker (but without offering the accommodation which would have turned them into inns). This competition had the effect of dragging many ale-houses 'up-market', although this increased respectability didn't prevent the criminal classes — the pickpockets, prostitutes, smugglers and highway robbers — from continuing to frequent the seedier houses at the bottom end of the scale.

Another change in the 18th century was in the amount of spirits being consumed, particularly cheap brandy and gin. While duty had to be paid on beer, spirits remained exempt for a good many years, so that the consumption of spirits increased from about half a million gallons in 1684 to eight million gallons in 1743 — an increase of well over a gallon per person per year. It took a succession of 'Gin Acts' to curb the dram shops and gin palaces and persuade people to turn back to the relatively healthy consumption of beer, ale and, increasingly, porter.

Porter was a specially blended mild beer which took its name from its popularity among London's market porters, and porter breweries soon sprang up all over the country — notably that of Samuel Whitbread in Chiswell Street in the City of London. This also led to another new development — the brewer's dray. Where once the ale-house keeper would have been expected to fetch the casks from the brewery himself, now the brewer made regular deliveries to all the pubs on his patch, a practice which eventually led to the 'tied house'. Although brewery-to-pub delivery was initially confined to the larger centres of population, horse-drawn brewer's drays inevitably found their way onto the streets and country lanes of Pembrokeshire.

Up to this time, and for many years to come, the easiest way to travel to Pembrokeshire was by sea, and little in the way of coaching inns had developed in the county. This changed in the late 18th century with the establishment of a packet service to Ireland from Hakin Point and also the emergence of Tenby as a fashionable sea-bathing resort. The coach road to Hakin Point ran by way of St. Clears, Llanddowror, Tavernspite, Narberth and Haverfordwest, and several coaching inns were established as posting stages along this route, including the Picton at Llanddowror, the Plume of Feathers at Tavernspite, the Golden Lion in Narberth, the Coach and Horses in Robeston Wathen and the Castle in Haverfordwest. On the road which branched south to Pembroke, there were the Milford Arms in Saundersfoot, the White Lion in Tenby and the Golden Lion and Green Dragon in Pembroke itself. These were all substantial buildings with good rooms and

The brewer's dray on its rounds in Pembroke. The Swansea Old Brewery Co. Ltd. took over the running of the Cromwell Brewery in Castle Terrace, Pembroke from local firm George's, before eventually giving way to Hancock's in 1928.

plenty of stabling, and as often as not had been built at the instigation of the local squire.

Many coaching inns were well-run establishments; some weren't. According to John Byng, writing in the 18th century:

> The innkeepers are insolent, the hostlers are sulky, the chambermaids are pert and the waiters are impertinent; the meat is tough, the wine is foul, the beer is hard, the sheets are wet, the linen is dirty and the knives are never clean'd!

It is to be hoped that Pembrokeshire's inns were run to a better standard, though most late 18th century travellers settled for describing them as 'middling' or 'tolerable' at best.

While the number of larger, well-appointed inns and public houses continued to increase, approved and licensed by the magistrates, there were still large numbers of smaller and humbler houses which operated in the grey area between ale-house and unlicensed 'shebeen'. In 1779, several people in Steynton, Pill and Hubberston were convicted of 'selling ale and strong beer without being licensed so to do', and as time went by it became apparent that gin drinking was once again on the increase and that the dodgier ale-houses were turning into dram-shops.

Various Acts were passed in the 1820s in an attempt to reverse this trend, culminating in the 1830 Beer Act. This was designed to encourage the consumption of beer at the expense of spirits — a move which would boost the country's agriculture and brewing industries and also improve health. Beer was widely considered to be a wholesome and health-giving drink, much more so than water which was often of a dubious quality, especially in

An advert for George Llewellyn Griffiths' steam brewery in 1906. The brewery is now the Castle Inn in Pembroke Main Street.

the towns. For example, when Milford Sunday School held a New Year's Day treat in 1818, nearly 200 children enjoyed a meal of roast beef and plum pudding 'and afterwards ale supplied by Mr. G. Starbuck and Mr. R. Byers' — Byers being the local surgeon.

The 1830 Beer Act duly abolished all duty on beer and brought into being the 'beer-shop' or 'beer-house'. For the cost of two guineas, any householder could obtain a beer-house licence which would permit the sale of beer and cider only, as opposed to the fully licensed public houses which could also sell wine and spirits. The result of this new legislation can be easily imagined — beer-houses by the thousand opened up all over the country. Former 'shebeens' entered the fold of legitimacy, while masons and blacksmiths, farmers, coopers and carpenters took the opportunity to sell beer as a sideline to their regular trade. Within a year of the Act coming into force there were 24,000 new beer-houses in Britain and the figure had reached 46,000 by 1836. In the twin towns of Pembroke and Pembroke Dock there were 45 beer-houses in 1840 while Milford Haven had 24. 'Everybody is drunk', reported Sydney Smith soon after the Beer Act came into force. 'Those who are not singing are sprawling'.

These new drinking premises were often called 'Tom and Jerry shops' after a pair of dissolute characters in Pierce Egan's serialised novel *Life in London*, or sometimes 'Kiddleywinks'. They were often badly run, and as the Haverfordwest weekly newspaper *Potter's Electric News* noted: 'Beer-shop owners prey upon labouring men who earn their money like horses — and then spend it like asses'. They also attracted a seedy clientele. 'The beer-shop keeper collects about him the very dregs of society. It is in these places that robberies are planned and crimes committed. The beer-shop keeper is too frequently the banker of the thief'.

Because of their very nature, beer-houses are difficult to research. The Beer Act made no provision for the keeping of records of licences, and numerous 'Kiddleywinks' came and went without leaving any trace other than a vague folk memory. Several of these were *ad hoc* affairs which opened to take advantage of such things as the arrival of gangs of navvies to build a road or railway and which closed again following their departure. Others lasted much longer, and there was hardly a street in Pembroke Dock which didn't have a beer-house or three to cater for the town's hard-drinking population of shipwrights, seamen and soldiers.

Running parallel with the spread of the beer-shop came the rise of Nonconformity and also the growing influence of the temperance movement. This movement had become organised as far back as 1828, and, ironically perhaps, had strongly supported the Beer Act and its aim of getting people to stop drinking gin. Its members pledged themselves to abstain from all spirits, except for medicinal purposes, and only to drink beer and wine 'in moderation'. This wasn't enough for some of the hard-line reformers who went even further and advocated total abstinence. These teetotallers, who often clashed with their more 'wishy-washy' temperance colleagues, embarked on high-profile campaigns aimed at persuading people to give up the demon drink altogether. Meetings were held up and down the country at which reformed drunkards in their Sunday best were paraded in front of the audience as living examples of the benefits of total abstinence.

One such character, who addressed a meeting in Ebenezer Chapel, Haverfordwest in January 1839, was introduced as 'a reformed drunkard from Milford'. He gave what was described in the *Welshman* newspaper as 'an exciting, though melancholic' account of himself, explaining that for 17 years he had 'served the monster intemperance'. During this time he had been notorious for his habitual drunkenness, but he had signed the pledge 12 months before and was now 'in every respect more happy than when he was in the habit of indulging in the intoxicating draught'.

In Narberth, a Total Abstinence Society was formed in 1837 and in 1841 the *Welshman* reported that there were 'numerous' total abstainers in the town of Pembroke whose battle-cry was: 'Honour to the Welsh water-drinkers! Destruction to the publicans and sinners of Cymru!' To begin with they were fighting a losing battle. The number of pubs and beer-houses continued to grow, and although the coaching inns were badly hit by the arrival of the railway, this was more than offset by the number of pubs created to serve the new form of transport, with Railway Inns and Railway Taverns being opened in every town and nearly every village on the line, from Johnston and Maenclochog to Jameston, Lamphey and Penally. Quarrying villages such as West Williamston, Ludchurch and Cilgerran were awash with pubs and beer-houses and it was said that every house in Hakin that wasn't a licensed pub was an unlicensed one.

Gradually, however, the tide began to turn. The Lord's Day Observance Society had been founded in the same year as the British and Foreign Temperance Society, and the two movements soon found plenty of common ground on which to campaign. They achieved some early success with the passing of the Lord's Day Act of 1848 which prevented pubs from opening before 1pm on a Sunday. Attempts to restrict Sunday opening still further in 1855 led to street riots in London; even so an Act was passed soon afterwards restricting Sunday opening to the hours of 1pm to 3pm and 5pm to 11pm. In Pembrokeshire, as in the rest of Wales, the campaign against Sunday drinking was spearheaded by the Nonconformists. Each wave of religious revival which swept across Wales was accompanied by a wave of temperance activity — in Cilgerran it was claimed that the thunder of one revival had turned the beer sour!

In 1860 came the first movement towards 'early closing' — a laudable scheme designed to give shop-workers in the towns a mid-week half-day holiday. Sports clubs, most famously Sheffield Wednesday, were formed in many places to provide 'healthful and innocent amusement' for young men with time to kill. Cricket clubs were formed all over Pembrokeshire; as one of the founders of the Pembroke club pointed out:

> If these young men are not on the cricket field, there will probably, many
> of them at least, be found in the pursuit of some vice or sensual pleasure
> — perhaps guzzling like brute-beasts in the pot-houses with which the
> town of Pembroke unfortunately abounds.

By the end of the 1860s there was a growing consensus that the beer-house had long outlived its usefulness and that the number of pubs in the country needed to be curtailed. The 1869 Wine and Beer-house Act brought all licensed premises under the control of the magistrates. This effectively meant that no new beer-houses were opened while many of the existing ones closed down, their trade not being sufficient to warrant the cost and effort of

---

LOT 53.
(COLOURED GREEN ON PLAN.)

THE LION HOTEL AND POSTING HOUSE,

BEING IN CONNEXION WITH THE SOUTH WALES RAILWAY,

Comprising Thirteen Bed Rooms, Two Closets, DINING and DRAWING Rooms, Parlour, Commercial Room, Farmer's Room, Two Sitting Rooms, Pantry, Cellar, Kitchen, Back ditto, large Yard, Greenhouse, STABLING FOR TWENTY-ONE HORSES, Two Coach Houses, Piggery, &c. No. 440 on Plan. In the occupation of Mr. John Jones, as yearly tenant, at £60. per Annum.

Two Rents to the Crown of 8s. and 2s. are apportioned, as between the Purchasers, on Lot 53.

LOT 54.
(COLOURED PINK ON PLAN)

A VALUABLE FREEHOLD ESTATE,

Situate close to the Town of PEMBROKE, in the Parish of St. MARY'S; comprising the

VICTORIA BEER SHOP and THREE COTTAGES,

No, 327 on Plan, containing 1R. 24P. Let on Lease to William Morgan for two lives, aged 56 and 52 years, at £7. 8s. per Annum

Two Pembroke hostelries, the Lion and the Victoria, came under the hammer in the 1850s when the Owens of Orielton estate were obliged to sell many of their properties to meet electioneering debts.

applying for a justices' licence. The Aberdare Act of 1872 added to the burden of legislation on the drinking trade, curtailing drinking hours, increasing fines for licensing offences, prohibiting the sale of liquor to under 16s and generally making life difficult for the landlord. (This Act was so unpopular that it was blamed for the fall of Gladstone's government two years later; Disraeli's administration increased the opening hours by 30 minutes as a mark of appreciation).

In Wales, Sunday opening remained the biggest bugbear of the temperance brigade. In Calvinist Scotland the pubs had been closed on the Sabbath since 1853, and when Ireland introduced Sunday closing in 1878, the Welsh campaigners were determined to be next. Temperance and chapel leaders claimed (with some justification) that the majority of people in Wales were behind them, although a public meeting held in Tenby in February 1880 to press for Sunday closing was 'miserably attended'. In the industrialised areas of Wales, the sabbatarians received powerful support from the iron-masters and the coal-owners who were fed up with half their workforce turning up for the Monday morning shift still drunk from the excesses of the previous day. Wales was ripe for Sunday closing, and when a private member's Bill, introduced by Flint M.P. John Roberts, received its third reading in August 1881, the Welsh Sunday Closing Act duly entered the statute books.

In Pembrokeshire, many of the big landowners were also active supporters of temperance, among their tenants, if not on a personal level. As a result, estates like Stackpole, Lamphey and Lawrenny were without a public house for many years, to the great benefit of pubs in villages like Maidenwells, Hundleton and Landshipping which were just over the border in neighbouring estates.

Towards the end of the 19th century and in the first part of the 20th century, efforts continued to be made to reduce the numbers of public houses and also to standardise their lay-out. Magistrates found themselves with the power to take away licences for petty offences or because the lay-out of a pub did not meet their approval. And since many of the magistrates were chapel deacons and temperance-supporting landowners themselves, they did not hesitate to use this power, even if it meant a family's loss of livelihood. Even this consideration was met by an Act of 1904 which established the principle of compensation for publicans whose licence had been suppressed through no fault of their own (although in practice most of the compensation went to the owner of the property, rather than the publican who was usually a tenant).

The first pub in Pembrokeshire to be axed under the compensation scheme was the St. Dogmells in Hakin, and the ruling was eventually responsible for the closure of nearly 100 pubs in the county, among them noted houses like the Albion on Tenby Harbour, the Tower Inn in St. David's, the Gun Tavern in Pembroke Dock and the Sailors' Arms in Lower Fishguard. However, the publicans did not go down without a fight. Pembroke Dock Licensed Victuallers Association was formed in 1909 'for combination to combat the forces acting against them' and the Pembrokeshire L.V.A. followed a year later with about 50 members. One of their aims was to obtain an 'impartial bench of magistrates' to adjudicate on the renewal of licences. All too often the magistrates would instruct the police to object to a certain licence, and then rule on the objection themselves — a 'disgraceful' situation according to Mr. S. McCulloch, the first president of the Pembrokeshire L.V.A.

However it has to be said that the magistrates often had statistics on their side. In the 1890s Narberth boasted 23 pubs for a resident population of just 1,200. And in 1912 there were 81 on licences and three off licences granted for Pembroke Borough, giving an average of one licensed house for every 190 residents compared with the national average of one for every 400. Thus Pembroke Borough had twice as many pubs per head of population than the rest of Britain in 1912.

The Defence of the Realm Act also took a toll on Pembrokeshire pubs, following the outbreak of the First World War. The Act meant the introduction of even tighter licensing laws aimed at preventing drunkenness among servicemen, dockers, munitions workers and the like. In Lloyd George's opinion: 'Drink is doing us more damage in the war than all the German submarines put together' — but as someone who had once pressed for total prohibition in Wales, he might not have been entirely objective. Opening hours were curtailed, while one of the daftest rules brought in by the Act was the 'no treating' law. Under this rule no-one was allowed to buy a round of drinks or even buy his mate a pint; this was thought to encourage excessive drinking. In 1916 James Gray, landlord of the eminently respectable Avondale in Hakin, was fined ten shillings for allowing 'treating' in the pub.

He was lucky not to lose his licence. With a mass of new rules and regulations to fall foul of, it was inevitable that many landlords found themselves in court; and when they appeared before the bench there would be the inevitable clamour from the temperance brigade for the pubs to be shut. Many were, and when the troops returned from the trenches it was often to find that their favourite local had been forced to close. Wartime 'casualties' in Pembroke Dock alone included the Foresters' Arms, the Albert, the Sun and the Duke of York.

Licensing restrictions were gradually lifted following the end of the war, although Sunday closing remained sacrosanct. The number of pubs continued

Three noted Pembrokeshire landlords from the 1950s are in the front row of this photograph. Left to right: Wiffie Vaulk of the Bush in Tenby, Jim Davies of the Cresselly Arms (where the picture was taken) and Tommy Nicholas of the Dragon in Narberth.
(Picture courtesy of Mr. Maurice Cole)

to fall, both as a result of the still active redundancy committee and the economic depression, while changing social habits (and weaker beer) meant the number of drunks on the street fell dramatically. In 1908, 99 people had been convicted of drunkenness in Pembroke Borough; by the 1930s the figure was down to half a dozen each year.

As attitudes changed, and people began to look upon the village pub as a convivial social centre rather than a den of iniquity, so support for the temperance movement began to wane. By the time the Second World War came, the tide had turned to the extent that calls for a return to the licensing restrictions of 1914 were dismissed out of hand. In his excellent history of brewing in Wales, *Prince of Ales*, Brian Glover quotes Quintin Hogg (later Lord Hailsham) as stating in 1939:

The Temperance Council must clearly understand that the national emergency is not a moment to introduce temperance propaganda under the cloak of national necessity. Beer is the innocent pleasure of many millions, especially those who bear the brunt today.

Such a sentiment — a million miles from that of Lloyd George 25 years earlier — shows how much attitudes had changed. The temperance movement was in retreat, although the redundancy committee continued to pick off pubs well into the 1950s — the Crown and Anchor and the Bell and Lion in Pembroke Dock were both closed in 1953.

With the post-war growth of tourism, inns began to be seen as an amenity and Sunday closing in Wales became increasingly regarded as anachronism and a hindrance to the industry. A new Licensing Act in 1961 paved the way for each county to decide by a referendum (held every seven years) if it wanted Sunday drinking. The three west Wales counties of Pembrokeshire, Carmarthenshire and Cardiganshire voted to stay 'dry' in 1961, but in November 1968, alone of the three, Pembrokeshire voted to become 'wet'.

The late 1960s and early 1970s also saw the opening of a number of new pubs in the tourist areas of the county, the Snooty Fox, the Lawrenny Arms, the Dial Inn and the Miracle Inn among others, and the enlargement and refurbishment of many more. Sadly, this refurbishment was often at the cost of the character of the old inn, and a pub guide of the time called *The Inn Crowd* shows (unintentionally) the widespread damage that was caused by the over-enthusiastic application of formica, leatherette and fake beams covered with equally fake horse-brasses.

Fortunately a good number of old Pembrokeshire pubs managed to avoid this kind of tasteless 'scampi in the basket' seventies makeover, so that the county still has a wide range of unspoilt taverns — from 'Bessie's' in the Gwaun Valley to the Charlton in Pembroke Dock and the Old Point House in Angle. And although well-established pubs continue to close — the Penry Arms at Pelcomb, the Royal Oak in Pembroke Dock and the York Tavern in Pembroke are all recent victims — a glance at the pages of this book will show that this is simply part of an on-going process that has seen pubs come and go throughout the centuries as taste and circumstances changed with the passing years.

CHAPTER TWO

The Angle Peninsula
ANGLE, RHOSCROWTHER, CASTLEMARTIN & STACKPOLE

At the westerly tip of south Pembrokeshire stands Angle — a remote and picturesque village, full of character and with a rich seafaring tradition. The village is a single street of fishermen's cottages and modern bungalows, behind which can be seen the medieval strip fields which reveal Angle's long history. Important medieval buildings include a fisherman's chapel, a dove-cote and the recently-restored three-storey Tower House.

Follow the village street westwards and you come to West Angle Bay, a sandy cove facing the entrance to Milford Haven. Thorn Island Fort just offshore was built in Victorian times to guard the harbour entrance and has now been converted into an hotel. Angle Bay to the east of the village is a shallow stretch of water much visited by waterfowl and a sheltered anchorage for fishing boats and other craft.

Angle has always held a special place in the annals of Pembrokeshire boozing, for it was on Thorn Island that the full-rigged iron ship *Loch Shiel* was wrecked in 1894, while bound for Australia from her home port of Glasgow. At night, and in treacherous conditions, the crew of the Angle lifeboat bravely helped the 33 passengers and crew to safety, but it was the events of the following morning which cemented the name of the *Loch Shiel* in local folk-lore. As the villagers wandered down to the beach to view the wreck they discovered case after case of 100 degrees proof whisky floating in on the morning tide.

Although customs officers raced to Angle they were only in time to secure about 60 cases of Scotch; one estimate had between 50 and 100 people on the beach swigging the whisky and carrying away thousands of bottles to be hidden all over the village (two turned up in a cottage roof as recently as the 1950s). Sadly there was a tragic element to this 'Whisky Galore' caper. A father and son drowned while trying to retrieve some of the whisky from the wreck itself, while on the north side of the Haven, which also received its share of the fiery flotsam, one young man drank himself to death.

As far as public houses are concerned, Angle has always been well catered for. The fishermen, oyster dredgermen and farm labourers who made up the resident population were good customers, and this trade was later augmented by the off-duty artillerymen manning the local forts. In the days of sail, vessels regularly had to anchor in Angle Bay during adverse weather, and, as one visitor noted in 1804, the village provided 'miserable accommodations for numerous passengers to and from Ireland and other places who are obliged to put in frequently to wait for the weather'. In more recent years, the growth of tourism has helped the village's two remaining pubs to survive.

The first mention of an inn at Angle occurs in the records of the landowning Cawdor family of Stackpole Court. In 1780, the Cawdor papers carried a reference to the **King's Arms** in Angle, but where this was is unknown. The list of licensed ale-house keepers for 1784 included four from Angle parish — George Bedford, John White, Henry Mason and Elizabeth Levett. By the time the 1795 list was published, Mason had disappeared, but the 1812 list still contained the names of Bedford, White and Levett, together with those of George Purser and Francis Purser — a healthy total of five ale-houses in a small village.

George Purser was the landlord of the **Mariners' Arms** from 1811 to 1828, but there is no indication of where it might have stood. Elizabeth Levett's inn was called the **Castle** and was the building which still stands to the north of the recently restored Tower House — now the Castle Farm. She was still the landlady when historian Richard Fenton passed through Angle during his tour of Pembrokeshire in 1810, but she had given way to Maria Levett by 1822. George Murphy took over as licensee the following year, but by 1841 the Castle was no longer an inn and was being run as a farm by Richard Davies.

John White kept the **Blue Anchor** (sometimes simply referred to as the Anchor) and he appears to have been the landlord from 1784 to 1828. The 1841 census showed 70-year-old Thomas White and his wife Elizabeth as publicans, presumably at the Blue Anchor, and for the next ten years the Whites shared the property with their daughter Mary and her husband, a butcher from Steynton called Richard Venables. By 1861 Venables had taken over the running of the pub, but he moved shortly afterwards to open the Hibernia, another local hostelry.

In July 1871 the pub passed to a widowed Frenchwoman by the name of Octavia Eleanore Maria Ball. She married a local farmer in 1884, after which the Blue Anchor seems to have closed; it is believed to have been a house with a single-storey cottage alongside, formerly numbers 53 and 54 Angle. These two properties were converted into a single house called 'The Brig' in 1969.

The former Dolphin Inn in Angle village.

The 1841 census showed two other publicans in Angle. Abra Abrams ran a pub a couple of doors away from the Blue Anchor while another was kept by 55-year-old Abraham John; the names of these ale-houses are not known.

A grocer named George Barger was granted a licence to open a pub in the village in 1864, and the landlady of the **Dolphin** in 1867 was Elizabeth Barger. By 1871 the Dolphin was being run by Thomas Jenkins who also had charge of the village post office. For some reason Mrs. Barger was back in charge by 1876, but the pub closed soon afterwards. It was located at what is now Old Dolphin House at the east end of the village, and the row of houses opposite — Dolphin Rise — takes its name from the old pub.

Being so far from any centre of population — and the long arm of the law — Angle pubs once enjoyed a reputation for flexible opening hours. George Griffiths was landlord of a cottage ale-house named the **Globe** in December 1867, and he was still serving merrily at 11.45 one evening when Police Superintendent George Evans from Pembroke burst in upon the scene. To make matters worse, Stephen Rogers, the parish constable, was one of those enjoying the landlord's hospitality and he was later fined 5 shillings for being 'drunk and riotous'.

Despite this misdemeanor, Griffiths obtained a full licence for the Globe at the Castlemartin licensing sessions in September 1868 and he remained the licensee into the 1880s. Octavia Maria Ball then entered the picture again. Even though her second husband had been 17 years younger than herself she was a widow again by 1889 and had returned to the innkeeping life, this time as licensee of the Globe.

The official Cadw (Welsh Historic Monuments) survey of the village states that the present Grade II listed Globe Hotel was built in 1904, being converted from two cottages, one of which was presumably the original ale-

An advert for the Globe Hotel in the 1970s.

house. This was part of the improvements carried out in the village by local squire, Col. R.W.B. Mirehouse, who had served in South Africa during the Boer War. This experience had given him a taste for colonial architecture and the new, three-storey Globe Hotel came complete with parapet, crenallations and a covered verandah-style walkway fronting the

The Globe has now been converted into private accommodation.

street. Landlord at the time of the alterations was Robert Husband, and he was followed by Dan Skone during whose time the Globe was used as a First World War hospital. Sgt. Major Paish was licensee in the early 1920s, while from 1927 to 1931 the landlord was George Rees.

Thomas Vallance ran the Globe from 1932 until the early 1950s, and he is remembered in the village as a radio repair man who would charge people's batteries while they enjoyed a pint in the tiny public bar. Mrs. Jean Williams took over in 1954 and was the licensee throughout the 1960s and early '70s. The Globe was bought by the Meymott Machine Tool Co. Ltd. in 1977 and was run for some years by Ron Pointon, but it closed in 1993 and after standing empty for several years was converted into private accommodation.

The **Hibernia** was opened in about 1865, and as with the Globe and the Dolphin this was possibly to capitalise on the trade generated by the building of the fort on Thorn Island. Its name is thought to derive from an Irish coin which was found during building work at the pub, and the coin itself, dated 1805, is still

An early postcard view of the Hibernia Inn at Angle.
(Picture courtesy of the Hibernia Inn.)

displayed in the entrance hall. (The statement by the authors of the *Dictionary of Pub Names* that you can see Ireland from the Hibernia suggests they might have been the victims of a bit of Angle 'Blarney'...).

The chap who opened the Hibernia was Richard Venables, formerly of the Anchor, and he handed over to a local fisherman named John Bamkin in 1867. Bamkin remained the licensee right through to 1901 when he was succeeded by Diana Bamkin. George Barger Rees took over as landlord in about 1914, and his family continued to run the pub until it closed in 1971. (Back in the 1860s, George and Elizabeth Barger of the Dolphin had looked after a nephew named William Rees, and subsequent Rees males all took the middle name of Barger).

The Hibernia Inn today.

As well as running the pub, George Barger Rees kept the garage next door, complete with petrol pumps. Charles Rees was the landlord from 1956 through the 1960s, but the pub was closed for much of the 1970s, being re-opened in 1979 by John and Mary Rees (no relation of the previous owners). Julian and Linda Hammond bought the Hibernia in 1986 and are still running it.

The Grade II listed **Old Point House** enjoys one of the finest settings of any pub in Pembrokeshire, being located on a headland overlooking the sweep of Angle Bay. Built in about 1700, but much altered since, it is a picturesque place full of character — and characters — and is regularly cut off by high tides which cover the approach along the pebble-bank shore. It has been the 'lifeboatmen's local' ever since the nearby station was opened in 1868, and generations of licensees have willingly opened their doors at all hours to provide the returning lifeboat crews with a warm fire and an equally warming drink.

How long it has been a pub isn't known, but James Nash held the licence and farmed the land from 1824 to 1828. John Nicholas was the long-serving landlord from 1841 to 1880 followed by his widow Martha who was still there in 1891. She employed Alfred Morse as a general labourer, and he eventually took over the business, being farmer and innkeeper from 1906 to 1935. He then handed over to William Andrew Morse who was there until 1958 when Mr. and Mrs. George Cooper became licensees and several of the Coopers' children have run the pub over the years.

The Old Point House closed for a time in 2001, but happily was re-opened in the spring of 2002 by Dougie Smith from Milford Haven.

The chunk of land between Angle Bay and the Pembroke River was once a relatively quiet rural backwater, but all this changed under the devastating impact of the oil industry in the late 1950s, with the tiny settlements of Popton, Bulwell and Pwllcrochan being lost to the tank farms, and Rhoscrowther becoming virtually a ghost village. Rather surprisingly the

20

The 'lifeboatmen's local' — the Old Point House at Angle.

parish of Pwllcrochan supported two ale-houses in 1784, one run by John Husband and the other by Thomas Aveston. The latter lived at **Holly Bush**, which was presumably the sign of his ale-house and which was near Pwllcrochan Church. From 1795 to about 1805 William Lewis kept an ale-house at Pwllcrochan, followed by Jane Lewis who carried on running the (sadly unnamed) pub until 1811.

James Waters kept an ale-house next to the shore at Bulwell from 1795 to 1813. This house was at one end of a rowing-boat link with Hakin and it had a couple of bedrooms for travellers. It appears to have been called the **Ferry House**, and it gained notoriety for its part in one of Pembrokeshire's most savage murders. The landlord was in the habit of sending a boat across to Milford Haven whenever supplies of beer ran low, and this was precisely what happened one morning in September 1812 when a young servant at the inn, James Dean, was instructed to row over to Milford town for a cask of ale from Starbuck's brewery.

Walters gave Dean a pound and some silver for the ale, together with some small change to buy tobacco in Hakin. There was also one passenger to be ferried across — a stranger by the name of John Bruce, who had been staying at the inn. Dean and Bruce went down to the nearby shore where they launched the smaller of the two ferryboats. With a few strong pulls on the oars, the tiny vessel glided out of the bay and into the early morning mist which shrouded the Haven. What happened next can only be speculated upon, but it seems that when they were a few hundred yards offshore Bruce attacked the defenceless youngster, cutting his throat with a knife and stealing the money from the pocket of the dying boy.

All this happened under cover of the mist and, but for a freak of nature, the murderer might have got away with his savage crime. But during and immediately after the struggle the drifting boat was carried along by the current and swept towards the shore. Just as the murderer was in the process of tipping his victim's body over the side, the swirling mist lifted long enough for a gang of quarrymen to witness what was going on. The alarm was raised, but Bruce was able to row off into the mist and make his escape — the blood-stained boat being found abandoned later that day.

Bruce was captured the following day, on the road between Templeton and Cold Blow, by a detachment of the Milford Volunteer Artillery, but because the murder was committed on the 'high seas' it did not come under the jurisdiction of the local courts. Instead, Bruce was sent up to London under armed escort to be tried at the High Court of Admiralty Sessions at the Old Bailey. In January 1813 he was hanged at Execution Dock in London, a newspaper report noting: 'He conducted himself with a propriety becoming his awful situation'.

The former rectory at Rhoscrowther was briefly converted into a pub-cum-guesthouse in the 1980s when it was given the name **Crowther Inn**. Some 130 years earlier there was a pub in the tiny hamlet of Wallaston. The **Wallaston Arms** was mentioned in a newspaper report in May 1854, but no further references have come to light. The pub may have been short-lived, but it didn't stop people in the area enjoying a pint; George Edwards of Wallaston Cross was fined 10 shillings for serving beer without a licence in 1865.

The Welcome Inn at Castlemartin was a fairly short-lived enterprise.

Being on the 'dry' Stackpole estate, Castlemartin was poorly served for pubs in the past and recent attempts to remedy the situation have been less than successful. The **Golden Plover** was opened in the old village school on the road to Warren in the early 1960s — the first time in 150 years that there had been a pub on the Cawdor-owned estate — but it only lasted a few years and is now an art gallery. The **Welcome Inn** on the other side of the village was converted from a former farmhouse in 1975 by George and Collette Bethwaite and soon established a reputation for good food. However the pub sank into a gradual decline following their departure and in May 2002 the National Park planning committee voted by six votes to four to allow landlord Mark Sanders to convert the inn back to residential use. Twenty-nine people objected to the closure of the village inn, but Mr. Sanders said that trade had dwindled year on year since he bought the pub in 1993 and it was no longer viable to keep it going. 'We're flogging a dead donkey', he told the local newspaper.

Standing just over the border, on the less sober-minded Orielton estate, the **Speculation Inn** was for many years the 'local' for Castlemartin and Warren. It stands on an important country junction, where the road from Pembroke splits into the Castlemartin road and the Angle road. How the pub got the name has been the subject of much speculation (so to speak), with one suggestion being that the property once changed hands as a result of a bet between local landowners. Perhaps more likely is the theory that whoever first opened this fairly isolated pub 'speculated' that he would be able to attract enough passing drovers and thirsty Castlemartin villagers to make the venture pay.

After being in the same family for some 90 years,
the Speculation has recently changed hands.

23

The 'Spec' seems to have opened in the early 1840s, and James Morris, a carter from Penally, was landlord from 1846 to the early 1860s when he left to open the nearby Elms pub just outside Hundleton. At Pembroke Petty Sessions in 1865 Thomas Lewis was granted a full licence for the Speculation, indicating that it must have been a beer-house before this date. Thomas Sayse was landlord in the 1870s, while from 1880 to 1891 Levi and Esther Williams were the licensees. At this time the 'Spec' was very popular with anyone desperate for a drink on a Sunday, being handily placed just outside the 'three-mile limit' from Pembroke.

William Henry Rogers, who also farmed at Summerton, was the landlord from 1901 to 1910; he was followed by Mrs. Sarah Rogers. When she left, the prospective new tenant was sent a letter of warning from the agent of the Orielton estate revealing that the squire, Col. Saurin, had received a 'very influential petition' urging him to close the pub. This the squire nobly declined to do, but the agent warned the new tenant that there were three things to be avoided at all costs:

Allowing farm servants to leave horses waiting outside or to waste their
time in working hours.
Allowing young men to frequent the house in the evening.
Allowing the house to be used directly or indirectly with rabbit-catching
or poaching.

The new tenant was Laurence Nelson. A landscape gardener from the Shetlands, he had worked at large houses all over Britain and in 1906 he became head gardener at Orielton. He married the head cook, who was from Castlemartin, and in 1915 they took over the tenancy of the pub. When the Orielton estate sold the 'Spec' in 1921 they paid £550 for it.

Despite the warning about rabbit-catching, the 'Spec' was a regular haunt of the dozens of men who made their living out of trapping rabbits on the Castlemartin peninsula. Each of these trappers had a 'collector' — a man with a van who would pick up the catch at a fixed point and transport it to the 'rabbit factory' in Pembroke. And what better place to arrange this rendezvous than outside the 'Spec'?

The Nelsons' daughter Lucy and her husband Jack Hunter took over as licensees in 1952, by which time the pub was popular with soldiers from the newly-established Castlemartin Camp. It is said that the squaddies would be marched from the camp to the inn by the R.S.M. and allowed in one at a time. They had to drink their pint of beer, and were then marched out again to make way for the next man. Peter and Margaret Thain, cousins of the Nelsons, took over the pub in 1967 and remained in charge for 20 years. When the Thains retired, Richard Nelson — Laurence Nelson's grandson — and his wife Ann took over and ran the pub until 2002, when their departure ended the long-standing family connection.

Under new owners, Jim and Miranda Doyle, the 'Spec' has been spruced up and given an Irish flavour, becoming noted for its live music nights and summer festival.

The **Elms** is just outside Hundleton on the Angle road. It was opened by James Morris, formerly of the 'Spec', in about 1865 and he still ran it in 1881 together with his wife Ann. Their daughter Mary Ann Morris eventually took over as landlady, running the one-room pub until it closed in about 1920. The house is still in the same family to this day. There is some suggestion that the nearby **Bushes** was once a pub as well; it certainly looks as if it might have been, but there is no evidence to confirm this and most records point to it having been a laundry serving the local 'big houses'.

The Elms, which stands at the western end of Hundleton village. The public bar was in the room on the right.

When the Elms closed, the village was without a pub for about 60 years, the locals having to decide between visiting The Wells in Maidenwells, the Salutation in Monkton and the Speculation. This changed in 1980 with the opening of the **Highgate**, a large and rather plush establishment which nowadays offers accommodation as well as being one of the main centres of social life in the village.

The Highgate Inn at Hundleton, a relatively modern pub.

25

A tailor called William Brace opened the **Ivy Green** in the centre of Hundleton in the 1850s, running it until his death in 1863. Thomas Williams then became the licensee, followed by his widow Phoebe Williams in 1876. When she died in the 1880s their son Austin was too young to take over the licence, so he helped his uncle George Lewis to run the pub for a few years. Eventually, in 1890, the 25-year-old Austin Williams became landlord in his

own right, but the pub must have closed in the 1890s because the 1901 census described him simply as a dockyard labourer. The Ivy Green was divided into two houses at some stage, and the village's church hall was built in part of the garden of the former pub in the 1920s.

The Ivy Green in Hundleton as it looks today.

Mary Harries, who lived at Bentlass, opened an ale-house in 1826. It was called the **New Inn**, but seems to have been short-lived. The **Sloop** was also down by the shore at Bentlass — one end of the rowing boat ferry link between the Castlemartin Peninsula and Pembroke Dock. Landlord Jos Williams collapsed and died in 1844 while inspecting his onion beds and the pub was run by a carpenter from Warren named George Lewis between 1851 and 1861. It appears to have been the building now known as Ferry House.

There exists an 1813 reference to the **Royal Oak**, Stackpole. Since the only licensed ale-house in the parish at the time was one at Stackpole Quay run by William James from 1811 to 1814, it follows that this must have been the Royal Oak.

The antipathy of the Cawdor estate towards the sale of alcohol meant that the village of Stackpole didn't have its own pub until the latter part of the 20th century when the estate was finally sold off. Local builder Mr. Terry Armstrong then obtained permission to convert the village's old post office on Jason's Corner into a pub — the post office itself having been created out of two even older cottages. The result was an attractive inn, which Mr. Armstrong named, with characteristic chutzpah, the **Armstrong Arms**. It has always had a reputation for good food and, following a pleasant refurbishment in the summer of 2002, the name was changed to the altogether more appropriate **Stackpole Inn**.

The attractive Stackpole Inn was once the village post office.

Like Stackpole, the village of Bosherston was without a pub for many years, the trippers who visited the nearby attractions of Bosherston Lily-ponds, Broadhaven Beach and St. Govan's Chapel having to settle for a cream tea in one of the village's numerous tea-rooms. This all changed in 1977 when, following a series of occasionally heated public meetings, the **St. Govan's Inn** was opened on the site of a former tea-room. It has since established itself as a popular village 'local' as well as catering for holidaymakers and for a growing number of rock-climbers, as the vertigo-inducing photographs on the walls indicate.

The opening of the St. Govan's Inn at Bosherston meant that the village was no longer 'dry'.

The Black Angel is a former cottage between Maidenwells and St. Twynnell's that was greatly altered and extended in the 1990s. Local tradition states that this was once a notorious 'shebeen'; there seems to be no record of it ever having been a licensed ale-house. Also the Satanic sounding name is not one that is likely to appear on a pub sign.

*This roadside cottage at Maidenwells
was once the Sun Inn.*

*The Wells in Maidenwells stopped serving
beer in the 1930s.
This is how it looks in 2003.*

At one time there were two pubs in Maidenwells village. This may appear excessive for a tiny hamlet, but the pubs drew plenty of customers who arrived by pony and trap, horse, cart and bicycle from all over the neighbouring Stackpole estate. Both pubs stood in the same short terrace and were just a couple of doors apart, the **Sun** being a cottage pub at no.1 Maidenwells. Samuel Smith, a retired farmer, ran the Sun from 1871 to 1880 when it passed to a mason named Thomas Jones who lived there with his wife Ann and their six children; how they found the room to live and run a pub in such a confined space is a mystery. Mrs. Jane Arlow was licensee in 1901 followed by Mrs. Leah Thomas who was the landlady when the Sun closed in 1907. It is now a private house and is still called the Sun Inn (except that the name is written in Welsh).

The Wells a few doors along has also kept its name, but in English this time. It was a much larger affair than the Sun and incorporated a grocery shop. William and Matilda Russell ran the shop and pub in 1871, while Matilda — from Kilkenny in Ireland — remained the licensee from 1881 to 1920, by which time she was 85. Miss L. Russell kept the pub from 1923 to 1932, but the Brewster Sessions in 1935 heard that the sign had been removed from the pub and that the bar had been converted into a sitting room. However the licence wasn't formally taken away until April 1946 when Jonas Daniel Maillard, freeholder, received £95 compensation and Anna Caroline Russell, lessee, received £15.

CHAPTER THREE

Monkton & Orange Gardens

Before the days of the oil refineries, anyone entering Pembroke from the Castlemartin Peninsula would do so by means of the ancient suburb of Monkton. This proudly independent community grew up in Norman times around the Benedictine Priory, of which the church of St. Nicholas, the Priory Farm and the Old Hall still survive. In early Victorian times the suburb began to spread westwards with the building of long rows of terraced cottages to house the workers in the nearby quarries and in the royal dockyard — a short ferry-ride across the Pembroke River. So far west did Monkton extend, in fact, that to Pembroke townspeople it seemed to reach to the end of the world — as indicated by names like Turk's Castle, New Zealand and India Row. Most of these solid Victorian terraces were removed by the borough council in the early 1960s to be replaced by a sprawling council estate, so that it is impossible in many cases to pinpoint where some of the old pubs once stood.

And there were plenty of these in 19th-century Monkton. As well as a large resident population of thirsty quarrymen and shipwrights, Monkton was also the first (and last) port of call for the farmers and drovers herding their flocks to market from the rich farmland of the Castlemartin peninsula. It was traditional to water the flocks at the old conduit in Monkton Lane, and if the sheep and cattle needed a drink, then so too did the drovers.

On arriving in Monkton, these Castlemartin countrymen would be greeted by the **Salutation**. The 'Sally' stood at the junction of Monkton Lane and the street known as Long Mains and appears to have dated from the early 1850s. The name 'Salutation' often appears on pubs at the gateway to towns — there was also one at the entrance to Haverfordwest. Originally however it referred to the biblical greeting of the Angel Gabriel to Mary: 'Hail Mary' or 'Ave Maria'. As the first recorded landlady of the 'Sally' was Maria Lloyd, a gentle pun may have been intended.

From the 1870s to the 1890s the Salutation was kept by a tailor from Haverfordwest called Thomas Williams and his wife Ann. They were

*The Salutation Inn, Monkton, shortly
before demolition.*
(Picture courtesy of Mr. David Waters.)

followed in the early years of the 20th century by William and Elizabeth Hill, in the 1920s by Mrs. Caroline Williams and later by the Chilton family. Billy Rossant was licensee from 1958 until 1964 when the Salutation was demolished as part of the redevelopment of the area into a council estate. This estate had its own purpose-built inn, the smart, functional **Priory**, which was erected on the site of the old Salutation but couldn't match the old pub for character. The Priory was never a rip-roaring success and closed after some 25 years; in early 2000 the building became a Pentecostal church, prompting newspaper headlines of the 'Last Orders to Holy Orders' variety.

At the other end of Long Mains, right on the shore, stood the **Ferry Side** ale-house, sometimes called 'Ferry House'. This was located in a building formerly known as 'Quarry Cottage' since it stood close to the oddly-named 'Catshole' limestone quarries. A rowing boat ferry crossed from here to the Pennar shore at the bottom of Imble Lane, a route much used by dockyard labourers who would no doubt break both their journeys at the Ferry Side. Landlords of this ale-house all seem to have shown a healthy disregard for the licensing laws, perhaps because the Ferry Side was in such a remote spot. Thomas Wells, landlord and stonemason, was fined £1 for late serving in 1871,

The Priory Inn, photographed in the 1980s, has since become a church.

30

and the inn was described by police as a 'badly conducted house' in 1873 when new landlord William Smith was forced to pay £2 10s. for serving out of hours — a stiff fine by the standards of the day. He soon left, and Charlie Harries was landlord from 1878 to 1884; perhaps surprisingly, bearing in mind the reputation of the inn, he seems to have stayed out of trouble with the law, but in 1887 the premises fell foul of the 1881 Sunday Closing Act when George Gwyther and William Hill were caught having a drink on the Sabbath. The fact that it was Boxing Day failed to impress the Scrooge-like magistrates who fined the two tipplers five shillings apiece. The Ferry Side closed soon afterwards; it seems to have been the building now known as Shore House.

Back in Monkton Lane, the next pub along from the Salutation was the **Rope and Anchor**. This mid-terrace beer-house was run between 1835 and 1844 by a widow called Ann Brown. Blacksmith Thomas Saunders and his wife Rebecca kept the pub from 1861 to 1867, and when Thomas died his widow married Charles Harris who remained landlord into the 1880s. The Rope and Anchor seems to have closed following his death and it is difficult now to pinpoint where it stood — not least because no proper system of naming and numbering the streets in Monkton was introduced until 1913.

Nor does anyone remember where the **Greyhound** was located, although it was probably in the old Bush Terrace, one of several terraces that fronted Monkton Lane. A short-lived beer-house, the Greyhound was notorious as a hangout for poachers who set their snares on the nearby Orielton estate. Thomas Williams was the landlord in 1867; he may have been the chap who later ran the Salutation.

All that is known of the **Farmers' Arms** in Monkton Lane is that it was kept by Abraham Lewis who died in 1835. Tradition has it that there was a **Carpenters' Arms** hereabouts as well, but it hasn't been possible to confirm this. No myths about where the **Dragon** stood however, because that was only demolished in the 1970s as part of a road widening scheme; a grassy area by the school car-park marks the spot. The Dragon was first mentioned in 1871 and was possibly erected on the site of an earlier Monkton Lane ale-house. Between the 1870s and

The Dragon in Monkton incorporated a shop and a bakery, and this photograph shows members of the Rock family with the bread van outside the pub.

the 1890s it was run as a pub-cum-grocery-shop by William Penney and his wife Sarah. Subsequently the Dragon was kept for some 40 years by the Rock family who also ran a small shop and bakery; John Rock was the baker and publican, the 'Miss Rocks' — Annie and Eileen — ran the grocery shop. Eileen Rock was herself the licensee from 1944 through to the 1960s.

The **Grapes** stood in Priory Terrace and was run between 1859 and 1868 by Thomas Phillips who was fined 2s. 6d. during that year for serving beer during the hours of divine service. He was followed by his widow Esther and their daughter Emma. William Johns held the licence between 1881 and 1909, but for some reason he did not bother to renew the licence at that year's Brewster Sessions. Priory Terrace was demolished in the 1960s.

The area where Church Terrace meets Monkton Lane is now a picture of respectability; there is nothing to show that this corner of town was once awash with pubs and ale-houses. In fact, apart from Point Street in Hakin this was probably the booziest neighbourhood in Victorian Pembrokeshire! The main reason for this was the presence here of the old conduit mentioned earlier — the trough of spring-water where drovers would water their flocks before heading out into the country. Another reason for the concentration of pubs hereabouts was the fact that this part of Monkton regularly hosted street sales of cattle and horses as well as the two great occasions of the May Fair and the 'Holroyd' or Holyrood Fair.

Writing about these fairs in the 1920s, Mr. A.G.O. Mathias recalled:

> The May and Holyrood Fairs at Monkton were at one time something to look forward to. You would see cattle on the pavements from the Old Hall to Bush Terrace, pens of sheep and pigs here and there; mountain ponies, too, were on sale. Many of the inhabitants during these fairs had to put up shutters to save their windows from being broken. There were shooting stalls with pipes twirling around to be shot at for nuts, sweets and fruit, and other stalls near the churchyard wall — and at one time in the churchyard and even in the church porch. At the 'Roebuck' you would see girls and boys dancing a jig to the tune of a fiddle, and you may take it they were thoroughly enjoying themselves in their own sweet way.

The **Roebuck** referred to by Mr. Mathias (who was a bit of an authority on old Pembroke pubs) seems to have stood on the corner of Church Terrace, where it meets Monkton Lane. William Williams and his wife Elizabeth kept the pub from 1824 to 1844. After William's death, his widow kept the pub going until the 1860s, with the occasional assistance of her son John, a sawyer, but when Elizabeth passed away the pub seems to have died with her.

A couple of doors down Church Terrace was the **Apple Tree**, the longest surviving pub in a terrace that once boasted five ale-houses in a row of barely

*An early postcard view of Church Terrace, Monkton,
which once boasted five pubs.*

20 properties. George Perkins was the landlord from 1835 to 1844 followed by his widow Mary. Between 1851 and 1861 Mr. Edward Rooks from Castlemartin and his wife Mary were roosting in the Apple Tree. They eventually left the pub and went into the grocery business; perhaps they were fed up with being fined for serving out of hours — a regular occurrence. John Stephens was landlord from 1866 to 1871, while Edward Jones was the colourful landlord from 1874 to about 1880.

An ex-Navy man, 'Ted of the Apple Tree' had been a member of the expedition which helped to suppress an uprising in 1869 when settlers on the Red River in north America rebelled against plans to transfer their land to Canadian ownership. In later life Ted used to drive a horse-drawn omnibus between Pembroke and Hobbs Point. 'Sixpence all the way, and cheap too!' he would declare. He was followed by John and Rebecca Rossiter and then by their daughter, Miss Eliza Rossiter, who was the landlady by 1891. Thomas Stephens was the publican from 1901 to 1912 and Albert Rabbetts kept the pub from 1920 until 1926. In that year the Apple Tree was given the chop by the licensing authorities who felt there were too many pubs in Monkton. They withdrew the licence, awarding compensation of £315 to be shared between Mr. Rabbetts (who went on to run the South Wales Hotel in Neyland) and the ground landlord, Sir Frederick Meyrick of Bush. Nowadays the Apple Tree is a private house which, happily for historians, still retains the old pub name.

The Apple Tree is now a private house.

A little further down the terrace were two tiny ale-houses next door to each other; the **New Inn** and the **Masons' Arms**. The New Inn was kept by James Vaughan and his wife Phoebe from 1824 to 1851 and later by George Morgans, a timber-yard foreman by day. It was a notoriously rough pub at one time; when police officers went there in 1864 to evict some after hours drinkers, one of the customers drew a knife. The man was promptly hit over the head with a truncheon after which a small-scale riot erupted which only ended when police reinforcements arrived. Morgans was also accused of running a 'badly conducted house' in 1866, but he must have cleaned up his act, because he remained there until his death in 1874, after which his widow Mary Morgans took over. She handed over the reins to John Brickle in 1878, but the New Inn seems to have closed soon afterwards.

The Masons' Arms was a fairly short-lived beer-shop, run as a sideline by stonemason John Tasker from 1858 to 1867. His widow Elizabeth was in charge by the time of the 1871 census, but there are no more recent references.

The final pub in Church Terrace was also probably the first to be opened. The **Brown Cow** near the top of Awkward Hill was recorded in 1816 when Mary Prickett was landlady. From 1824 to 1830 the licensee was Elizabeth Hitchings and in 1835 it was James Williams. The landlady in 1844 was Ann Stephens who ran a grocery shop in tandem with the pub, as did Mancunian Joseph Lockett who was the landlord in the 1860s. It seems to have closed by 1871, as Mr. Lockett was a described in that year's census return as a clerk in the Dockyard and there is no mention of an inn. The building later became a grocer's shop and is now a private house.

All these pubs would have taken part enthusiastically in the old Monkton tradition known as 'Tapping Sunday'; this was in the days when all the pubs brewed their own beer. When one of the big fairs was approaching a great deal of extra beer would need to be brewed, and naturally the barrels would have to be tapped and the beer tasted a few days in advance, just to check that it was all right. By tradition this beer-tasting always took place on the Sunday before fair day, and 'Tapping Sunday' became renowned as a day of roaring drunkenness in Monkton — much to the disgust of the local vicar and churchwardens who fought long and hard to end the practice.

Where the **Coach and Horses** and the **Red Cow** were in Monkton is not known. The Red Cow is briefly recorded between 1803 and 1806 when James Lloyd held the ale-house licence. The Coach and Horses was a much more prominent inn in its day and may have been one of the two pubs recorded in the parish in 1784; it was certainly up and running in 1799 when Richard Howells was landlord. He was followed in 1813 by his widow Theodosia, who remained the landlady until 1833. The Pembroke Corporation accounts for 1827 include the entry: 'Paid Theodosia Howells her Bill for Ale for Holyrood Fair'. William Millard was landlord in 1835 but there is no further reference. According to A.G.O. Mathias, writing in 1929, this ale-house was at 'Trevor Cottages' (wherever that was) and had a horse-block or 'upping-stock' outside. 'In the time of Cromwell it was the parsonage', he wrote.

A noted character in Pembroke in the first half of the last century, Arthur George Owen Mathias was actuary to the Pembroke and Pembroke Dock Savings Bank in the Main Street. He was an amateur naturalist who encouraged owls to roost in the attic of the bank and every morning he fed the swans on the Mill Pond. An enthusiastic local historian, he was a familiar figure in his Bullnose Morris, setting off with his dog Meg on archaelogical excursions that probably did more harm than good to the sites he excavated.

In 1929 he compiled an interesting if rather fanciful list of former Pembroke pubs for inclusion in the *West Wales Guardian* — a list which might have been more useful to today's historians had it not simply described the pubs as being 'now Mr. Welby's house' or 'now Wm. Howells'. This list included a further three pubs in Monkton which don't appear in any of the records (though that isn't to say they never existed). These three included the **Bushes**, which Mr. Mathias placed 'opposite the cemetery', and the **Ferryboat Inn** which allegedly dated from the days before Monkton and the Westgate were connected by bridge.

> One of the oldest hostelries [in Pembroke] was undoubtedly the Ferry Boat Inn, Awkward Hill, which was still a going concern in Cromwell's time. Its last landlord was a John Gwenilla.

wrote Mr. Mathias; he placed the Ferryboat at Prospect House.

A third pub, the **Old Flag** in Bridgend Terrace, was described by Mr. Mathias thus:

> Ye Old Flag with its canopy over the front door at Bridgend was a bit of old Monkton. In the 18th century a John Tennant was landlord and he was followed by James Phillips who afterwards kept a grocer's shop.

A grocer named James Phillips did indeed live at the 'Flag', Bridgend Terrace, between about 1844 and 1881, and though there is no record of the building being used as a pub or beer-house in his day, it may well have been licensed in previous times.

It is remarkable that of all the many ale-houses that once flourished in Monkton, only one still survives. That is the **Victoria** in Bridgend Terrace which, as its name indicates, dates from just after the coronation year of 1837. David Thomas and his wife Elizabeth kept the Vic. between 1840 and 1851, leasing it from the Owen family of Orielton. Following the break-up of

Still going strong, the Victoria is the last survivor of Monkton's many pubs.

the Orielton estate, the Vic. was sold by auction in 1857, and the landlord from 1867 to 1884 was a carpenter named David Evans. In 1891 the pub was kept by Robert and Elizabeth Hay. Thomas Griffiths ran the Vic. from 1901 to 1912 and in the 1920s the landlady was Mrs. Mary Griffiths. George Onions was there in 1939 and among the longer-serving post-war licensees was John George Davies who ran the pub from 1945 to 1962 before handing on to Billy Scourfield.

Adjoining Monkton is the tiny suburb of Orange Gardens, half a dozen streets of 'comfortable cottages for respectable mechanics' which was built from the 1860s onwards by Isaac Williamson, agent to the Owens of Orielton. He named his new suburb 'Orange Town' in honour of the Owens' election colours, but the locals always called it Orange Gardens. And because even respectable mechanics need a pint sometimes, a pub was built on the corner of Thomas Street and South Row — the **New Inn**.

Catherine Lewis may have been the first licensee; she also ran a grocery shop at the New Inn by 1871. The licence passed from her to James James in June 1872; two months later he was fined 20 shillings for serving late. Next came George A. Brewster, who was regularly in trouble with the law for selling beer outside permitted hours, and then William Bate. Walter Golesworthy held the licence from 1914 to 1920 followed by Mrs. Sarah Golesworthy and later by William and Sarah Evans.

*Licensee Walter Golesworthy stands at the doorway of the New Inn,
Orange Gardens — now the Black Rabbit Club.*

Shortly after the Second World War the tenancy of the New Inn was taken over by Charlie and Bessie Waters, who had previously been at the Old Cross Saws. By this time the New Inn was popularly known as the 'Black Rabbit' — a nickname which derived from a trick played by a local landowner in order to catch the poachers who were helping themselves to the rabbits from his fields and selling them to a dealer in Pembroke. Night after night the landowner patrolled his fields and woods, but the poachers were always too slippery for him and he was never able to catch them. So he laid a trap. Somehow he was able to obtain a rabbit that was coal-black, and on one fine and moonless evening, perfect for poaching, he released the rabbit into his field. Next day he went down to the rabbit-dealer in Pembroke and waited. Sure enough, an hour or two later, two men from Orange Gardens turned up with a sack each of dead coneys which they tipped on the floor, and there, on top of the pile, was the black rabbit.

In 1957, Hancock's Brewery decided to close the New Inn; the licence wasn't renewed and the building was sold as a private house. Tenants Charlie and Bessie Waters bought the property and a week later re-opened it as a members' club — the Black Rabbit Club. It proved a great success with Orange Gardens people, especially as they were now able to enjoy a drink on a Sunday — a privilege they had been denied when their local boozer was restricted to pub hours. The Black Rabbit Club is still open, but much changed from the cottage pub, and cottage club, it once was.

1	Dragon
2	Apple Tree
3	Victoria
4	New Inn
5	Railway
6	Eastgate
7	Hope
8	Maltsters
9	White Lion
10	Commercial
11	Rifle Corps Arms
12	Royal Oak
13	Red Lion
14	Old Cross Saws
15	Butchers' Arms
16	York
17	Bush
18	Lamb
19	Union Tavern
20	Green Dragon
21	Stag's Head
22	Oddfellows
23	Castle
24	Old King's Arms
25	White Hart
26	Lion
27	West End Vaults
28	Royal George
29	Red, White and Blue
30	Waterman's
31	Army and Navy
32	Castle and Dragon
33	Black Horse

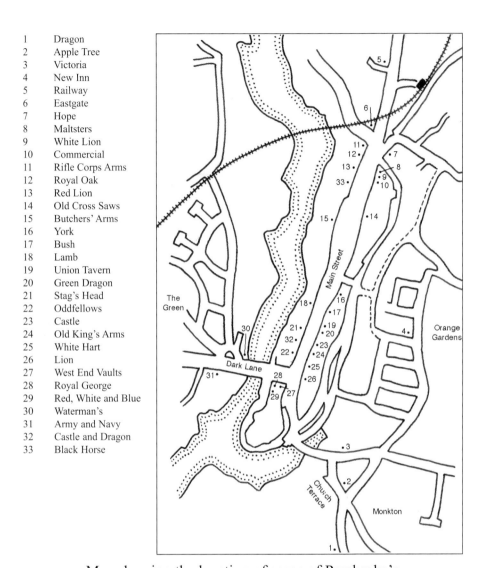

Map showing the location of some of Pembroke's
more notable pubs

38

CHAPTER FOUR

Pembroke East

The town of Pembroke was built in Norman times along a narrow limestone ridge, on either side of which were tidal branches of the Milford Haven estuary. A magnificent castle guarded the seaward end of the ridge, and towers and walls completed the imposing fortifications of the town. It was a flourishing place in medieval times, thanks to a lucrative monopoly on sea trade, but it suffered down the centuries due to the loss of this trading monopoly and the ravages caused by the Black Death and later by the Civil War, when Cromwell himself supervised a siege that lasted for two months.

By 1725 the town was back on its feet, so much so that Daniel Defoe was able to describe it as 'the largest, richest and most flourishing town of all South Wales'. Much of this wealth came from Pembroke's renewed importance as a port, with regular trade links with Bristol, Ireland and further afield. A Customs House was opened to deal with this growing trade, and thriving merchants built elegant Georgian houses along the Main Street, replacing the humble dwellings that had survived from medieval times.

There had always been ale-houses in the town, particularly around the town quay and market-place. But it wasn't until the 18th century that any real record was kept of these early pubs. A list of those licensed to keep ale-houses in Pembroke, dated September 1784, recorded the following nine names: William Duggan, George Miller, Henry Amson, William Streck, Richard Jenkins, Hugh Williams, John Furlong, George Williams and Aaron Game; sadly the records do not indicate which ale-houses they kept.

By 1795 the list of ale-house keepers ran as follows: Aaron Game, David Millingchamp, William Watkins, John Lewis, William Duggan, Benjamin James, William Jones, Arnold Morgans and John Williams. (a chap called David Jones also ran an ale-house out at Stoops Lake, near Nash). The opening of the Royal Dockyard in nearby Paterchurch in 1814 gave a tremendous boost to the drinking trade in Pembroke, as did the arrival of soldiers and marines to guard the new shipyard. As Pembroke began to grow beyond the town walls, so the number of inns and ale-houses increased — to 18 by 1830, to 25 by 1850, and to around 50 by the late 1860s, with a hefty chunk of those being in Monkton.

At East End Square, four roads fan out into the Pembrokeshire countryside. At one time this square stood outside the town's medieval east gate and would have been the point of arrival for road travellers from Tenby, Lamphey and further afield. Weary wayfarers who arrived after the gate was shut for the night would be unable to enter the town, so there may well have been early inns here, to cater for these benighted arrivals. In later years, the regular horse and cattle fairs for the parish of St. Michael's, held in the street here, coupled with the annual Michaelmas Hiring Fair, gave rise to a concentration of pubs and inns in the East End nearly equal to that of Monkton on the opposite side of town. The opening of Pembroke station just to the east of the Square in 1863, and the subsequent building of several terraces of cottages and houses alongside the roads to Lamphey and Holyland brought added prosperity to the area in Victorian times.

The **Railway Inn** on the Upper Lamphey Road is a street corner pub built close to the town's old ropewalk, where the ropes and rigging for the locally-owned sailing ships would have been manufactured. The Railway seems to have opened in the late 1860s, and the pub has benefited over the years by being handy for both the train station and the town's cattle market. In the 1870s it was owned by local brewer Robert George who installed a succession of tenants, including Irishman John Guilthrap, who was landlord from 1878 to 1901 and who had a reputation for bending the laws over

The Railway Inn was once the 'local' for the cattle market.

Sunday drinking. On one occasion in 1898, two policemen hid across the road from the Railway and counted nearly 20 people sneaking in for a Sunday morning sleever of Mr. Guilthrap's beer; he was duly fined £10 for the offence.

Albert Dunn was the landlord from 1914 to 1923, while Mrs. Dunn subsequently held the licence until she retired in 1936. Narberth brewers James Williams bought the Railway at auction that year for £1,300 and installed William Smith, formerly of the nearby Royal Oak, as landlord. At this time the village of Lamphey was 'dry' and so the Railway was adopted as the 'village local' — especially on Saturday nights. Jack Skeels, who took over in 1958, is probably the best remembered of the post-war licensees and the Railway is still a James Williams house today.

There was once a pub on the Lower Lamphey Road as well, but only for a short time. Twice-widowed Rebecca Evans lived at Rose Valley in the 1860s. Still only in her 40s, and with a large brood of children to bring up, she tried to make ends meet by opening a beer-house which she called the **Rising Sun**. It is impossible to identify exactly where the Rising Sun was located, but when the landlady was fined for keeping her pub open during prohibited hours in 1860 she was described as 'Rebecca Evans, Alleston'. The pub seems to have been short-lived, although a trade directory for 1867 gives Hugh Matthews as landlord of the Sun, Pembroke, which may or may not have been the same place.

On East End Square itself stands the **Hope**, an out-and-out beer-house when William Colley was there in 1844. Stonemason Thomas Colley ran a beer-house in the town in 1850-55, which was almost certainly the Hope, while Morris Phillips was the landlord from 1861 until his death in 1873 at the remarkable age of 93. The licence then passed to his widow Jane, a mere whippersnapper of 69 at the time, who was still the licensee in 1881. Another elderly lady was there in 1891 — Elizabeth Gibbs, aged 70.

The Hope came within a whisker of being shut down by the licensing authorities in 1909 when it was recommended for closure by the town's magistrates. The

The long-standing Hope Inn on East End Square.

41

Pembrokeshire Redundancy and Compensation Committee had been in operation since 1905, suppressing pub licences throughout the county and compensating the breweries and, to a much lesser extent the licensees, for loss of earnings. But it was in 1909 that the system really began to bite, with Pembroke Borough magistrates in the forefront of the campaign to reduce the number of licences. Spurred on by figures showing that 99 people were convicted of drunkenness in 1908 — 10 of them women — they determined to close eight pubs in the two towns.

Of the four Pembroke pubs recommended for closure, one was the Hope where the landlord was George Thomas. It was Police Superintendent W.G. Thomas who urged the magistrates to close the inn. He described it as follows: 'On the ground floor there is a front parlour and in the rear of that a kitchen, with cellar behind. Both rooms are used for drinking purposes and also domestic purposes'. The officer added that there were eight pubs in the vicinity of East End, and suggested that the Hope, with its basic facilities, was not required and would not be missed.

Local solicitor F.S. Reed mounted a valiant defence of the Hope, disagreeing strongly with the last comment by the police superintendent. 'There is more beer drunk there of a night than in any other house in the town', he declared. Describing the Hope as 'an old beer-house before the 1869 Act', he went on:

> There should be two classes of house in every town — a first-class hotel and a house where the working classes can go. The licensee here is doing an enormous legitimate trade and the true judges of the necessity of a house are the customers who go there!

He could have saved his breath. The magistrates were in no mood to listen to arguments and decided to refer the Hope to the next meeting of the redundancy committee — effectively passing a death sentence on the pub. But a few months later, when this committee finally met to rubber-stamp the closure decision, things had changed. The nearby Commercial Inn had closed of its own accord, so that Hope landlord Thomas was able to argue, successfully this time, that there was no need to close his house as well.

George Thomas went on to hold the licence for over 43 years until his death in July 1935. At that time he was the borough's oldest licensee and in his obituary it was said that he had an 'unblemished record' as a publican. This conveniently overlooked the fact that he was fined £5 in December 1900 for selling bottles of beer in contravention of the Sunday Closing Act.

A tiny pub which has always had a loyal following, the Hope has had more than its share of 'characters' behind the bar in recent times, notably Fred Smith in the 1950s, Norman Peachey in the 1970s and disc-jockey-

A view of the East Gate Hotel in 2002.

cum-cricket umpire Graham Price in the 1990s. Recent alterations and extensions have actually enhanced the Hope's attractive Main Street frontage — not something one could say about too many Pembrokeshire pub make-overs.

Across the square from the Hope is the **East Gate**. In 1844 this was a grocery shop known as Turnpike House, run by an Irishman called John McCarthy. A few years later he added a bar, probably in the Irish style with groceries for sale at one end of the counter and ale and porter at the other. John and his wife Sarah called it the **Rose and Crown** and they were still there in 1861. In 1868 the licence of the Rose and Crown passed from the recently deceased George Hughes to his widow Naomi. She married again, and her second husband, John Devote, was the landlord in 1871.

Local magistrate William Hulm then entered the picture. Spotting that Pembroke did not have a railway hotel, Hulm redeveloped the Rose and Crown to serve that purpose, but was obliged to call it the East Gate Hotel to avoid confusion with the recently opened Railway Inn up the road. A former police constable called Sidney Peter Gedge was the first licensee of the East Gate, having previously been master of the local workhouse at Riverside until he was forced to leave under something of a cloud. (He had been using the workhouse inmates as 'slave labour' to dig his private vegetable patch). He later left to run the Royal George on Pembroke Quay and subsequent tenants included Richard Miller and John Ogleby. Miss Elizabeth Price was the landlady from 1901 to 1909 and Richard Devote was behind the bar in the

43

1920s, after which the licensee was the long-serving Roland Greenhow, who remained there until the early 1960s.

A pub with a strong sporting tradition, the East Gate was the watering hole of choice for Pembroke's rugby and cricket fraternity in the years before the rugby team opened its own clubhouse on the Crickmarren ground — and afterwards as well, especially when Eifion Morgan and then John Evans were licensees in the 1960s and '70s. Nowadays it is a popular live music venue.

On the Main Street corner directly opposite the East Gate stood the **Rifle Corps Arms**, which seems to have been under the wing of the White family of Cosheston who were prominent local brewers. Henry Lewis held the licence in 1867, while the landlady in 1869 was Martha Evans whose cavalier attitude to the law led to the pub losing its licence. In the 1870s the Whites applied several times for the licence to be reinstated and transferred to a new, more respectable tenant, but the magistrates steadfastly refused each request. Although the press reports do not actually spell it out, the impression is that the Rifle Corps was something of a den of iniquity where more than just late drinking was carried on. It may well be that the pub was known as a hang-out for the East End prostitutes — a colourful bunch who included Mad Maggie and The Sergeant Major.

Across the Main Street from the Rifle Corps Arms were three pubs in close proximity. On the corner at the top of Goose's Lane stood the **Maltsters' Arms**. A maltster, naturally enough, called John Jones is known to have kept the Maltsters' between 1840 and 1861 before it passed into the hands of the Thomas family. George Thomas held the licence in 1867, followed briefly by James Thomas in 1870 and then the hard-working Charles Thomas. Charles, who was licensee from October 1870 to 1884, sold groceries in one part of the building, dealt in glassware and china in another room, and still had energy left in the evening to pour the pints for his regulars.

Thomas Thomas was the landlord from 1901 to 1907 followed by Mrs. Marion Gilbert, described as 'a widow in unfortunate circumstances'. The pub was closed and referred for compensation in the purge of 1909. Despite offering 'good accommodation', according to the police officer who recommended closure, it was doing only a 'nominal trade'. Compensation of £175 went to Buckley's Ltd., with £25 going to Mrs. Gilbert. The building was later known as Coronation Stores.

Next door to the Maltsters at 141 Main Street was the **White Lion**. Like the Green Dragon further along the street, the sign may have been taken from the heraldic device of the Earls of Pembroke. This was always a busy pub during the fairs that completely took over the street outside, particularly the Michaelmas cattle and hiring fair. In 1864, for example, it was estimated that

An early postcard view of the east end of the Main Street, showing the Royal Oak on the right and the former Maltsters' Arms on the left, next door to the former White Lion.

14,000 people attended this fair, the numbers boosted by the recent opening of the railway from Tenby. Henry Lewis kept the pub in 1840 followed by his widow Elizabeth in 1851, while Elizabeth Wiggin, a widow from Narberth, was the landlady from 1861 to 1874. The White Lion was offered for sale in July 1877 by 'the trustees of the late Thomas Codd' — no doubt the Sageston maltster. Charles Canton was landlord in 1884 and James Penney was there from 1901 until his retirement in 1905.

John Frederick Neil purchased the White Lion at an auction on the premises in March of that year, but in May 1916 the building was sold to a Mr. Sudbury who converted it into a grocery shop, later to become well known as Beesley's Stores. The landlord at the time was John James who had been there since 1907 and who then moved across the road to run the Royal Oak.

Of the third pub along this row nothing now remains. That's because the **Commercial** stood on what is now the forecourt of the petrol station. Catherine Miller was the landlady from 1871 to 1876 having succeeded her late husband Edwin who had been there since 1867. Mrs. Miller ran the pub with the help of her daughter Caroline, but it seems to have been a far from ladylike establishment in their day and Mrs. Miller in particular was renowned for her fiery temper. Daniel Gommer, a Dorset man, was landlord from 1879 to 1890 and Fred Hargreaves was the landlord in 1901. Thomas

45

Wrench ran the pub in 1906, but the licence was allowed to lapse in 1909 and by 1929 a fishmonger was using the premises.

With the ropewalk nearby, it followed that several ships' chandlers should set up shop in the East End; the 1874 trade directory lists Charles Asparase, Patrick Bohane, John Campodonic, Jacob Devote and Peter Lanning as 'marine store dealers, East End'. This was an occasionally shady business, because the rope and tar, sail-cloth, wooden oars and brass fittings supplied by these dealers had often been recycled from vessels wrecked on the treacherous Pembrokeshire coast. Sometimes this process was above board, so to speak, the authorities having held official auctions where the dealers could bid against each other for the cargo and fittings from a wrecked trading vessel. On other occasions, however, the stricken ship would have been stripped of its valuables long before the official authorities got to know of its existence. There is little evidence that Pembrokeshire people actively engaged in wrecking — luring vessels onto the rocks with false signal lights — but if a shipwreck did happen in the neighbourhood then they were not averse to helping themselves to anything useful that could be scavenged from the wreckage. In time, some of these looted goods would turn up in the various East End chandleries, no doubt after some surreptitious deal had been concluded in a dark corner of one of the local ale-houses.

Perhaps one of these was the **Three Cups**, which was kept by William Rossant in 1844. He was a member of a well-established family of local

The Royal Oak as it looked in 2002.

shoemakers and is known to have lived in St. Michael's parish, but his ale-house seems to have been short-lived and the site cannot now be identified. Nor is it known where the **Swan** was located. This was a much earlier establishment, being run by William Watkins between 1795 and 1802, and now long forgotten.

Happily the **Royal Oak** at no. 140 is still thriving — the last survivor of four pubs which once occupied a short stretch of the Mill Pond side of the street. The Royal Oak is a bit of a puzzle, because although it seems to be a well-established inn with a coach arch and stable-yard behind (now a beer garden), there are surprisingly few references to it in the records. John Duggan was known to be at the Royal Oak in 1835, but he had become a hairdresser by 1840 and there are no further mentions of the pub until 1861 when a labourer named Benjamin Phillips and his wife Martha were running it. They were still there in 1891, but when they left the pub changed hands fairly regularly. From 1927 to 1936 William Smith was behind the bar, but he left to take over the nearby Railway Inn and David John was licensee during the war. Postwar licensees have included ex-Navy man J.F. Horrigan, former Milford Haven councillor Kenneth Wade and Gareth Jones who was there in the 1970s.

A couple of doors along was the **Red Lion**, part of which is nowadays a fish and chip shop. Located just inside the town walls, the Red Lion belonged at one time to the Cawdors' Stackpole estate and

The former Red Lion Inn is now a fish and chip shop.

probably takes its name from the *lion guardant gules* on the Cawdor coat of arms. It dates back to at least 1795 when John Lewis held the licence. He was still serving ale in 1810, but Morgan Morgan is recorded as being at the Red Lion in 1820. Local ship-owner James Williams was the licensee between 1828 and 1830, but by 1835 Henry Lewis was in charge; probably he was the chap who opened the White Lion across the road a few years later. Licensee by 1840 was John Rees who seems to have run the place as a beer-house until his death in 1858, while William Morris and his wife Eliza were behind the bar from 1867 to 1884.

The Heart of Oak Benefit Society met here in 1859, while another friendly society called the Friendly Helpmate Society used the pub as its registered office in the 1880s. By this time the Red Lion was being rented from the Cawdor estate by local brewer Robert George, and it seems to have been one of the better-run pubs in a part of town that could occasionally resemble the Wild West. Former licensee of the Odd Fellows at the other end of the main street (see chapter 5), Thomas Henry Rogers, was running the pub in September 1888 with the help of his wife Margaret, but when they left in 1891 the Red Lion's fairly blameless life-span came to an end.

Somewhere near the Red Lion was the **Carpenters' Arms**. Benjamin Marchant is recorded as being its tenant in 1834, leasing the property at an annual rent of £3 8s. He was still the licensee in 1844, while in 1858 he is described as a 'retailer of beer, Pembroke' — evidently running the Carpenters' Arms as a beer-house with the help of his wife Mary. He handed over to Isaac Lloyd from Manorbier in 1860, but the pub closed a few years later. A.G.O. Mathias placed the Carpenters' Arms 'two doors above the Red Lion' — without indicating which direction he meant by 'above'.

The **Black Horse** at no. 118 is remembered in the name of the walkway leading down to the Mill Pond, created on the site of the former pub. Boot and shoe-maker Charles Morris ran the pub as a sideline between 1840 and 1852 (when it was described as an 'unruly house' which kept late hours). George Harries became landlord in 1858 followed by Ann Harries in 1868. John Devote, formerly of the Rose and Crown, was licensee from 1878 to 1891; he and his wife Naomi were also china-dealers. A basket-maker named Carl Lohr was the landlord from 1906 to 1923, while George Onions was the last licensee. He didn't bother to renew the licence in 1934, subsequently moving to the Victoria in Monkton, and the pub never re-opened.

By 1958 the Black Horse had long been empty and the building had become 'unfit for human habitation'. The borough council of the time was happily pulling down Victorian houses in Monkton, Bankers' Row and at St. Michael's Square, and simply added the Black Horse to the list of victims — replacing it with public conveniences and a walkway to the Mill Pond.

Pembroke's East End was certainly full of characters. In the summer of 1854 a small band of Russian Gypsies turned up in the town, complete with dancing bear and a rather shabby wolf on a leash. The show they put on for Pembroke's Eastenders emptied the beer-houses as a crowd gathered in the Square, clapping and cheering. One onlooker, who had spent too much time

The Black Horse inn can be seen between the second and third trees from the left in this old postcard view.

in the Black Horse or the Red Lion, went a stage further and decided to congratulate the dancing bear by shaking hands with it. The bear responded with a friendly bear-hug — too friendly, because the poor chap nearly had the breath squeezed out of his body before the bear could be persuaded to release his grip!

With a dozen inns and ale-houses crowded into a small area — plus a few brothels — the East End could be a rough and rowdy part of town; in 1846 the *Pembrokeshire Herald* described it as 'that not very quiet and peaceful locality, commonly called or known by the name of East End'. Respectable people from the 'posher' end of the street tended to steer well clear, especially at night, and not without good reason. John Partridge was a wheelwright who kept an unnamed beer-house near St. Michael's Square in 1833. On one occasion a disturbance began in the beer-house involving a woman named Ann Gwyther and her husband Henry — one of several petty crooks who lived around the East End. The disturbance escalated into a drunken brawl and ended when Ann Gwyther stabbed John Harris, a constable who was trying to arrest her husband. Harris was lucky to survive the attack, which left him smothered in blood, and at the next assizes Ann Gwyther was sentenced to death for the crime. This was later commuted to transportation and she spent nine years in New South Wales before returning to Britain.

In Victorian times there were at least three more pubs on the north side of the Main Street between the Black Horse and the start of the East Back at Wesley Chapel. Of course, these three did not include the present-day **Coach House**, a purpose-built pub-cum-restaurant which dates from the late 1960s and which housed the town's folk club for a number of years as well as being popular with German Panzer troops enjoying an evening away from the tank training camp at Castlemartin.

None of the three former pubs along this stretch can now be identified with any accuracy, having been little more than houses which happened to sell beer. First of these was the **Milford Arms** which probably stood on the site of the present St. Michael's Square car-park. The Milford was a rough pub, even by East End standards, and in 1861 the landlord, Benjamin Jones, was fined 10 shillings for assaulting P.C. Jones by throwing a chair at him. By 1863 the licence was held by James Walsh who seems to have installed John McCarthy, former licensee of the nearby Rose and Crown, as barman. This failed to improve the pub's unsavoury reputation and in 1864 the local magistrates decided enough was enough and refused to renew the licence. (Pembroke also had a **Milford Tavern** in the early 1800s, run by John Gullam, but this seems to have been a different place altogether).

When the two-storeyed house at no. 102 Main Street was demolished in 1957 to help create the present car-park in front of the church, the workmen discovered a sign saying 'public bar' beneath the layers of paint on one of the internal doors. This long-forgotten pub must have been either the Milford Arms or the **Pelican**. Boot and shoe-maker George Rowlands was landlord of the Pelican from 1835 onwards, but the pub does not seem to have survived his death in 1848.

The **Blacksmith's Arms** was nearer the East Back and enjoyed a brief hey-day in the 1840s. John Wade was one of seven blacksmiths in the town in 1844. He and his wife Esther had six children and it may have been the need for extra cash that prompted them to open the Blacksmith's Arms. The beer-shop doesn't seem to have been a great success, however, and appears to have been closed by 1850. A lease dated 1930 referred to 'a house and garden on St. Michael's Square, formerly the Blacksmith's Arms, now known as Milford House'; it was occupied by William Devote.

One pub that does remain open on St. Michael's Square is the intriguingly-named **Old Cross Saws**. Various theories exist as to how this name came about, several of them connected with the old preaching cross which used to stand hereabouts in medieval times. Another possible answer is that the pub was once called the Crossed Swords — the symbol of the Cutlers' Guild — and that the name became slurred into Cross Saws over a

The Old Cross Saws may take its name from a medieval preaching cross which once stood outside.

period of time. This was always one of the better-run pubs at this end of town, partly because it was on the fringe of the East End proper, and partly because it remained in the same family for many years. As a sign of this respectability, the Court Leet and View of Frankpledge for the manor of East Pembroke and the Court Baron of Pryse Pryse, Lord of the Manor, were held at the Old Cross Saws in the 1840s.

A widow named Catharine Millard was landlady here from at least 1830 until her death in 1858. Her daughter Martha then took over and ran the Old Cross Saws until 1884. John Thomas, a solicitor's clerk from Boulston, kept the pub in 1891 and Robert George Tucker was the landlord in 1906. Following the death of licensee Mr. F.G. Harwood in 1912, his widow Mrs. Emma Harwood took over, and she was still running the pub in 1932. John Henry Goverd then ran the pub until his death, aged 73, in 1937 after which Tom Phillips took over. When the pub came up for sale in 1953, an advertisement noted that it had been recently renovated 'at considerable cost'. It contained three licensed rooms and boasted a three-pull beer engine.

A Buckleys house, the Old Cross Saws remained a compact, three-roomed local until fairly recently, but was expanded and enlarged in the 1980s while remaining substantially the same in outward appearance. A popular pub with rugby supporters, it was run for 21 years by Bud and Frankie Small who retired at the end of 2001.

Because Catharine Millard is the first known licensee of the Old Cross Saws, it is tempting to conclude that the unidentified ale-house run by George

Miller or Millard between 1784 and 1810 in the parish of St. Michael's was actually the Old Cross Saws. However, Mr. Richard Rose in his book *Pembroke People* has unearthed an 1819 reference to George Millard of the Sun Inn somewhere in the East End of Pembroke, which rather knocks that theory on the head.

At Wesley Chapel the road splits into two for 100 yds. or so before meeting up again at the top of the New Way, and at one time there was at least one pub on each route. On the East Back stood the **Butcher's Arms**, known locally as the **Pig and Whistle**, in what is now Slate House. This beer-shop was kept by a butcher, of course, called James Morris, who was there between 1835 and 1844. It was later occupied by Lewis Truscott, a bit of a rogue who crops up in connection with several pubs further along the street. The Butcher's seems to have stopped serving beer by the late 1850s and has been a private house ever since.

On the other branch of the highway, the Main Street proper, were the long-forgotten **Prince Albert** in Hamilton Terrace, the **Horseshoes**, which was mentioned in connection with a court case in 1837, and the **Elm** run by hat-maker Abraham Griffiths in 1835. None of these can now be pinpointed with any confidence, though the latter must have stood close to the magnificent elm tree which dominated the centre of town for hundreds of years. It was beneath the elm that the town stocks once stood, where local drunks would be forced to languish until they sobered up.

CHAPTER FIVE

Pembroke West & The Green

Historians believe that Pembroke was built in two distinct stages — hence the two parish churches of St. Mary's and St. Michael's. The dip in the Main Street at the top of the New Way, which may once have been the defensive ditch that marked the boundary of the first stage of development, now marks the boundary between the parishes. Historically, St. Mary's has tended to be the commercial centre of the town, being where the market-place, the quays and the custom house used to be. The banks, the bigger shops and many of the gentry town-houses were located here, as were the town's main coaching inns.

The **York Tavern** wasn't one of these principal inns, but it was certainly one of the most historic of the town's hostelries. Legend has it that there were once secret passages leading from the rock-hewn cellars of the York, one of which ran underneath the castle and on to the priory at Monkton. There is even a rather dubious tradition that Cromwell spent a night at the tavern following the surrender of the town's Royalist defenders, while a more trust-worthy tale concerns John Wesley who is said to have preached on several occasions in the old chapel meeting house which still stands in the garden of the former tavern.

Old though the building undoubtedly is, the pub's name was almost certainly of a much more recent vintage. Most pubs called York or Duke of York were named after the chap in the nursery rhyme — Frederick, the son of George III, who commanded the English army in Flanders in 1795. It seems likely that a soldier returning from the Flanders campaign to take over the tavern named (or re-named) it in honour of his former commanding officer — a fairly common practice. Perhaps this soldier was Benjamin James who is recorded as being at the York between 1795 and 1803. Richard Eynon was the licensee from the 1820s to 1838, while his widow Anne subsequently held the licence until at least 1857. The tavern was sold by auction that year by the landowning Owens of Orielton, at which time the 'York Hotel'

The York Tavern shortly before it closed in 2002.

comprised four bedrooms, four rooms on the ground floor, cellar, coalhouse and brewhouse. In 1861 the landlord was John Rodney from Llawhaden, a gardener by trade, while George Tracy held the licence between 1865 and 1867.

For the next 50 years the landlord was a carpenter and joiner from Monkton named William Jenkins. 'Billie the York' was a tremendous character who brewed all his own beer in the old chapel in the garden and who still had all his own teeth when he died in 1918. 'Good ale is far better than a bad cup of tea' was one of his favourite sayings. Following his death the York was taken over by his daughter Elizabeth Maud Jenkins who became known as 'Maudie the York' in her turn and who was still behind the bar well into the 1950s, being succeeded in 1957 by Iestyn Griffiths.

A newspaper reporter who visited the York in 1953 recorded:

> There is a tavern in the town of Pembroke where you can find sawdust on the floor, a tiny-paned bow window and an atmosphere of peace and well-being.

The pub changed little over the following half-century, for much of which time the York was run by Ruth and Billy Morgans — inevitably known up and down the Main Street as 'Ruth the York' and 'Billy the York'. They retired in April 2002 after 38 years in business and sadly the historic pub has remained closed ever since and looks likely to remain that way.

Further along the street was the **Bush Inn,** which was probably in the building which now houses Brown's café. Mary Trewent was the landlady in 1830 while wheelwright William Paget was the landlord from 1844 to 1846. Stonemason Richard Jones from Lawrenny and his wife Louisa kept the pub between 1850 and 1861, and Louisa ran the pub on her own from 1867 to 1884. Michael O'Hara and his wife Margaret subsequently kept the

Bush, but it closed in 1892. There was also a beer-house next to the Bush, in one of the buildings demolished when the Post Office was built. It was run by Elizabeth Blethyn in the 1850s, but the name hasn't come down to us.

Opposite the Bush was the **Lamb**, a beer-house where the landlady was Bridget or 'Biddy' Scourfield. Following an assault case in 1849, the *Pembrokeshire Herald* reported:

> The complainant and the defendants, with many others, had been drinking and playing cards at a Tom and Jerry shop called the Lamb in Pembroke until a very late hour.

A drunken brawl broke out, as a result of which the complainant, William John, lost the sight in one eye. His assailants were fined £1 each, but John didn't escape a tongue-lashing from the magistrate:

> You go to a low beer-house and there you continue drinking and playing at cards and using language of a disgusting nature from five o'clock on a Saturday afternoon until half past one on a Sunday morning. I trust this will be a warning to you to refrain from similar acts.

Mathias had another tale to tell about the Lamb:

> A young man who had been imbibing freely, but not wisely, at the Lamb, had been persuaded into marrying a sister of Biddy's. Now Biddy's sister was not what you might call prepossessing, and when he came to see her with clearer eyes he was not too pleased with his bargain. He there and then wished his spouse goodbye, never to return.

The Lamb stood where Lowless and Lowless now have part of their solicitors' offices — the lower part, on the left as you look at it from the street.

Back across the road again, and just west of the Post Office is the building which until fairly recently housed the Electricity Board Showrooms and is still part of the Power Station Club. But back in the 1840s this was the wildest and wackiest tavern in town. Officially it was called the **Union**, but everyone knew it either as 'Oriels' — after the licensees — or more usually as the 'Green Mead' since it stood near the site of an old duck-pond called the Green Mead Pool. The Union was kept by a father and son, both named George Oriel, with the father being in charge from about 1800. It is thought that the pub opened that year, taking its name from the Act of Union which united Britain and Ireland. In 1821 the Union was recommended as being one of the best three inns in town (alongside the Green Dragon and the Golden Lion) in John Cary's *Itinerary*.

The elder George Oriel was certainly a popular chap, and his establishment had a large and loyal following. In his *Historical Sketches of Pembroke Dock*, George Mason recorded the visit of the Duke of Clarence to the town in 1827 to launch a ship named in his honour:

> At Bush Hill the horses were taken out of the carriages and three hundred of the Greenmead Boys of Pembroke drew the carriages to Pembroke under the management of the — at that time — well-known George Oriel.

Oriel had been a member of the Castlemartin Yeomanry — he may have helped round up the French at Fishguard in 1797 — and the troopers continued to support their old comrade's pub for many years afterwards. Sometimes they supported it too well; there were reports of troopers being so drunk on parade that they slid off their horses in a stupor. 'I've seen the drummer beating the kettle-drums with his head and the cornopean player holding his trumpet upside down', recalled a former Yeomanry trooper some years later.

Part of the popularity of the Union or 'Green Mead' stemmed from the fact that the inn had a large room at the back where theatrical entertainments of a fairly basic kind were staged — burlesques and early music hall acts. These were very popular with the town's lesser tradesmen who couldn't really aspire to the concerts and banquets held in the ballrooms of the Dragon and the Lion. George's son, George Oriel junior, was in charge by 1835 and had a reputation for being a notorious practical joker. On one occasion he apparently arranged to have one of his more boring customers shot with a blunderbuss at point-blank range. 'I am dead!' cried the man as his shirt-front turned crimson with gore — only to discover that the blunderbuss had been loaded with a harmless charge of cotton waste and ox-blood.

George Oriel died in 1852, and on 19 February 1858 the following entry appeared in the *Pembrokeshire Herald*:

> Oriel's House, Green Mead Pool. This old house, once so celebrated in its locality as the 'Garrick Head' or 'Coalhole' in London, where in days of yore certain inhabitants of this town were wont to assemble to regale themselves, sing and play practical jokes, and where many ludicrous scenes have been enacted, has been for some time untenable and in a few days will have passed away, the site having been taken by Messrs. John Morris and Sons. for the purpose of erecting and carrying on their business. Workmen are already employed in pulling down the old building.

It appears, as so often happens, that the landlord 'made' the pub. The eccentric George Oriel was an impossible act to follow and when he died the spark went from the Union and it closed soon afterwards. John Morris, the new occupier of the site, was a boot and shoe maker.

A new pub, the **Cavalier Inn** has recently opened a few doors along from the old Union, while one of the town's three **Spirit Vaults** was once located in the building that is now Barclays Bank. This was run by wine merchant Daniel Shewen Thomas in the 1850s and '60s and later by his widow Elizabeth who kept it going into the '80s. It was 'a house noted for the excellence of its beer and stout' according to Mathias.

The chemist shop at 31 Main Street — known for many years as 'Treweeks' and later as 'Mendus' — was at one time the **Old White Hart.** Before 1817 it was owned by the Owens of Orielton, but in that year they sold it to local maltster and brewer John Whitta. The sale documents record that the Old White Hart was 'formerly in the occupation of John Duggan, innkeeper, deceased' and it seems to have been no longer an inn by the time Whitta took over.

Next door to the Old White Hart is where the town's corn market was located in the 18th century, with the town hall above it. In 1823, this building was also acquired by John Whitta, who bought it for £189 from the mayor and corporation, and it seems that he converted it into a house and shop with a brewery behind. When Whitta died in 1827 he divided his estate into nine equal parts to be shared out among his nine children. One of these children, Elizabeth, married a wine and spirit merchant by the name of Thomas George and throughout the 1840s he gradually bought up all the part-shares in the Main Street property held by his brothers-in-law and sisters-in-law.

The result was that the building became the headquarters of the George family business, a highly successful enterprise that involved the sale and supply of ale, stout, wine and spirits over a large area. When Thomas George died in 1866 the business passed to his son Robert, an energetic and enterprising businessman whose name was soon emblazoned across the shop front. Mayor of Pembroke from 1879 to 1882, he described himself as

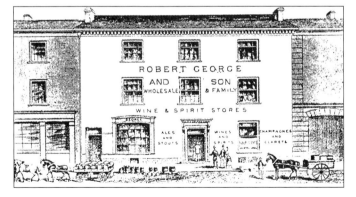

Robert George's wine and spirit store in the Main Street, depicted in 1893.
(Illustration courtesy of Mrs. M. Phillips.)

'The Cromwell Brewery is fitted with a capital modern plant of the most improved construction' reported a guide to Pembroke in 1893. Owners Messrs. Robert George and Son described themselves as: 'Family Wine and Spirit Merchants, Brewers and Maltsters, Hop, Seed and Manure Merchants'.
(Illustration courtesy of Mrs. M. Phillips.)

'wholesale wine and spirit merchant, maltster, brewer, hop and seed merchant and agent for artificial manures'. It was Robert George who was responsible for opening the extensive Cromwell Brewery on the site of the derelict custom house almost opposite the castle entrance. 'The mild and pale ales of the Cromwell Brewery are always sent out in the finest possible condition and command universal approval' declared an 1880s advertisement. He also operated another of the town's **Spirit Vaults** (sometimes called **George's Hall**), but whether this was in the Main Street or at the brewery is hard to say.

In 1896, George's merged with the Swansea Old Brewery, which was in turn taken over by William Hancock's in 1927. Cromwell's Brewery eventually closed and is now the Haven Christian Centre, while the elegant former wine and spirit stores at number 29 Main Street still displays a plaque bearing the name of Robert George.

The NatWest Bank next door was at one time the **Green Dragon** — in its day the most fashionable coaching inn in Pembroke. The name was well chosen, since the sign was taken from the coat of arms of the Earls of Pembroke. It was mentioned in *Pugh's Hereford Journal* of January 1771, when Henry Phillips of the Green Dragon, Pembroke, 'begged leave to inform his friends and customers that he has lately refitted his house in a neat and elegant manner, where Gentlemen and travellers may be provided with proper accommodations and very good beds'. He added that he had half-a-dozen horses for hire, for any distance, at threepence a mile, and that there

was 'a large Lamp at the door, well lighted in the Winter season'. The Green Dragon was described as a 'middling' inn by a traveller in 1791, and seems to have been run by William Jones between 1795 and his death in 1803. He evidently improved the place, because it was recommended as the best hostelry in Pembroke by the *Cambrian Directory* of 1800 and as 'the principal house of public entertainment in Pembroke' by a visitor in 1804 (although he did think the inn had witnessed better days).

In October 1805 the following advertisement appeared in the *Cambrian* newspaper:

Pembroke's NatWest Bank was at one time the Green Dragon coaching inn.

> Green Dragon Inn, Pembroke. Mary Jones takes this method of returning her sincere thanks to the public for the very liberal favours conferred on her during her residence at the above house and to request a continuance of those favours for her successor Mr. James MacIntire whom she begs leave to recommend as a person properly qualified to conduct the business.

MacIntire and his wife Anne ran the Dragon for the next 13 years, though not all of their customers went home happy. In August 1818 Lord Cawdor of Stackpole had 'a very bad dinner' at a meeting of the Farmers' Club which gathered at the Dragon once a month. The MacIntires left soon afterwards to open a small hotel in Tenby (and immediately became bankrupt) and the lease of the Green Dragon was advertised along with seven acres of meadowland — the freehold being held by Daniel Roberts of Loveston.

The new licensee was John Upton who spent some time altering the place to his satisfaction before re-opening the inn. At a concert in the ballroom in 1821, attended by many of the local gentry, 'the superior execution of the Misses Owen of Orielton on the Harp and the Pianoforte drew forth the wonder and admiration of all present'. By 1823 the inn was being run by Mrs. Mary Jones (presumably a different person from the one mentioned above) and her husband Thomas, while in 1828 the *Carmarthen Journal* again advertised that the 'Capital Inn and Posting House' called the Green Dragon was shortly to be let. According to the advert, the inn possessed 'every convenience for carrying on an extensive business'. The lease had become available because the landlady, Mrs. Jones, was retiring.

Edward Pritchard was the man who took up the lease, having been 'the obliging and respected landlord' of the Nelson Inn at Milford Haven for some years as well as a noted breeder of enormous pigs! The housewarming party he held to announce his arrival at the Green Dragon attracted most of the great and the good to the 'fine and tasteful ballroom'. It seems that Pritchard oversaw the running of both inns until about 1832, when ill health obliged him to hand over the running of the Dragon to William Lover. Mr. Lover, a former butler to Carmarthen M.P. John Jones Esq. of Ystrad, had previously been in charge of the Thomas Arms in Llanelli. He remained at the Green Dragon for seven years, leaving in 1839 to return to Llanelli. During his time in Pembroke he presided over the festivities in October 1836 which marked the transfer of the Irish packet service from Milford Haven to Hobbs Point — a significant boost to the towns of Pembroke and Pembroke Dock. By 1840 the Royal Mail was arriving at the inn at two o'clock each morning, departing at 10.30 each night.

John Jones kept the Green Dragon between February 1840 and 1851 and carried out various improvements before moving, with his wife Esther, to run the rival Golden Lion down the road. For many years the Green Dragon had vied with the Golden Lion to be the smartest inn in town, and at the Pembroke mayor-making of 1828 a 'sumptuous dinner' was provided by the Lion, while a Quadrille party at the Dragon that evening was 'numerously and beautifully attended'.

Pembroke Farmers' Club diplomatically held its dinners alternately at the two establishments, while the Dragon was also popular with benefit societies — at various times it was the headquarters of the Odd Fellows, the United Friends Society and the Loyal Order of Ancient Druids. By 1852 Francis J. Michael was the innkeeper and the following year he was advertising 'Post horses, neat flies, cars, phaetons etc., roomy stalls and loose boxes' at the Dragon. He also farmed the 50 acres of land which by then went with the property.

Mr. Michael kept the Dragon until 1868, in which year the inn closed. The railway had arrived in Pembroke by this time, making coaching inns virtually a thing of the past, and the opening in 1866 of the splendid new Assembly Rooms just along the Main Street, with its ballroom built to hold 600 people, must have been another nail in the coffin. The Dragon closed its doors and was converted into a bank. It is still a bank today, although its former use is clearly revealed by the archway through which the mail coaches once clattered into the stable yard beyond.

The **Castle Inn** a few doors further along is a relatively recent pub, opened on the site of a former brewery and maltsters run since the 1870s by George Llewellyn Griffiths and known as the Pembroke Steam Brewery before it was taken over by James Williams during the First World War. The brewery had a tiny tap-room sometimes known as **Griffiths' Brewery** and also as the **Spirit Vaults.** Brewing ceased in the 1920s, but the Spirit Vaults continued to operate until the last war when Mrs. Jane Andrews was licensee. By 1952 Mr. Ronald Stock, landlord, and Western Inns (Pembroke) had acquired the premises, and in March that year they were granted a licence to open the Castle Inn. The Castle has since become Pembroke's most cosmopolitan pub, especially in the 1970s and 1980s when it was a regular port of call for visiting Norwegian sailors and German soldiers.

There were also a handful of ale-houses on the rather less desirable Mill Pond side of the street. (The properties on the Commons side had south-facing gardens, many of them backing onto the once-fashionable Parade, which is why the

1960 advert for the Castle Inn.

The Castle Inn was formerly a brewery.

fine Georgian houses and the main coaching inns were all on the south side of the street).

From the Lamb, where Biddy's sister was left still sobbing after being jilted, it was just a few steps along to the **Prince of Wales** at 42 Main Street — the first of two pubs of that name in the street. A widow named Elizabeth Rainsford dispensed the ale here in 1857, the year that the five-room property was auctioned off by the Orielton estate; it seems to have been a short-lived enterprise.

Half-a-dozen doors along was another **Prince of Wales**. This was of a much later date, but also was never a great success. It seems to have been opened in about 1906 by Mr. James Nice Vaughan, who had arrived in the area in 1858 to run the canteen at the barracks in Pembroke Dock. He later worked for over 30 years as manager for Robert George, the Pembroke brewer, before opening a pub in his own right. When he died in 1913 the licence passed to Rosa Louisa Vaughan, but when she departed there was a regular turnover of licensees and the pub went quickly downhill, gaining a reputation for drunkenness and little else. In October 1916 this Prince of Wales not unexpectedly lost its licence under the redundancy ruling; as the magistrates were told: 'One man failed at this house and another gave it up'. The property was owned by Richard Ormond and leased by the Swansea Old Brewery who shared a compensation package of £450. The building became part of the Star Supply Stores in later years and more recently was lost in the building of the Kwiksave store, nowadays a seconds clothing shop.

The **Sloop** also stood hereabouts; according to Mathias it was at no. 28 — the building now occupied by Margaret's china shop. The only reference is in the 1861 census which shows the Sloop being kept by George Eynon, mariner, and his wife Elizabeth. This was at a time when the number of licensed premises in Pembroke and Monkton was at a peak. Apparently, however, not even the presence of 50 inns and beer-houses was enough for the town's hardened drinkers. As an exasperated police sergeant told the local magistrates in 1858:

> It is impossible to control drunkenness in this town, because as soon as the licensed houses close at night, there are low fellows who move on to the unlicensed places to drink and play cards until the early hours.

Opposite the Green Dragon at number 24 was the **Stag**, sometimes known as the Stag's Head. Local councillor William Eynon opened the Stag in 1835, having moved from the White Hart further down the road (he evidently had a thing about deer). He was followed by John Eynon, presumably his son, who died in 1844 at the age of 33. His widow, Ann, who took over as landlady, then married another Eynon — Richard, son of the licensees

*Two former Pembroke inns frame this view from the 1890s —
the Green Dragon on the left and the Stag on the right.*

of the York Tavern. In 1867 the licence passed from a Mrs. Nicholas to John Truscott, 'he having married the good lady'. Sadly Mr. Truscott was declared bankrupt in 1868; the licence passed to John Butler, and from 1871 until 1878 the pub was kept by Jane Butler.

Mrs. Elizabeth Mary Griffiths kept the pub from 1881 — when she was a widow of 29 — to 1923. It was a flourishing little inn by this time, with a billiard room on the first floor, four bedrooms on the second floor and a brew-house at the back. Despite being one of Pembroke's more popular locals (or perhaps because of that fact) the Stag was culled by the licensing authorities in 1928 with compensation totalling £492 paid out. The building later became well known as Bagshaw's home decorating and fishing tackle emporium but is nowadays Redwing Travel.

A short stagger from the Stag, at 16 Main Street, was the **Castle and Dragon**. Joseph Powell was licensee in 1872 followed by his widow Mary. She subsequently married Philip Shears from Tenby who held the licence from 1879 to 1884 and also acted as an agent for W. & A. Gilbey, wine and spirit merchants. John Lewis was the landlord in 1889, in which year the licence was not renewed. The building was later occupied by bakers H. & A. Hall.

The **Picton Inn** a couple of doors further west seems to have been demol-ished in 1866 to make way for the town's assembly rooms — later the site of Haggar's cinema and now a nightclub. Named after General Sir Thomas Picton of Haverfordwest, who led a cavalry charge at Waterloo while wearing a top hat, the Picton was kept in the 1850s by a tin-worker called John Jones and later by his widow Martha.

This part of town must have been thick with inns and alehouses in the early part of the 19th century, but most traces have been lost due to demolition and rebuilding. The construction of the present town hall and the removal of a number of properties at the top of the Dark Lane between 1867 and 1871, coupled with the supermarket development in the late 20th century, swept away a number of buildings which once housed ale-houses that are now remembered only as names in early trade directories. These may have included the **Castle** where Thomas Gwyther was landlord in 1835 and the **Plough** kept by Eliza Phillips. Both of these could have been located near the old clock tower, as could the **Bee Hive** and the **Freemasons' Arms** which both appear in Pigot's 1844 directory and the **Clarence** which was in existence between 1835 and 1840.

The **Odd Fellows Arms** was definitely here, having been opened in September 1848 by Charles Woodward. He was previously the Relieving Officer for the local Poor Law district, when he often had his windows broken by disgruntled paupers and vagrants unhappy at their treatment under the Poor Law regulations. Opening a pub must have seemed an easier option for Woodward and his wife Charlotte, and they were still there in 1851 when a parade of Odd Fellows through the town ended with a dinner in the lodge room at the inn. Joseph Hitchins was the landlord from 1858 to 1871, describing himself as 'maltster, brewer and retailer'. One regular, if unwelcome, patron of the Odd Fellows at this time was Catherine Griffiths, better known in Pembroke as 'Kitty the Hen'. She was frequently arrested for being drunk and riotous and beating up her husband (the original hen-pecked husband?). George Hitchins, a draper by trade, followed his father as licensee in 1873. By 1884 Thomas Henry Rogers was in charge, but he left to run the Red Lion at the other end of town, and the Odd Fellows closed in 1891. The pub was next door to the town clock, in part of a building later occupied by Simon and Sons and now a supermarket.

An early view of the Old King's Arms. To the left of the inn can be seen the '39 steps' which once led up to the town's courthouse.

The reason there were so many hostelries in this section of the town is in part a familiar one; just as the parishes of Monkton and St. Michael's held cattle, pig and horse-fairs in the street, so too did St. Mary's — though on a much smaller scale. These fairs were held from the top of the Dark Lane along to the Green Dragon, so that on fair days the Main Street was so thronged with horses and cattle, sheep and pigs, drovers, dealers and cheap-jacks that all traffic came to a standstill. No doubt this raucous hubbub was frowned upon by the gentry peering down from their Georgian houses, and St. Mary's street-fairs seem to have gradually disappeared in favour of the fairs in the other, rather less fashionable parishes.

However, there was plenty of other trading going on to keep a score of ale-houses in business. The town's cornmarket was held underneath the new town hall, where the official weights and measures were kept, while outside was the meat shambles with its line of butchers' stalls. And on Saturdays the provision market came alive as the country people poured into town to sell butter, cheese, eggs and vegetables, and perhaps buy farm tools, candles and clothing.

One inn that was handily placed for the market — too handily sometimes — was the **King's Arms**, which still stands next to the town hall. This old coaching inn was presumably the place referred to in the Mompesson accounts of 1617 and 1620. A chap called Sir Giles Mompesson had the bright idea of licensing inns throughout Britain, and in 1617 he was granted a patent

which gave him the authority to do so — an inn, as opposed to an alehouse, being somewhere that provided accommodation as well as beer. Unfortunately Sir Giles used his position to line his own pockets, so that after only four years the patent was revoked and he was thrown into the Tower of London. Fortunately there had been time for his agents to visit Pembrokeshire on at least two occasions, because his surviving account books

The Old King's Arms as it looked in 2002.
The ground floor window on the right is where
a coach arch once led to the stable yard.

65

for 1617 and 1620 contain three entries for the county, one of which is for the King's Arms in Pembroke where the landlord was John Williams.

David Millingchamp, a saddler from Cardigan, was landlord between 1795 and his death in 1809 when the King's Arms was taken over by Joseph Hitchings. In 1815 Mr. Hitchings retired from running the inn and the sale of furniture that accompanied his departure lasted two days; among the items sold were four-poster beds, card tables and an eight-day clock. The King's Arms seems to have gone downhill at this period, not least because the meat shambles was right outside the front door. The stench and blood must have been off-putting to say the least, and there are stories of visitors to the inn having to shoulder their way between rows of pigs' carcases to reach the front door. This would probably not have worried Thomas Cadwallader, a local butcher, who appears to have been the licensee in 1818.

The inn is not mentioned at all in the trade directory for 1830, though by this time a new town slaughterhouse had been built on the Commons, ending the nuisance in the street outside. Although John Morris is recorded as being licensee of the King's Arms in 1835, it seems to have stopped being an inn shortly afterwards and for a time was run as a saddler's shop by Thomas Richards.

In about 1845 he reopened the inn, but called it the **Bunch of Grapes**, perhaps to avoid confusion with the King's Arms in Pembroke Dock. In 1846 the *Pembrokeshire Herald* reported:

> On Tuesday last the members of a club designated the Pembroke Provident Society paraded the town of Pembroke preceded by the Pembroke Cavalry Veteran Band and proceeded to the house of Mr. Richards, the Bunch of Grapes, where they partook of their annual dinner.

The following February the *Herald* carried a more startling story:

> Rebecca Again! About two o' clock in the morning of Saturday last, a number of men, some with faces blackened, forcibly entered the premises called the Bunch of Grapes in Pembroke, and after securing a man who was placed there to watch a quantity of goods which had been seized under a distress for rent and impounded there, succeeded in carrying them away, nor has any tidings of them been discovered or of the parties implicated. Ten pounds reward has been offered for the discovery of the offenders.

This appears to be the only recorded example of the Rebecca rioters being active in Pembroke town, although it smacks more of a copycat crime than the real Rebecca. The Bunch of Grapes was kept by Thomas Richards from 1844 to the early 1850s, but it seems to have been little more than a sideline for him.

It was John Miller, a butcher from Monkton, who restored the inn's fortunes in the late 1850s. He renamed it the **Old King's Arms,** presumably because this is what everyone called it when it masqueraded as the Bunch of Grapes. The Old King's Arms soon became popular with farmers on their visits to town, and by the 1880s the Pembroke Farmers' Club held its get-togethers here, the Old King's Arms having succeeded the Green Dragon as the main rival to the Lion. The grandly-named Pembroke British Oak Friendly Benefit Society also had its registered office there, and for a time the courtyard at the back of the inn also served as the town's butter-market.

John Miller retired in March 1883, to be succeeded by Thomas William Young, an auctioneer and appraiser. At his house-warming dinner 'some seventy good men and true placed their legs under the mahogany which literally groaned beneath the good things provided — salmon, turkeys, roast beef, legs of wether mutton, tongues, fowls &c. &c.'. When Mr. Young died in the influenza epidemic of 1892, his widow Mrs. M.A.Young took over as land-lady and she was still there in 1906. Mrs. Flora Davies held the licence from 1914 to 1923, while in 1936 the local police surprisingly made a bid to have

the place closed down, Sergeant Williams stating that the premises were 'not needed for the neighbour-hood'. However the inn survived, the licensee at the time being Edward Mathias who remained there until his death in 1938, when he was succeeded by his son, another Edward Mathias. By 1953 the inn was being managed by Trevor White and boasted a *chef de cuisine* in M. Bernard Blaizot; it advertised 'unsurpassed cuisine and wines at reasonable prices in the romantic atmosphere of one of the most famous old hostelries in Wales'.

The present high reputation enjoyed by the Old King's Arms owes much to Mr. George Wheeler, who ran a rabbit-skinning factory and leather-tannery at the 'back of town' between the 1930s and 1950s before taking over the inn in 1957 and carrying out a programme of gradual renovations and improvements. His widow, Mrs.

The Kings Arms in 1960 was the place to visit!

67

Shirley Wheeler, still oversees the running of the hotel. The old coach-arch has gone, but the King's Arms still has a solidly 'old-fashioned' look and the atmosphere of a true coaching inn. Of special architectural note is the staircase, an excellent example of the so-called 'Chinese Chippendale' style; there is a similar staircase in the Royal George on the Quay.

A couple of doors west of the King's Arms was the **White Hart** where William Eynon was the landlord from 1830 to 1835. in which year he opened the Stag just up the road. Mary Truscott seems to have been the next licensee, followed by James Truscott who kept the inn until at least 1861, by which time he was 77. James Truscott was one of the great characters of the town. A Cornishman by birth and a smuggler by nature, he was living in Pembrokeshire by 1808 when his son Lewis was born in Lamphey. By 1810 he was running a pub in Monkton, probably the Brown Cow, but he later moved into St. Mary's parish where he took over the now long-forgotten **Plough Inn**, supplementing his income with a healthy amount of bootlegging. He even put together his own smuggling gang, whose members must have spent many a moonless night transporting casks of brandy from lonely south Pembrokeshire coves to secret cellars beneath the Plough.

The last of Jim Truscott's smuggling escapades came in March 1834 when he was nearly 50. Together with two of his sons, William and John, and fellow smugglers George Howells and James Williams, Truscott was waiting in the dead of night on the shingle at Bentlass Ferry for the arrival of a cargo of contraband tobacco. Also waiting in the darkness, however, was the well-armed crew of the *Skylark* revenue cutter, and as soon as the last bale of tobacco had been landed and loaded onto the waiting horses, the preventive men sprung their trap. The gang was surrounded and Truscott (described in newspaper reports as 'an old fox') and three of the other smugglers were immediately captured.

The only one to make a run for it was William Truscott, but in his panic-stricken flight he rushed blindly into the black and icy waters of the Pembroke River. As he floundered desperately in the river, calling for help, the nearest revenue man levelled his pistol and fired a shot at him. That the shot missed did not matter; 19-year-old Truscott drowned anyway, and at the inquest that followed in Pembroke Town Hall the revenue officer responsible was condemned as being 'highly reprehensible, cowardly and cruel' by a jury which included William Lover of the Green Dragon.

The four surviving smugglers were hauled before the magistrates in Haverfordwest. John Truscott, being just 15, was released without charge. The three others were imprisoned pending the payment of £100 each in fines and it was not until November 1834 that James Truscott was released. By this time the Plough seems to have been taken over by Eliza Phillips, so the large tribe of Truscotts moved into the White Hart when William Eynon moved out.

The Truscotts still seem to have kept up their smuggling links, though James' days of active service in the 'free trade' were over. His youngest son Thomas Truscott, then 19, was called to give evidence at a court case in 1846 after a cache of contraband whisky was discovered in a warehouse on Pembroke Quay. While denying any involvement in the actual smuggling, Thomas was forced to admit that his father, who ran the White Hart, was usually in the market for smuggled whisky — 'provided it was good stuff' — and that he had been sent down to the quay to sample the product.

James' first wife Jane died in 1830 at the age of 47, having given birth to 12 baby Truscotts. At some stage the old rogue married again and in 1866 there is a reference to Mrs. Truscott of the White Hart Inn — possibly the widow Frances who was 30 years younger than the doughty James. The White Hart had closed by 1871 and become part of Samuel Willing's grocery shop; Willings' Passage now marks the spot.

Two doors from the White Hart, facing down the Dark Lane, is the **Lion Hotel**, formerly the **Golden Lion Inn**. This impressive former coaching inn was called the **New Inn** when it was opened in about 1800 and also seems to have been called the **Castle** at one stage. It was built for the Owens of Orielton House who eventually re-named it Golden Lion after their family crest and it was used by the Owens as their campaign headquarters during many bitterly-fought election campaigns.

The Lion Hotel in the 1920s.

A trade directory for 1811 revealed that the three best inns in town were the King's Arms, the Green Dragon and the Castle, the latter being kept by George Dawkins. As it is known that by 1817 Mr. Dawkins was running the Golden Lion, it seems to follow that the name of the inn changed during the interim. (The well-known golden lion above the porch may also date from this

Lion Hotel
PEMBROKE
Telephone: PEMBROKE 236

A.A.   R.A.C.
★ ★

★   First Class Accommodation
            for a most Comfortable Stay

Terms on Application to
the Manager
                    ★
            FULLY LICENSED

Boating - Yachting - Fishing - Shooting - Bowls - Tennis - Golf

Caterers for Pembroke Rotary Club

A 1960 advert for the Lion Hotel.

time). Following George Dawkins' death in 1818, the inn was kept by Charles and Sarah Worcester. In 1819 it was the scene of a splendid ball held to mark the launch of the 74-gun warship *Belleisle* at Pembroke Dockyard. The ball 'was graced by many fair votaries of Terpsichore and honoured by many brave companions of Nelson and Wellington' according to the *Carmarthen Journal*. Charles Worcester was still in charge until about 1828 when he handed over to his son-in-law Thomas Thomas who remained in charge until August 1839.

Next on the scene was Mr. William M. Roberts. A licensee for 35 years,

The golden lion still gazes down from the Lion Hotel.

Roberts had previously run the Castle Inn at Llandovery and the White Lion in Tenby and he obviously knew his business because the 1840 Nicholson's *Cambrian Travellers' Guide* recommended the Golden Lion as one of the best two inns in town (The other was the Dragon). In 1841 Mr. Roberts was succeeded by his daughter Mary and she remained remained the 'worthy young land-lady' until 1850. During this time the Golden Lion was able to offer patrons 'Good Stabling with lock-up Coach Houses, good Chaises, able Horses and attentive Drivers'.

In 1851 the licensee was John Jones, formerly of the Green Dragon, who paid an annual rent of £60 to the Owens of Orielton House, the owners of the Lion (and half of Pembroke as well). But the Owens had managed to blow the family fortune in various election campaigns, so in August 1857 the Lion came under the auctioneer's hammer. The sale catalogue shows that the inn then comprised:

> Thirteen bedrooms, two closets, dining and drawing rooms, parlour, commercial room, farmers' room, two sitting rooms, pantry, cellar, kitchen, back kitchen, large yard, greenhouse, stabling for twenty-one horses, two coach-houses, piggery &c.

Licensee John Jones was a highly respected figure in the town, and appears to have retired in about 1865 when he moved to London. When he died in 1873, the shops in Pembroke all closed on the day of his funeral as a mark of respect.

The Lion was advertised as 'family and commercial hotel and posting house' when William James was the innkeeper between 1868 and his death in 1897, and a trade directory of 1880 revealed that the Golden Lion was still the 'principal hotel' in Pembroke. It was during the later years of Mr. James' reign that the 'Golden' was dropped from the name — and certainly the Lion seems to have lost some of its glitter around the turn of the 20th century, so much so that in 1910 the official receiver was called in to investigate the affairs of licensee William Walter Peacock who had gone bankrupt with a deficiency of just over £1,000.

However George Henry Bowen boasted excellent cuisine and a motor car for hire in 1920, as the 'motoring age' gave a new lease of life to many old coaching inns and as the newly-restored Pembroke Castle began to attract more and more tourists to the town. The building has seen a number of changes since the war, including the purchase of the adjoining Westgate House in 1949 which was incorporated into the hotel for a time. Sadly the old coach arch has been blocked up, but the Lion still remains a lively hostelry and its golden mascot still stares proudly down from his perch outside the first floor ballroom.

Westgate House itself may once have been licensed. Mr. A.G.O. Mathias' list of old Pembroke pubs included the **Fox** at Westgate House; possibly this had some connection with the Fox Brewery run by George Butler in 1858. William Williams ran the **Westgate** according to a trade directory of 1844.

It is possible that the **Globe Tavern** was somewhere near here. In 1838 the following advert appeared in the *Welshman* newspaper: 'To be let. All the commodious Dwelling House, Shops, Gardens, Skittle Ground etc. called the Globe Tavern, situated in the centre of the much-admired and improving town of Pembroke'. Particulars were available from Mr. P. Duggan on the premises — presumably local shoemaker Philip Duggan. Oddly enough, for such an important-sounding place I have been unable to track down any other reference.

Another pub which has proved infuriatingly difficult to pin down is the long-lost **King's Head.** In 1783, Aaron Game took out an ale-house licence for a house in St. Mary's parish and he still held a licence in 1798; there is some evidence that it went under the sign of the King's Head. There is a further mention of an inn of this name in a lease of 1820 (although this may well be a mistake for the King's Arms), while to confuse matters still further the King's Head described in an 1835 trade directory as being run by Ann Davies may be another place altogether.

There must have been a number of other licensed premises between the top of the Dark Lane and the old west gate of the town, but again it's no longer possible to pinpoint where they stood. The **Angel**, kept in 1830 by auctioneer, corn merchant and brewer John Marshall, was somewhere here. Somewhat surprisingly, the Angel was described in Pigot's trade directory of 1830 as the principal inn of the town and at one time the coaches for Carmarthen and Tenby left from outside this establishment. The **Golden Cross** is thought to have been in this area as well, taking its name from an old market cross near the entrance to the Long Entry car-park, where once foreign merchants would transact their business. William Phillips ran the Golden Cross from 1830 to 1835. **Cromwell's Tavern**, now the only pub in the area, is of 1970s vintage and was formerly known as Cromwell's Kitchen.

Also in this area, perhaps opposite the Long Entry, was an ancient inn known as the **George**, references to which go back to 1710. In that year a lease was entered into between Charles Bowen of Camrose and Thomas Bowen, a Pembroke mercer, for a property known as the George which lay 'between the house of Richard Cuny, gent., on the west side and a lane called the Dark Lane on the east side'. The occupant at the time was John Barras or Burras. Between 1784 and his death in about 1800 the licensee was Richard

The West End Vaults at the top of the Dark Lane.

Jenkins and he appears to have been succeeded by his widow Mary. There are no references after about 1805.

The Dark Lane, or Northgate Street, leads down to the Mill Bridge and was once a steep, narrow and dangerous thoroughfare, especially when the old North Gate was still standing at the bottom. This didn't matter so much before 1814, as only a relatively small proportion of traffic passed this way, but the mushroom growth of Pembroke Dock, coupled with an increase in trade at the quay, suddenly meant that the Dark Lane became very busy indeed. Carts and carriages regularly collided on the narrow hill, or overturned while taking the tight corner at the top and tipped their loads of corn, lime and sometimes passengers onto the muddy road; in February 1860 a petition was drawn up urging the authorities to take action.

After a protracted debate — eerily similar to recent discussions about a Pembroke by-pass — it was decided that a number of properties on the Main Street corner would have to be demolished and the roadway raised at the bottom to make the hill less steep. The wide pavement outside the entrance to St. Mary's Church and half way down the hill indicates where the buildings were removed in 1867, some of them, no doubt, former ale-houses. Further demolition work in 1871 revealed a fine 'Flemish' chimney attached

The Dark Lane with a customer just leaving the Mariners' Inn.
A couple of doors further down was the Globe, while
the Waterman's Arms is across the bridge on the right.

73

to one of the buildings. An attempt was made to preserve the chimney, but when workmen stripped off the ivy, it collapsed into the street, narrowly missing a group of onlookers.

Even after the alterations, the Dark Lane still possessed a healthy quota of licensed premises. Indeed, a police officer told the local magistrates in 1909: 'Standing on top of the Dark Lane any person can see twelve licensed houses in a small area'. On the top corner, on the castle side, was the **West End** — perhaps built on the site of the old George inn. The pub was owned by William Williams of Tenby and the licensees in the 1870s included Henry Statton and Richard Miller. Miss Caroline Buttress Gover was publican and wine and spirit merchant from 1880 to 1906. In 1924 the West End Vaults, then owned by Mr. Gibbon Williams of Cardiff and leased by Narberth brewers James Williams, was closed by the licensing authorities; compensation was reckoned at £325. In recent years the West End has housed a bookmaker's premises.

Just below the West End was the **Mariners Arms**. Mary Jacob was the landlady in 1830, while John George, a joiner from Narberth, kept the pub from 1835 to the 1860s. There is a suggestion that the Mariners began life on the opposite side of the road, and that when this building was threatened with demolition during the road improvements, the pub moved to new premises across the way. John George, who evidently arranged the move, was followed by his son James who was still at the Mariners when it closed in 1909 — another victim of that year's purge on public houses by the local magistrates. In vain did Mr. George argue that his family had been at the Mariners for 80 years without a blemish on the licence. The magistrates agreed with Police Superintendent Thomas that the building 'was not structurally suited to being a public house' and closed it down, with the owner of the property, John Harcourt Powell, receiving £135 compensation, and publican, James George — who had lost his livelihood through no fault of his own — getting just £15. The George family continued to live in the building up to the last war, but it was boarded up and subject to a demolition order by the late 1940s when it was described as a single-fronted, six-roomed house with doors only 5ft. 6ins. high and 2ft. wide. Along with the former butcher's shop next door, it was knocked down in the 1950s and replaced with unsightly advertising hoardings.

It seems likely that the original Mariners was the same place as the **Three Mariners**, described in the Harcourt Powell estate papers for 1778 as one of five properties in the Dark Lane owned by the estate. The tenant at the time was John Davies.

It was the licensing magistrates who closed the **Globe** as well. This stood between the Mariners and the Royal George and seems to have been opened by James Mason in the late 1860s. Mrs. Elizabeth Saies from Rhoscrowther was the landlady of the Globe from 1870 to 1884. She ran a grocery business from the premises and also fattened a few pigs; in 1880 she was charged with 'keeping swine so as to be a nuisance and injurious to health'. By 1891 the licensee was a house decorator called Harry Edgell, who ran the pub with his wife Harriet. Dockyard pensioner David Owen held the licence from 1902 until 1911 when the magistrates decided that the Globe was surplus to requirements and suppressed the licence. Brewers James Williams, who had owned the property since 1890, were paid £350 compensation.

With four pubs almost in a row, the Dark Lane was a hard-drinking and fairly rowdy part of town, where brawls involving marines, soldiers, cattle drovers, local men (and women) and the crews of coasting vessels were commonplace. Indeed it is said that on fair days and market days these pubs would be so full of beer-swilling drovers that the spilled ale would be flowing out under the street doors and down the gutters into the mill-pond.

The fourth and last of the pubs in the street is the only one still surviving. The **Royal George,** on the corner of the Dark Lane and the Town Quay, once rubbed shoulders with the old North Gate. There must have been an ale-house in this prime position for hundreds of years, but the present building seems to date from the 18th century. It probably takes its name from the *Royal George*, a ship of the line which was launched in Woolwich in 1756 and which sank at Spithead in 1782 with the loss of 800 lives.

A prosperous local ship-owner and merchant named George Hurlow

ROYAL GEORGE
WINE AND SPIRIT VAULTS
QUAY, PEMBROKE.

S. P. GEDGE, Proprietor.

***

Wines and Spirits of the Choicest Brands

Luncheons provided for Families, &c.

Sitting-Room, Beds.—Good Accommodation.

PLEASURE BOAT FOR HIRE.

You could hire a pleasure boat at the Royal George when Sidney Gedge was landlord in 1880.

kept the inn for several years from about 1797. From the early 1820s to the early 1840s the licensees were a father and son, both named William Bowen, who also operated the nearby mill on the bridge. At his death in 1838, the elder Mr. Bowen was described as a 'peaceable, honest and industrious old inhabitant of Pembroke'.

Another miller, Thomas Jones, was landlord from 1844 to the 1860s and he also seems to have been a commercial brewer in a small way, as well as fathering a large brood of children. The Royal George closed as an inn during much of the 1860s and early 1870s; it is believed to have been used by the Jones family as a private house during this time. However, it was reopened in 1874 by George Hurlow Scale, formerly a farmer at Eastington, Rhoscrowther and the grandson of the earlier George Hurlow. His brother John Scale became landlord from 1876 to 1878.

Former workhouse master Sidney Peter Gedge, who was running the East Gate in 1875, had become licensee of the Royal George by the summer of 1878, and Jane Gedge, 46, was the innkeeper in the 1881 census. The George was sold by auction in 1905 to Mrs.

The Royal George in the 1950s.
The building to the right of the inn
was once the Red White and Blue.

Elizabeth Vittle who held the licence for a time before leasing the pub to various tenants. One of these was Ernest Holden, who quickly departed in 1912 after being fined for watering down his whisky. He was replaced by Samuel Farrant, formerly of the Dumfries in Pembroke Dock, who paid £10 a year rent but struggled to make a living, only selling half a barrel of beer each week. Mrs. Vittle sold up around about this time and Thomas Griffiths was landlord by 1914.

The George changed hands with bewildering frequency in the 1920s and there were seven different tenants in the space of eight years — many of them, for some reason, from Monmouthshire or Glamorgan. Lieut. J. Galloway R.N. steadied the ship; he was at the helm for much of the 1930s. Following his death in 1943 the pub was run by his widow Lydia who subsequently remarried. Her second husband was a Polish seamen named Mr. K. Dylewicz who was still running the pub in the 1980s, the Royal George being renowned as the only pub in town to have the Warsaw Concerto on its jukebox. The pub was a warren of small rooms and passageways at this time, and the tiny bar, reached through a door from the Dark Lane, seemed to be trapped in a 1950s time warp. The pub was given a drastic mock-Tudor makeover in the 1980s which smartened the place up but took away much of the scruffy charm and character of the old boozer.

The Royal George provided a full service in 1960.

During the years that the Royal George was closed as a pub the licence was transferred to the **Red, White and Blue,** a patriotically-named if somewhat rowdy beerhouse on the quay, which regularly figured in the dealings of the local petty sessions. It opened in about 1864 in a building that adjoined the Royal George, being also owned by Mr. Jones the miller. In 1866 the landlord was W.H. Truscott, who suffered a tragic bereavement when a wagon returning from haymaking and carrying 14 women and children overturned at the foot of Westgate Hill, injuring many of the passengers and killing his daughter, Dorcas. He gave up the pub the following year in favour of one of his relations, Lewis Truscott, formerly of the Stag. Lewis Truscott, son of smuggler Jim, was something of a rogue

The Royal George on Pembroke Quay.

77

in his own right and had several brushes with the law in his youth. He worked variously as a tallow chandler and butcher, lived for a time at Staines in Middlesex, and then returned to Pembroke to follow his father into the licensing trade.

He remained at the Red, White and Blue until 1872 when the licence passed to George Hurlow Scale. When Scale moved, a couple of years later, next door to reopen the Royal George, he closed the smaller pub. The building later fell into disrepair and was eventually demolished in 1961 and replaced by a toilet block.

There must have been several more ale-houses around the quay at one time, not only to cater for the crews of visiting trading vessels, but also to welcome travellers arriving on the turnpike road from the horse-ferry crossing at Pembroke Ferry and later from the new town of Pembroke Dock. There would have been ale-houses huddled under the town walls on either side of the North Gate and also on the opposite shore, across the Mill Bridge. As so often, all that is left are the names of these early hostelries and their licensees, but not their precise location; indeed, in some cases it is only the nautical sound of a pub's name that has prompted me to place it in this area at all. These salty-sounding inns include the **Anchor** kept by John Jones from 1797 to 1805, and an almost certainly different **Anchor** where carpenter and joiner George Price was the landlord in 1835. There was also a **Ship** where the landlord in the 1830s was William Jones and a **Jolly Sailor** which was kept by Jane Lewis in 1835.

The **Waterman's** is still with us, on The Green side of the Mill Bridge. Mathias was of the opinion that this was one of the oldest pubs in the county, possibly being a ferryman's cottage in the far-off days before the Mill Bridge was built, but the present building seems to date from the beginning of the 19th century. A boatman from Angle called John Belt ran the Waterman's until his death in 1835, and he may have given the pub its name. His widow, Elizabeth Belt, carried on running the pub until 1864, by which time she was 87. She might have carried on even longer but for an unfortunate accident when she was knocked down outside the pub by John Bramble's four-horse omnibus on its journey from Tenby to Hobbs Point. She was seriously injured and gave up running the pub soon afterwards, dying the following year. A newspaper report stated that she had lived in the house 'more than half a century', perhaps dating the pub to about 1810.

George Price was the landlord from 1868 until 1871 and a widow named Fanny Price held the licence from 1878 to 1881. She was a sister of 'Billy the York' and when she married for a second time her new husband, George Thomas took over the licence of the Waterman's and held it till 1901. The pub then changed hands fairly frequently before Billy Neil took over in 1921. He

*The Waterman's looks in rather a sorry state in this early
20th-century postcard. Further up the hill the wagon
is passing the Army and Navy on the left.*

was aged 21 years and three weeks, and since you had to be 21 to hold a pub licence in those days he was the youngest licensee in Britain at the time. A member of the Neil family who ran the Rising Sun in Pembroke Dock, he was a virtual teetotaller and in the 42 years he kept the pub his annual consumption of alcohol was a glass of sherry at Christmas.

In 1963 the licence passed to his son John Neil who gave the pub a major

*In the doorway are Harry Collins and his wife
Minnie who kept the Waterman's Arms in the
years leading up to the First World War.*
(Picture courtesy of Mr. John Neil.)

facelift in 1977. For many years it had been a fairly dowdy looking establishment, but the renovations allowed the Waterman's to take full advantage of its fine riverside setting. Mr. Neil ran the pub until his retirement in 1988, but the Waterman's stayed in the same family because it was purchased by his cousin David Morgan who ran it for the next ten years. It is still a thriving concern.

The Waterman's as it looked in 2002.

Across the road and a little further up, the first house in the row beyond the entrance to Croft Court was the **Army and Navy.** This was originally called the **Royal Exchange**, but in September 1866 James Belt — probably a son of the Waterman's couple — successfully applied to change the name. (In fact, the official name of the pub was the 'Navy and Army', but no-one ever called it that). Charles Joyte from Exeter, a former drill instructor with the Pembroke Rifle Corps, was the landlord from 1869 to 1874 while an Irishman named Thomas McNally was there from 1876 to 1884. He claimed to have been one of the 600 at Balaclava. Since Mr. McNally was 47 in 1881 he would have been 20 at the time of the Charge of the Light Brigade, so it is possible. The landlord in 1891 was William Bate, Thomas Rogers was there in 1901 and Thomas Prickett was landlord in 1906, having crossed the bridge from the Globe Inn.

Between 1911 and 1914 the pub was run by John and Beatrice Usher who later managed the town's cinema. The Army and Navy was closed by the licensing authorities in 1924, with compensation of £384 being shared unevenly between the owner, Swansea Old Brewery (who took 90 percent) ,and the licensee. It is now a private house.

Two other ale-houses are known to have existed in this western part of the Green in Victorian times, one being the **Royal William**, where the landlord from 1827 to 1840 was a Cornish stonemason named Samuel Hallett. The **Pembroke Dock** beer-house was in existence from 1840 to 1855 when it was run by Samuel Harbour and his wife Elizabeth. Interestingly the owner of the Army and Navy in the 1870s was Miss Ellen Harbour of Bristol, so perhaps the Pembroke Dock stood on the site of the future Army and Navy.

Like Monkton, the Green was much altered in the 1950s and 1960s by the demolition of numerous buildings and the creation of a large council housing estate, which makes tracking down any of the other beer-houses which may once have stood on the lower slopes of Golden Hill an impossibility. The **Masons' Arms** and the **Unicorn** both feature as licensed houses in the Green in Mr. Mathias' list, while in September 1867, Elizabeth Hall of the **Golden Inn,** Golden Hill, applied to have her inn-keeper's licence renewed. For some reason this was was refused. The **Bank Tavern** may also have been in the Green. In 1862 the landlady Margaret Jones was charged with assaulting Elizabeth Belt - presumably the 82-year-old landlady of the Waterman's.

These ale-houses were probably *ad hoc* affairs, opened to take advantage of the building work which extended the railway from Pembroke to Pembroke Dock. This was a difficult piece of engineering which necessitated the construction of five road bridges as well as an embankment across the upper reaches of the Mill Pond and the excavation of a tunnel 450 yards long under Golden Hill. This labour intensive job involved many hundreds of hard-working, hard-drinking navvies in the early 1860s. The pubs and brothels of the town's East End would have benefited greatly from this dramatic increase in custom, and no doubt anyone with a cottage near the navvy camp in the Green would have opened it up as a short-term beer-house to muscle in on the trade.

The **Shoulder of Mutton** is an old name for part of the Green, and as this was once a fairly common pub sign — especially when there was a butcher in charge — there might well have been an early ale-house of this name located here.

1	Shipwright (King's Arms)
2	Waterman's Arms
3	Sloop
4	Crown and Anchor
5	Three Horseshoes
6	Globe (Albion)
7	Old Lion
8	Milford Arms
9	Swan Inn
10	Flying Boat (Commercial)
11	Rising Sun
12	Rose and Crown
13	Gun Tavern
14	Queens
15	Royal
16	Bell and Lion
17	Royal Oak
18	White Hart (Royal William)
19	Navy Tavern
20	Market Tavern
21	Olive Bar
22	Clarence
23	Victoria
24	Duke of York
25	Farmers Arms
26	Prince Albert
27	Ivy Bush
28	Crown Stores
29	Dock Gate
30	Navy Inn
31	Steam Hammer
32	Charlton
33	Royal Marines
34	Talbot (Blenheim)
35	Pembrokeshire Arms
36	Lamb and Flag
37	Imperial (Pestle & Mortar)
38	Burton Brewery
39	Albert
40	Bird in Hand
41	Salutation
42	Alexandra Vaults
43	Star
44	Prince of Wales

45	Three Crowns
46	Bush Hotel
47	Bush Tavern
48	Greyhound
49	Three Tuns
50	Railway Hotel
51	Dumfries
52	Criterion (Bombay)
53	Pier Hotel
54	South Wales
55	Welshman (Railway)

56	Setting Sun
57	Caledonia
58	Wheatsheaf
59	Myrtle Tree
60	Britannia Arms
61	Red Rose
62	Cambrian
63	Prospect Tavern
64	Temple Bar.

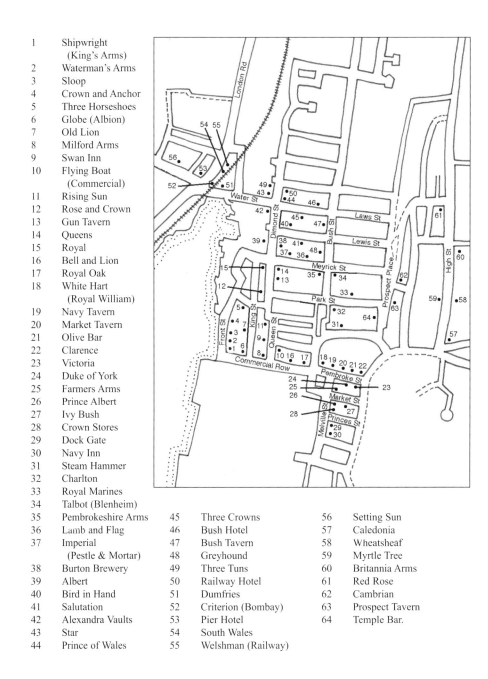

Map showing the location of some of Pembroke Dock's more notable pubs

CHAPTER SIX

Pembroke Dock
FRONT STREET & KING STREET

Pembroke Dock, or Pater as it used to be called, set its stall out early as a hard-drinking town. In *The History of Pembroke Dock*, Mrs. Stuart Peters quoted from an old diary which claimed that of the first five houses built in the town, two were pubs. One of these was built for the oddly-named Mr. Honeydear in what is now Front Street (the first four houses in the new town are thought to be numbers 25 to 28 of the present street). The other pub was the long-vanished Globe (previously Albion), built soon afterwards on what was to become the corner of King Street and Commercial Row; this was described by a local solicitor in 1909 as the 'first and oldest public house in Pembroke Dock'.

Both of these pubs were built in the summer of 1814, as the first terraced streets of the town began to take shape alongside the new naval dockyard, which had been established by the Admiralty on shoreland purchased from the Meyrick family of Llanion and Bush. Previously, the dockyard had been further downstream at Milford Haven, and during its removal to its new site and for some time afterwards the Milford-based shipwrights, carpenters, clerks and labourers continued to travel back and forth each day by boat. This didn't suit everyone, so building soon began on terraces of houses and cottages to accommodate the work force close to the slipways and workshops that formed their place of employment.

It is generally agreed that the first three streets to be laid out were Front Street and the two streets running behind and parallel to it — King Street and the western part of Queen Street. North Brewery Street and Commercial Row were begun soon afterwards, the latter being extended southwards to form Pembroke Street. The chief route into Pembroke lay this way, and cottages duly grew up alongside this road to form Bellevue Terrace and the long straggle of High Street. Properties branching off Treowen Road formed a

Dockyard workers stream out of the dock gates — many of them heading for Pembroke Dock's plethora of pubs.

little community which later grew into Pennar, while to the east of Pembroke Street was built Brewery Row, later renamed Charlton Place.

As the dockyard expanded and shipwrights and their families flocked to the area, notably from Portsmouth and Devonport, so more streets were added to the town — Park Street, Nailers' Lane (renamed Wellington Street) and Clarence Street. The latter was originally called Friday Street because the market traders all parked their carts along here on that day. It was renamed in honour of the Duke of Clarence (later William IV) who visited the shipyard in 1827.

The market hall was built at the bottom of Pembroke Street in 1826 and this became the commercial hub of the town; Market Street, Princes Street and Melville Street were begun in about 1830. As the names Brewery Row and Brewery Street indicate, the town had its own brewhouse and malthouse from a very early stage, and by 1818 Richard Lilwall's Royal Pembroke Dock Brewery was up and running in the area that is now Albion Square.

Since the dockyard needed to be guarded, a system of forts was built around the Haven, with an impressive limestone barracks that overlooked the town being constructed in the 1840s. This meant a large number of soldiers and marines being garrisoned in and around Pembroke Dock, which in turn meant plenty of trade for the pubs; seven new licences were granted for Pembroke Dock in 1848 alone. It could also mean a good deal of trouble, especially in the years following the Crimean War, when the garrison was composed entirely of militiamen. 'At that time the military authorities were not so particular as now,' wrote Mrs. Stuart Peters in 1905, 'and the militia were oftentimes a very rough class of men who were much given to practical joking and disquieting pranks'. A typical 'prank' occurred in July 1861 when about 50 servicemen stormed into the Castle Inn in Clarence Street and proceeded to smash every glass, bottle, clock and ornament in the house.

Pembroke Dock continued to spread in classic Victorian grid-iron style, with streets intersecting at right angles — often with a pub on the corner. The Charlton, the Commercial (now the Flying Boat), the Milford Arms, the Alexandra Vaults and many more were classics of their kind, usually with a doorway set into the corner of the building and with a long bar on which lines of drinks would be set up ready for the influx of thirsty dockyard workers when the evening hooter blew. Many of these pubs would also be packed at six in the morning as well, as labourers who had to walk or row to work from villages many miles away stopped off for a quick breakfast of bread, cheese and porter before 'clocking-on'. Since regulations prevented anyone employed in the dockyard from keeping an inn, licences were often held by women — the wives, or even mothers, of dockyard workmen.

As the town grew, so did the number of pubs and beer-houses, from the two original hostelries in 1814 to nearly 60 in the 1850s. The number continued to rise until the Wine and Beer-house Act of 1869 effectively killed off the smaller cottage ale-houses, of which there were many in the town, especially in the older part around King Street. So while Front Street boasted nine or ten pubs in the 1860s, this was down to four by the 1870s (although plenty of places continued to operate as illicit beer-houses).

The evening hooter sounded for the last time in 1926 when the naval dockyard, which once employed over 2,000 men, closed, plunging the town into depression. Several pubs shut at this time, and those which didn't usually changed hands on an almost annual basis in the economic turmoil of the time. The redundancy and compensation committee had previously made itself unpopular by closing a number of thriving Pembroke Dock pubs like the Gun Tavern, the Foresters, the Landshipping and the Sun — so much so that in 1908 the Pembroke Dock publicans responded by forming a branch of the L.V.A. 'for combination to combat the forces acting against them'. After 1926, the picture changed and the committee suddenly found licensees almost begging to have their struggling businesses closed — with a compensation pay-out, of course.

Of the pubs which weathered this storm, eight, including the Prince Albert, the Crown Stores and the Criterion, fell victim to the German air-raids of the 1940s, although a few were later rebuilt. In the 1960s and 1970s the oil industry, and particularly the construction of the refineries and power station, brought the good times back to Pembroke Dock, and for a few years it was possible to imagine what the pubs were like during the hey-day of the dockyard, as construction workers and steel-erectors lined the long bars and downed their pints. But those heady days are also in the past, and in recent years the Navy Tavern, the Bush Hotel, the Prospect Tavern and the Royal Oak have all closed for business.

There have been a few attempts to pin down the history of Pembroke Dock pubs. Mr. H.H.R. Reynolds was a friend of Arthur Mathias, and his *Some Old Inns and Reminiscences of Pembroke Dock*, published in 1939, was a response to the latter's history of the pubs of Pembroke. A rather rambling mish-mash of memories and anecdotes, it is sometimes innaccurate but always entertaining; the fact that Mr. Reynolds was a life-long teetotaller doesn't appear to have diminished in the slightest his affection for the old Pembroke Dock pubs and the characters who frequented them. Mr. Reynolds and his wife were killed in the Blitz by a bomb which also destroyed the **Three Crowns** inn next door to their house in Laws Street.

Several articles appeared in the *West Wales Guardian* in the 1960s, repeated and updated in the 1980s, under the heading *The Inns and Taverns of Old Pater*. They were written by local solicitor and historian Mr. James Meyrick Owen, who drew heavily on the work of Mrs. Stuart Peters and Mr. Reynolds, while adding a number of useful recollections of his own. More recently, *Pembroke People* by Mr. Richard Rose included valuable information on some of the early Pembroke Dock pubs and their licensees. However, to quote Mr. Rose: 'When one attempts to give a comprehensive list of each licensed house that once existed in the town, they seem to be endless...'

Considering that there were more than 15 licensed houses in Front Street alone at various times, plus another 15 in nearby King Street, the task of identifying all the pubs in Pembroke Dock is indeed a daunting one. Add to this the fact that many of these pubs have undergone name-changes, that names are duplicated (and even quadruplicated in the case of the Commercial), and that some pubs have moved addresses, then it really does seem an impossible undertaking. But at least we can start on fairly solid ground, at the corner pub in Front Street which for most of its life was called the **King's Arms** before its name was changed to the **Shipwright** following a recent refurbishment.

There is a reference in the *Carmarthen Journal* in July 1824 to 'the dwelling house, yard and garden, called and known by the sign of the King's Head Inn, situate in the town of Pater, late in the occupation of John Harris', which may be a mistake for the King's Arms, since no King's Head appears to be mentioned elsewhere. The licensees of the King's Arms in the 1830s were butcher Thomas Roch and his wife Jane, who in 1840 moved to take over the Globe in Commercial Row. George Mason, in his *Historical Sketches of Pembroke Dock*, recorded that during Mr. Roch's time at the King's Arms, 'in the bar parlour, the elite of the little town met each evening to discuss the passing events with dignity and decorum'.

From 1841 until his death in 1850 the landlord was Richard Phelps, who must have watched with interest as work began in 1849 on the imposing Gun Tower outside his front door. His widow Ann was followed as licensee by James Dean who kept the pub in the late 1850s and early 1860s. He was a master seaman and a member of the Dean family who owned a shipyard at Burton Ferry where they also ran the Jolly Sailor pub.

At some stage, perhaps in the early 1870s, the pub was acquired by Pembroke brewer and maltster, George Llewellyn Griffiths, who let it to various tenants, including several members of the Chappell family from Dorset who seem to crop up in connection with most pubs in Pembroke Dock at one time or another. The pub was later let to William Horn, and it was he who held the licence in 1889. One day, during the summer of that year, two policemen lurking in the Gun Tower kept the house under observation from 8 a.m. until dusk and counted over 80 customers visiting the pub. This would have been fine, except for the fact that it was a Sunday and the pub was meant to be closed. Not surprisingly, the magistrates refused to renew Horn's licence at the next Brewster Sessions, and by 1891 the landlord was Stephen Mathias.

From 1901 the landlord was Joseph George Phillips. He struggled increasingly to make the business pay, was twice fined for watering down his spirits, and gave up altogether in 1914 to go and work in the dockyard. He

The Shipwright in Front Street was formerly the King's Arms.
The front door used to be set into the corner, but in 1914
it was moved to its present position facing Front Street.

87

was replaced by Benjamin Rees who seems to have been more successful and was still there in 1923. The depression caused by the closure of the dockyard was probably responsible for the fact that the pub changed hands regularly in the late 1920s and early 1930s. James Rixon was licensee during the war and Thomas Mellor was there in the 1950s.

At high tide the water washes to within a few yards of the King's Arms, and the pub has always been frequented by boatmen, especially local fishermen and pleasure-boat owners. This has helped to make it a lively place, especially during the 1970s when Pat and Mary McDermott were behind the bar. And while it might be regretted that the name of such an historic inn should have been changed recently, at least the new sign is highly apt, and as the Shipwright the pub has been given a new lease of life with the emphasis very much on food.

The Shipwright is the last survivor of a string of pubs and beer-houses along Front Street, all of which would have benefited from the construction of the Hard in 1827. This was the chief landing area of the town until the building of Hobbs Point, and even afterwards it was the place where the market boats landed, bringing produce from the north side of the Haven and oysters from Llangwm to the town's nearby Market Hall. The ferry-boats from Neyland and Llanstadwell used the Hard, while trading sloops and ketches were regularly beached there to offload their cargoes. When the tides allowed, dockyard workers from 'up the river' would leave their boats tied up there during the day and then row home at night. All of which meant a regular supply of customers for the King's Arms, not to mention the remarkable number of other pubs and beer-houses along the terrace.

Two doors along from the King's Arms, at number three Front Street, was the **New Inn** where Thomas Griffiths was the landlord from 1835 to 1844; he may have been there much longer, because there is a reference to a Thomas Griffith, innkeeper of Pater, as far back as 1821. The New Inn had closed by 1850, but it reopened in about 1860 under a different name — the **Sailor's Return**. In 1861, Mrs. Ruth Davies of the Sailor's Return died a terrible death, reaching for something from the mantlepiece her dress caught fire and she died from the burns; it is said that the headline in one newspaper read 'Death by Crinolene'!

Mary McCarthy kept the pub in 1867, but by 1871 it had become the home of John McCarthy and his wife Sarah — the couple responsible for opening the Rose and Crown (now the Eastgate) in Pembroke 20 years earlier. The 1871 census merely described him as a 'labourer', so he seems to have given up the licensed trade, and by 1881 he was a 'retired labourer'. With seven grown-up children living at home and all bringing in a wage he could afford to take it easy.

Next door to the Sailor's Return, at number four, was the **Waterman's Arms** which was kept by Ann Rees in 1841. It appears from the name to have been the ferrymen's pub and it was kept in the late 1840s by James Bishop, a boatman with a fiery temper. One day in 1847 Bishop attempted to drive some 'loose women' out of his pub by threatening them with a red-hot poker. Some soldiers from the barracks intervened to restrain the landlord, and one of them, a Bombadier, was burnt by the poker. Bishop later prosecuted one of the soldiers for assault, but the case was thrown out when the bench heard from various witnesses that the landlord had been 'violent in the extreme' and that he had hit a sailor over the head with the poker.

Even so, Bishop was still the licensee of the Waterman's in 1852, but by the time of the 1861 census the landlord was a Llangwm man named David Herbert who changed the name to the **Milford Haven**. It was subsequently taken over by David Williams, but had become a butcher's shop by 1871 — no doubt a victim of the Wine and Beer-house Act.

Confusingly, there were once two, and possibly three, Shipwrights' Arms in Pembroke Dock, two of them in the area of Front Street, and none of them the pub which bears name Shipwright today. The 1830 trade directory records two pubs of that name, one kept by Walter Stodden, who lived in King Street, and the other by William Handford; this may have been in Front Street. From 1844 to 1850, Jane Davies was licensee of the **Shipwrights' Arms** in Front Street, while the 1861 census placed the Shipwrights' firmly at no. 6 Front Street, when it was one of four pubs in the space of six houses. The licensee was Sarah Dean, the wife of shipwright George Dean — another member of the Burton family of ship-builders, mariners and innkeepers. This pub was closed by 1871.

The **Hearts of Oak** at no. 7 seems to have opened in the late 1860s, possibly taking its name from a benefit society. The licence passed from Martha Mills to George Lawrence in 1870, while Sarah Harries held the licence from 1871 to 1875 followed by Richard Hall, a dockyard pensioner, who was still there in 1884. Esther Furlong was fined twice in 1894 for opening out of hours — crimes which appear to have hastened the pub's demise.

In 1830 Jane Twigg kept the **Sun Inn** somewhere in Pembroke Dock, followed by Richard Twigg from 1835 to 1840. Since Richard Twigg was living at no. 10 Front Street in 1841, there is a good chance that this was the place. The Sun had become the **Prince Albert** by 1844, in honour of the young queen's new husband, but the pub was closed by 1851.

John Bradley, publican and ferryman, lived at no. 11 at the time of the 1851 census and publican Elizabeth Williams lived at no. 12 in 1841. No pub names were recorded in either case and there is nothing to show whether the pubs they were running were at their home addresses or elsewhere in town.

At no. 13 was the **Milford Arms** where Henry Cooper was landlord in 1840 and Mary Cooper was the landlady between 1841 and 1844. It later became the **Sloop**, being run by Thomas Jones and his wife Elizabeth — more often by the latter, because Thomas was a seaman and was away from home for long periods. The Sloop was open between the early 1850s and 1870, but had closed by the time of the 1871 census; Thomas Jones had become a coal-merchant by this time.

At no. 16 was the **Mariners**, built as a private house in 1815 by dockyard shipwright Abraham Hall. The passing of the beer-shop act probably persuaded him turn the house into a pub which he ran from the early 1830s until his death in 1851. His neice and housekeeper Louisa Rees took over as landlady and she was still there in 1858, although the pub had closed by 1861.

The **Crown and Anchor** began life at 19 Front Street but moved to no. 17 in the 1860s. Ellen or Elinor Thomas ran it as a beer-house in the early 1850s before it was taken over by James and Mary Welsh in 1858. After a few years they moved the pub two doors along the street, taking over a former grocer's shop. James died in August 1873, but his widow Mary was still there in 1891, aged 70, although in the 1881 census she was described as being blind. The landlord from 1901 to 1914 was Charles E. Price while Mr. E. Hudman kept the pub in the 1920s and 1930s and Jane Hudman was there at the start of the war; it was widely known as 'Hudmans' at this time. The Crown and Anchor was one of the last pubs in the county to fall victim to the redundancy ruling, losing its licence in July 1953. William 'Billy' Rees, who had been licensee and leaseholder since 1943, received £154 compensation.

The **Brown Cow** at no. 39 was a short-lived beer-house where John Davies was the landlord from 1858 to 1861.

The **Shamrock and Harp** next door at no. 40 was opened by Henry Webber in about 1864, the licence passing to Henry D. Lloyd the following year. Being a blacksmith, and evidently one who worked with ships, he changed the name to the **Chain and Anchor**. Henry Lloyd and his wife Elizabeth ran this small and fairly spartan pub until 1889 when he was fined a fiver for opening on a Sunday. This gave the local temperance movement the ammunition it needed to try to get the place closed, any landlord with a conviction to his name being liable to lose his licence. In the event, Lloyd managed to spike their guns by getting the licence speedily transferred to his sister Ellen. The pub was still going in 1891 when it was being run by another member of the family, Thomas Lloyd and his wife Maria, but it had closed by the turn of the century.

At no. 44 was the **Paterchurch Inn**, a name full of poignant memories for landlord William White who opened it in about 1860. In his younger days he had worked with his father Francis White who had farmed the pleasant and productive Paterchurch Farm, and he might have expected to take over the farm in due course. The dreams were shattered one day in 1814 when William looked up from his plough to see a boatload of men disembark on the nearby shore and begin staking out the land for the new dockyard. Where William was ploughing is now Albion Square and Paterchurch Farm stood some way to the west.

Francis White was forced to cede some land to the Admiralty almost immediately, and when the dockyard expanded in 1822 he lost the rest, moving with his family to Windsor Hill Farm near Pembroke. William White became a haulier, eventually moving back to Pembroke Dock where he opened the pub in Front Street called after the old family farm.

By 1867 the Paterchurch had become the **Masonic** and was being kept by Lyon Benn. A retired jeweller and watch-maker, Benn was a staunch freemason and had been Worshipful Master of the local lodge in 1849 — hence the new name. But it didn't last long, and like many another Front Street pub had closed by 1871.

Other Front Street pubs are impossible to pin down. Margaret Radford ran the **Pilot Boat** in 1844, while another pub along here may have been the **Hibernia** where Maria Allen was landlady in 1835. Peter Williams kept the **Packet** from 1830 to 1840 and that too may have been in Front Street.

Connecting Front Street with King Street and Queen Street was Gravel Lane, a short street of few houses, but possessing a well-established and well-conducted pub, the **Three Horseshoes** at no. 3. This was run as a beer-shop by John Merriman from about 1840 to 1870, in which year he applied for, and was granted, a full licence. As might be expected from the name of the ale-house, Mr. Merriman had been a blacksmith in Pembroke Dock since 1828. He made anchor chains for the local boatyards and in later years he also ran a coal-merchant's business.

Of the old Gravel Lane and King Street, which ran behind and parallel to Front Street, not a trace now remains, the old terraces having been swept away and replaced by new houses and a day centre, with the Western Way traffic now roaring along the route once occupied by the railway spur to the dockyard. In its earliest days, King Street must have been solidly respectable; the town's first school was here and a number of prominent businesses grew up among the workers' houses. It was not to last and by the 1850s, King Street had become the rowdiest street in the town, where regular fist-fights between drunken sailors, local hard cases and soldiers from the nearby barracks often escalated into full-scale riots. This was particularly true during and immediately after the Crimean War, when the town was garrisoned by the militia — reservists only liable for service on home soil and not as disciplined as the front-line troops.

Both Reynolds and Owen, in their accounts of Pembroke Dock's former pubs, glossed quickly over King Street, merely listing a few names before hurrying on gratefully to more salubrious surroundings. It is hard to blame them, since much of King Street seems to have degenerated into a seedy mix of beer-shops and cheap lodging houses, both of which were the regular haunt of prostitutes. A police officer noted in 1909 that there were 55 houses in King Street with a pub at either end; at one time there had been as many as 15 drinking dens in the street.

On the seaward side of the Commercial Row junction stood the **Globe** with its typical street-corner entrance. It was described as the oldest pub in town at the Brewster Sessions of 1871, and in 1909 a local solicitor stated during a court hearing that the Globe was the 'first and oldest public house in Pembroke Dock' and apparently produced documents to back this up. These statements tend to confirm that this was indeed the place referred to in the diary mentioned by Mrs. Stuart Peters as being the fifth house built in the town, 'a public house for Mr. Phillips at the west corner of King Street'.

The inn seems to have been known as the **Albion** for at least part of its somewhat chequered life — certainly when it was kept by John Murphy in 1844 and then by Catherine Lawrence, formerly of the New Caledonia in Wesley Row, from 1847 to 1852. It seems to have been closed for a while before Matthew John reopened the pub as the Globe in the late 1860s, after which it changed hands regularly until John Fulcher from Cambridge became landlord from 1879 to 1891; he was followed by his widow, the oddly-named Lettice Fulcher who was still there in 1901. Mrs. Elizabeth

A rare photograph of King Street showing part of the Globe Inn on the left.
(Picture courtesy of Mr. John Hogg.)

92

Baker was the landlady in 1906 and Henry Baker was landlord from 1909 to 1914.

In 1909 a police officer described a visit to the Globe:

> I found on entering from the corner a small bar. Going through a passage I entered a tap-room facing King Street. At the rear of the premises I found a large smoke-room and a small back yard. There was accommodation upstairs for 18 sailors and others.

Edward E. Perkins kept the pub in 1923 and he was still there the following year when the Globe was forced to close under the redundancy ruling; it was owned at the time by Messrs. Bowling and was the last-ever as well as the first-ever pub in the street.

Boatman Walter Stodden from Saltash lived at no. 3 King Street for many years. He ran the **Shipwrights Arms** in 1830 and the **Sailor's Return** in 1835 — possibly different names for the same place — but seems to have given up the licensed trade by 1841.

Another King Street pub with which Matthew John and his wife Ann were involved was the **Old Ship** which was somewhere near the Globe. They ran it as a beer-house, usually in Ann's name, from 1858 until 1870 when they were granted a full licence. In 1879 the licence of the Old Ship was transferred to the nearby **Bridgewater Arms** — possibly the three-storey building next to the Globe which was previously the Sailor's Return. A groom from Staffordshire called Henry Rowley was the landlord from 1879 until its closure in about 1903.

The **Black Horse** was recorded as early as 1820 and seems to have been a terraced cottage pub. James Hancock was the landlord in 1830 followed by a sawyer named Thomas Hancock from 1835 to 1840 and Daniel Evans in 1844. Elsewhere in the street, stonemason George Isaac kept the **Dolphin** from 1830 until his death in 1836; he may have built it, too, since in 1818 he took out a lease from the Bush estate on two plots of land in King Street. Landlord of the Dolphin in the 1850s was Joseph (or possibly James) Parratt.

The **Old Lion** at no. 11 was one of the town's oldest public houses, and one which enjoyed a rough and ready reputation in later years. In May 1816 the Meyrick estate granted a building lease for the Old Lion in King Street to a carpenter named John James. The lease then passed to the Starbuck family — presumably the Milford Haven merchants and brewers — and Mr. Richard Rose has unearthed an 1818 reference to David Price of the Old Lion, Pater, who was taken to court by George Starbuck for non-payment of his quarterly rent.

Abraham John was the landlord from 1835 until his death in 1844 and Maria Rixon kept the pub in the 1850s. The Old Lion was a popular haunt of soldiers and marines from the town's barracks, and was consequently much frequented by certain kinds of women as well. The celebrations to mark the turn of the year in 1866 became so wild and and boisterous that William Morris, who was then the landlord, was fined five shillings for keeping a disorderly house. The commandant of the local garrison subsequently issued an order prohibiting all soldiers from visiting the pub and Morris later lost his licence altogether.

In September 1876 the Old Lion was caught up in a riot involving soldiers of the 54th Dorsetshire Regiment who were celebrating their last night of duty at the local barracks before being posted to Ireland. After an evening of heavy drinking and fighting around the town, the soldiers congregated in King Street with its array of pubs and beer-houses. Ten of them pushed their way into the Old Lion and did their best to wreck the place, smashing glasses and throwing chairs through the windows. Eventually the rioting soldiers were rounded up by the local police, who were aided by military patrols from the barracks and a gang of locals who fancied a scrap. Over 40 soldiers were arrested and ended up spending the night in military cells.

Ann Thomas was in charge of the pub at the time, and she was regularly in trouble for serving after hours. In 1877 her son-in-law, James Supple from Chatham, applied to take over the licence, but this application was strongly opposed by Superintendent Thomas: 'Inasmuch as the house has always been very badly conducted and the man Supple, who is very well known to the police, is not a fit person to be entrusted with the running of a public house'. Despite the police objection, the licence did indeed pass to Supple, and he was still there in 1890, evidently having managed to keep his nose clean. The following year the pub licence was not renewed and the Old Lion became a grocer's shop, no doubt to the relief of the local constabulary.

Richard Rose records that James Webb was landlord of the 'Milville Inn, Pater' in 1820, while Michael Woodcock kept the **Melville Inn** in 1830. Since he is known to have lived in King Street, it is possible that the Melville was here. John Wilcocks appears as licensee in the 1835 trade directory. The pub was named after the Rt. Hon. Robert, Viscount Melville, First Lord of the Admiralty from 1812 to 1827 and a key figure in the establishment of the dockyard.

There have always been close links between Lawrenny village and this part of Pembroke Dock — both places were involved in shipbuilding, and a number of people from the Lawrenny area moved to the dockyard town in its early days. They included John Allen, who founded the school in King Street and whose daughter married John Merriman, the Gravel Lane publican and blacksmith. Ann Davies, another Lawrenny girl, opened a beer-house in King

Street in about 1860 and named it after her home village. The **Lawrenny Inn** survived until about 1874.

It's rare to find a full complement of equine footwear in a pub's name, but there was once a **Four Horseshoes** in King Street. Thomas Williams, who ran the pub in the 1850s and 1860s, also had a blacksmith's business around the corner in Commercial Row.

Two pubs in the street with a confusing history are the **Launch** and the **Ship on Launch**. Elizabeth Dally was at the helm of the Launch in 1844, but the following year the licence passed to John Arla. He died in 1847, aged 73, and his wife Elizabeth Arla took over as landlady and was still in charge at the time the 1852 trade directory was compiled.

The Ship on Launch was kept by a seaman called Charles Allen according to *Robson's Commercial Directory* of 1840, but Martha Rogers was the landlady from 1844 to 1848. 'It is not a common public house; it has a spirit licence', she rather snootily informed a court hearing that year. Sadly, the Ship on Launch does seem to have been rather common, even by the King Street standards of the day, and it was regularly mentioned in court as a place where stolen goods were recovered or where fights broke out. Eliza Evans took over from Martha Rogers in 1849, but failed to raise the tone of the place. 'This house is one conducted in a very improper manner and a sharp lookout will be kept on it in future', warned the magistrates that year.

By the following year their patience had run out, and having heard from the agent of the Bush Estate that the house was 'a great nuisance', the magistrates took the brave decision to close it down — brave, because the court was packed with rowdy supporters of Eliza Evans who repeatedly directed 'unseemly and harsh remarks' at the bench. In the 1851 census, Eliza is listed as 'shopkeeper'; the confusion arises from the fact that she appears to have been the daughter of John and Elizabeth Arla who kept the nearby Launch.

Annoyingly for historians, publicans in Pembroke Dock seem to have taken great delight in duplicating the names of their premises, so it is no surprise to find two pubs in King Street, both called Foresters - the Foresters Inn and the Foresters Arms. The Ancient Order of Foresters was a Friendly Society which went in for all sorts of semi-secret rigmarole, and had an inner circle known as the Ancient Order of Shepherds. The society was established in Pembroke Dock in the 1840s, and on special occasions the members would parade around the town, gamely dressed in tunics of Lincoln Green with ostrich plumes in their hats and carrying toy hunting axes.

Trying to disentangle the history of these two King Street Foresters has been something of a nightmare. The key to the problem is a local butcher named Isaac Nicholas who was at the Foresters Arms in 1858 but had moved

95

to open the rival Foresters Inn or 'New Foresters' by 1868. This **Foresters Inn** was at the eastern end of King Street, at no. 51, and Nicholas seems to have been well suited to running a pub in the street; he was fined 15 shillings in March 1873 for being 'drunk and riotous'. Perhaps as a consequence of this he gave up the business the following year, the licence passing to James Wade. In 1877 the licensee was Daniel Davies who ran the pub until 1884. Mrs. M.A. Bradley was there in 1891, and the Foresters Inn subsequently changed hands several times before it was closed in 1915 under the redundancy ruling; by this time it was a James Williams house.

The **Foresters Arms**, or 'Old Foresters' was at no. 46; it was where the society first met in the town in about 1845 before eventually moving to the Royal William. Margaret Davies was landlady of the Foresters Arms in 1852, Isaac Nicholas was there by 1858 and John Davies was landlord in the 1860s. In October 1878 the licence passed to Mrs. Ann Morris, and she was still the landlady in 1894 when the magistrates decided not to renew the licence.

Other King Street pubs were the **Butchers Arms** where James Marony was the landlord in 1867 and the **Stag**, where the licence was transferred in October 1847 from Sophia Williams to William Maclin.

CHAPTER SEVEN

Pembroke Dock
QUEEN ST., COMMERCIAL ROW, BREWERY ST., WELLINGTON ST., & CLARENCE ST.

Queen Street began life as 'Upper Row' and initially ran as a single south-facing terrace from Commercial Row to just beyond the junction with Brewery Road. As Pembroke Dock grew in the 1830s and '40s, so Queen Street was extended in an easterly direction, the new development being a much more commercial affair than the old terrace of workers houses, having business premises on both sides. By the 1860s Queen Street ran from Commercial Row to Meyrick Street and it had become one of the main commercial arteries of the town.

The **Milford Arms** was on the corner of Queen Street and Commercial

Nowadays a laundry, the Milford Arms had a classic street-corner entrance door. The terrace to the right once boasted a number of pubs including the Golden Lion and the Landshipping Inn.

Row where the laun-derette is now; it still has the classic street-corner entrance of so many of the town pubs. In the 1850s and '60s the Milford was the scene of many a lively scrap between shipyard workers and soldiers from the barracks. Trying to keep order in 1858 was landlord William Jones, but the pub-cum-lodging house passed to Thomas Owen the following year.

In 1862 Owen, his wife Mary and step-daughter Margaret Evans, were tried and acquitted of beating up an engineer from H.M.S. *Lucifer* who was trying to leave without paying his bill. In 1866 Owen was twice fined for serving out of hours; he gave it up as a bad job soon after and handed over to a butcher named William Nicholas who was followed in 1877 by his widow Mary Nicholas. The pub closed in 1884 and became a butcher's shop.

The short terrace to the east of the Milford Arms contained numerous hostelries. The fourth house along was once the **Golden Lion**, but as usual the name was often shortened to 'Lion'. Martha Morgan was the landlady in 1830 but carpenter and joiner Josiah Davies, a prominent freemason, was drawing the ale between 1835 and 1844. Jane Davies was landlady in the early 1850s and Thomas Hurlow from Lawrenny and his wife Mary were licensees from 1858 to 1870. By the mid 1870s the pub was closed and they were running a watchmaking business.

Two doors further along was the **Landshipping Inn** at 11 Queen Street. This was known as the **Narberth Arms** when it was opened in the 1850s by David John of Llanboidy, but the name was changed when Thomas Davies, a former coal-miner from Hop Garden, Landshipping, took over the pub and lodging house in the 1860s, running it initially with his wife Rebecca.

The pub gained some notoriety in 1868 when a local man, James Thomas, knifed a soldier, one James Gafney, during a fracas in the back-yard. Gafney lived and Thomas was acquitted of malicious assault at the next quarter sessions. The pub survived an attempt by the local magistrates to have it closed in 1909 and Thomas Davies, the son of the previous licensee, was still there in 1914. Frederick Williamson held the licence in 1923, in which year the pub finally did have its licence taken away under the redundancy and compensation ruling. The court was told by a police officer that the Landshipping was 26 yards from the Commercial, 60 yards from the Royal Exchange and 50 yards from the Swan, and in his opinion that was more than enough pubs for the area.

Next door to the Landshipping was probably the site of one of the town's three **Globe** inns. It was run for just a few years in the 1850s by George Thorn. On the corner of this terrace, at no. 21, was the **Plough and Harrow**; in fact, at one time the four corner properties on this crossroads were all pubs or beer-houses. The Plough and Harrow was kept in the 1850s and '60s by Joshua Huzzey, but was closed by 1871 and the building is no longer standing.

Across the road is the **Flying Boat**, formerly the **Commercial Inn,** the name having been changed in the 1960s to commemorate the wartime flying boat squadrons based in the nearby dockyard. It is thought to have been origi-inally a cobbler's shop (and possibly a beer-house), being extended in the

1850s into a fairly substantial inn by Walter Griffiths from Laugharne who had previously kept a grocery shop on the diagonally opposite corner. As well as turning his former shop into a pub, the Swan, he also ran the Commercial from 1858 to 1875, offering accommodation and stabling for

The Flying Boat was once the Commercial Inn.

commercial travellers. Miss Emily Potter from Devonport held the licence in the 1880s and Lionel Brooks was the landlord in 1891. It is said that the 'Tichborne Claimant', the subject of the most celebrated impersonation case in English law, once stayed at the Commercial and, inevitably, that he left without paying his bill!

John Williams was the landlord from 1901 to 1906, in which year the inn was taken over by Tom Barger. Liverpool-born Barger had previously enjoyed a 30-year career in the music-halls, where he was renowned as a comedian, female impersonator, quick-change artist, ventriloquist and vocalist. When he left the boards, he took over the licence of the Commercial, also becoming proprietor of the town's Queen's Theatre which he ran for a few years before turning it into a roller-skating rink. It later became White's Picture Palace.

When he died in 1912 at the early age of 56, his widow Mrs. Martha Barger took over the licence. As with many Pembroke Dock pubs there was a tremendous turnover of licensees in the 1920s before Mrs. Beatrice Heck arrived; she kept the Commercial until the Second World War. Among the best-remembered of the post-war licensees were Cliff John in the 1950s and Joe and Kath Charman who are credited with having changed the name of the pub in the mid 1960s. There were fears for the pub's future when it was closed for a couple of years in the late 1990s, but happily it was reopened by Colin Edwards and the interior — with its interesting collection of Sunderland flying boat memorabilia — remains unchanged.

On the opposite corner at the bottom of Clarence Street stood the short-lived **London Tavern,** kept in 1858 by George Griffiths and in 1861 by plasterer Henry Burgess; it still has the typical canted corner where the door would have been. And the fourth pub on this junction in the 1860s was the

Swan Inn at 23, Queen Street. Happily the Swan is still with us, a rare survivor of the multitude of cottage pubs which once flourished in this network of terraced streets. When Walter Griffiths opened the Commercial he also turned part of his former grocery shop into the Swan and installed Henry Banner from

The Swan as it looked in 2003.

Carew to run it. Mr. Banner eventually left to open the New Swan in Pennar and the pub was taken over by an Army pensioner named Walter Arrowsmith. When he in turn moved on to the King's Arms in Front Street, Mr. Griffiths took over the running of the pub himself and he was still there in 1884, by which time he was nearly 80.

William Evans was the landlord from 1891 to 1901, while Jesse Jenkins kept the Swan from 1906 to 1914. At this time the Swan had the reputation of being the first pub in town to open each morning, serving its first customer at around 5.30 a.m. For many years after the war, the Swan was also the meeting place of the town's R.A.O.B. club. Harry Perry was the popular licensee from 1922 to 1961; he was reputedly the only teetotal publican in the town. Since his day there have been several changes of licensee, with May and Wilf Harries, who were there in the late 1970s and early '80s, being the longest-serving.

The **Lamb**, where Levy Williams was the landlord in the early 1840s, was also in this area, perhaps a couple of doors from the Swan.

Moving eastwards, there is a kink in the road at the junction with Brewery Street. This area was once known as Queen's Square and it formed the boundary between the original Queen Street and the eastern extension originally called New Road. Two pubs stood on this square, the Sun and the Rising Sun. The **Rising Sun** at no. 43 was so-called because it faced east, being in the centre of the short terrace where Queen Street makes a double bend. It was opened in September 1866 by William Gwyther from Cosheston who kept the pub until 1891, while Charles Smith was there in 1901. For 20 years the pub was run by the Neil family, during whose tenure it gained some notoriety for its unwitting involvement with a local brothel described as 'a hot-bed of infamy' and 'the blackest spot in the history of Pembroke Dock'. This brothel was at 31 Queen Street, and the Rising Sun was apparently used as an unofficial 'waiting-room' for soldiers and sailors intent on patronising the house of ill-repute. The brothel was closed following a police raid in 1913, while the Rising Sun fell victim to the redundancy ruling in 1929 when the licensee was Mr. R.S. Bailey.

The **Sun** at no. 49 was a slightly older pub. William Morris was the landlord from 1858 to 1861, but by 1866 it had been taken over by a young bootmaker from Newport, Gwent called John McBean. He ran the pub until the 1880s, and his widow Mrs. Mary Ann McBean followed him as landlady until 1906. Their son, Arthur Stewart McBean, a former dockyard worker, then took over. He died in 1917, just before the pub was declared surplus to requirements by the redundancy committee.

The Sun is no longer standing, and neither is the building which once housed the **Royal George** at no. 53. This pub stood on the corner of Queen Street and Gravel Lane, and Sarah Bevan was the landlady from 1844 to 1852. In the mid 1850s it was taken over by Jane Hancock, the widow of Thomas Hancock who had at one time run the Black Horse in King Street. William and Frances Frith kept the grocery shop and pub collectively known as the Royal George in 1864, evidently as tenants of the widow Hancock, but it was closed by 1870.

The **Devonport** was located three doors to the west of the Rose and Crown in Queen Street East. It was kept in 1851 by Amelia Nicholls from Devon and she was followed by a Greenwich pensioner called Joseph Harries who was the landlord from 1858 to 1867. The Devonport was a notorious haunt of 'unfortunates' as the newspapers of the time coyly referred to prostitutes.

The Rose and Crown in an early postcard view.

Gamely coping with the good times and the bad, the **Rose and Crown** is still a thriving Pembroke Dock local. It must have opened in the early 1840s, and on Christmas Eve 1844, the Loyal Prince Albert Lodge of Odd Fellows held its inaugural meeting there; the society later established its own lodge room at the inn. William Llewellyn was licensee at the time and in 1845 the *Pembrokeshire Herald* reported:

101

We are happy to find a spirited individual, Mr. Llewellyn, landlord of the Rose and Crown, Pembroke Dock, is establishing a horse-boat communication between that place and Neyland whereby horses, carriages &c. may be conveyed across the Haven at all hours of the day and night. The boat is of large dimensions, of beautiful mould, and in every way qualified for the duties of transit.

The Rose and Crown in 2003.

The enterprising Mr. Llewellyn was followed in the 1850s by Richard Llewellyn who was still there in 1861 and who was the owner of a splendid parrot. Thomas Thomas, bandmaster of the Pembroke Yeomanry, was landlord in 1875, after which there were various licensees before Jack and Margaret Emment took over in the 1890s and steadied the ship; photographs from that time show the outside of the pub looking a bit like a Wild West saloon. Fred Fenge became the landlord in 1906, having moved from the Albion on Tenby Quay, William Roberts was landlord in 1914 and William John Grey was there from 1923 to 1931. Mr. and Mrs. Matthew Glaister were in charge during the war, while Ernest Peach was landlord in the 1950s and '60s. For the past 20 years the licence of the Rose and Crown has been held by Len and Irene Thomas, and the pub is still going strong, having seen off most of its rivals in the past 160 years.

One of these rivals was the **Odd Fellows Arms** on the other side of Queen Street — the 11th house from the Meyrick Street corner. Thomas Warlow was the landlord from 1858 until 1864, when the local magistrates refused to renew the licence. They heard that people living in the vicinity of the Odd Fellows were being continually disturbed by 'broils and fighting' outside the pub in the early hours of the morning.

The **Gun Tavern** was the 5th house from the corner, also on the south side. The licensee in 1861 was a Chelsea pensioner named James Wadell who probably thought up the name. The licence passed in 1867 to Simon Thomas who was still landlord in 1872. William Stewart then took over and kept the

The Gun Tavern had a replica gun on top of the pub sign.

pub until his death in 1878. His widow Mary succeeded him, and when she remarried the licence passed to her second husband James Adams. In 1889, however, it was reported that Adams had 'run away', and the licence was transferred to Mary's daughter, Mary Jane Stewart. However, when the magistrates heard later that she was only 16 they hurriedly changed their minds and reinstalled her mother as licensee.

John Thomas held the Gun from 1901 until 1914, while in the 1920s the licensees were Albert and Catherine Venning. In 1925. the Gun was finally silenced by the authorities, who were keen to reduce the number of licensed houses in this part of Pembroke Dock. They declined to renew the licence and made an order for compensation to be paid to Mrs. Venning, who was both the licensee

Albert Venning stands in the doorway of the Gun Tavern.
(Picture courtesy of Mr. Vernon Scott.)

and leaseholder, and also to the Meyricks of Bush who owned the freehold. Compensation was set at the relatively high figure of £1,050, reflecting the level of trade at what was a popular gathering place of the town's shop-owners and professional men.

An early view of Queen Street showing the Queen's on the left and the Royal Edinburgh on the right.
(Picture courtesy of Mr. Roger Davies.)

The **Queen's**, on the junction of Queen Street and Meyrick Street, had a typical Pembroke Dock street corner entrance with its door set in the angle, but before it became an inn it was for many years a saddler's shop run by Thomas John. It was listed as an hotel in 1875 when Anne John was the landlady. She was followed between 1878 and 1884 by Anna Sharpe and then by William Neil. Martha and Blanche Davies, two sisters from Rosemarket, both in their twenties, ran the pub in 1891, Richard Bone was landlord from 1906 to 1912, and seasoned Pembroke Dock licensee, Jack Nicholson, was landlord in the early 1920s. He was later followed by Bob and Alice Whisby.

Mrs. Annie Gill, formerly of the bombed-out Criterion, took over after the war, while the best-known post-war licensee was Norman Wren who

held the licence in the 1960s and also ran a hairdressing business nearby. The Queen's closed in about 1988 and is now a toyshop.

The **Royal**, on the corner of Queen Street and Meyrick Street, was an imposing place in its heyday, with stables and coach-houses, numerous bedrooms, kitchens, pantries, large cellars and various public

The Queen's in its present guise as a toyshop.

104

rooms, including a bar, smoke-room and coffee room. It was opened in 1849 by John Llewhellin, who had previously run an inn of the same name at Hobbs Point. The housewarming dinner was held at the 'comfortably and commodiously fitted-up establishment' to welcome new landlord. 'The wines were very choice, having been procured from a first-rate London house', reported one newspaper.

George Dawkins took over the Royal in 1866, but it seems to have closed for a while and was used as a private house for six or seven years before Mrs. Lettice Isaacs leased the property from the Bush Estate in 1873 and reopened it as an inn. The Royal was taken over in 1882 by William B. Price of the Crown Stores in Melville Street who was starting to assemble a portfolio of Pembroke Dock pubs. He changed the name to **Royal Edinburgh** in honour of the Duke and Duchess of Edinburgh, who paid a visit to the town to launch the turret ship *Edinburgh* which had been built in the dockyard. 'It was a cold and wet night in that year when Mr. Price officially opened the doors', wrote Reynolds. 'The late Mr. Milligan Phillips of Haverfordwest handed out some good bottles of champagne through the window. In the bar was a blazing fire and many toasts were given and drank'. James Shenton was licensee in 1906 while new proprietor John Griffiths confidently advertised in 1913:

The Royal Edinburgh in its heyday in the early 1970s.

> The house has been renovated and decorated throughout, the commercial, smoking, coffee and dining rooms are replete with every comfort and there is a daily luncheon at 1.15pm. For the convenience of commercial men, all trains and boats are met.

Ethel Egerton held the licence in the 1930s, while in 1953 Mr. D.J. Walters announced the opening of a new cocktail bar and lounge. The Royal Edinburgh was one of the town's main social centres at this time, being a meeting place of the local freemasons — 'square and compass' symbols can still be seen above the Queen Street entrance to the building. It was also the headquarters of Pembroke Dock Quins R.F.C., a relationship which was cemented when 6 ft. 4 ins. rugby player Wilf Gunter took over in the 1960s and a 'Quins Bar' was created. In recent years the premises have been 'down-

The Royal Edinburgh was in its heyday in this 1960 advertisement.

The masonic window at the Royal Edinburgh.

sized' somewhat, with part of the old hotel becoming a shop. The name has also been changed back to the original one of Royal Inn.

Commercial Row gained its name from the number of businesses which grew up on this busy thoroughfare, which was built in the 1820s to run from the 'Hard' at Front Street to the market hall. According to Mason: 'Some of these commercial houses were very important in their day, such as Trewent's drapery, Clougher's book-shop and Nathaniel Owen's Royal Oak hotel and general shop'. The street began as a scattering of workers' cottages at the Front Street end and met up with the commercial properties around the junction with Queen Street.

As the town's main business street in the 1850s, Commercial Row was the first in town to be lit by gas. There was also an attempt made at that time to turn into it a fashionable promenade, with a row of shady trees and benches along the dockyard wall. Military bands played, as couples in their Sunday best ambled along arm-in-arm, window-shopping or perhaps stopping for refreshment at one of the street's numerous hostelries. These tended to be rather more 'up-market' than the general run of beer-houses tucked away in the streets behind.

On the corner with Albion Square is the building which once housed Moore and Co.'s chemist shop, established in 1825. In common with many other druggists, Joseph Moore ran a pub as a sideline — as did Cornelius Williams when he took over the business in later years. In order to be allowed to sell certain alcohol-based patent medicines, such as the popular Colman's Malt Extract, it was necessary for a chemist to obtain a wine and spirits licence. And having obtained the licence, many chemists decided to take advantage of the fact by serving alcoholic drinks. This was usually done in a one-room bar tucked away behind the shop, and it was often the case that only the chosen few would be invited into this inner sanctum to smoke a pipe, sup a glass or two of beer or porter and generally put the world to rights. The drinking den attached to Moore and Co.'s was called the **Bee Hive** in the 1870s, but although it still held an 'on licence' right up to 1962, few of the more recent chemists seemed to take advantage of the fact.

The **Royal Oak,** mentioned earlier, was two doors along at 26 Commercial Row. Nathaniel Owen was landlord of this notable inn from 1830 until his death in 1854; he also ran an ironmongery, grocery and post office business for part of that time. Mason described the Royal Oak as being somewhere where accommodation for horse and man could be had, plus everything 'from a pennyworth of tin-tacks to a mangle, a bun to a sack of flour, and refreshments of all sorts'. Mary Owen, Nathaniel's widow, was the landlady from 1858 to 1861.

The signboard of the Royal Oak was said to have been painted by a once-famous, but sadly anonymous, artist who had fallen on hard times, and who carried out the commission in return for a bed and meal in the inn — but since that story is told about any number of pubs up and down the country it needs to be taken with a good measure of salt. Much altered, the building is now part of a First Aid centre, though what appears to be the old coach arch of the inn is still in evidence.

Further down, at about no. 17 was the **Globe** — one of several pubs of that name in the area. This was located here from the early 1840s to about 1855. Butcher and local councillor Thomas Roch, formerly of the King's Arms in Front Street, was landlord from 1844 till his death, aged 50, in 1846. His widow Jane then took over and still kept the pub in 1852; she was described as a spirit merchant in the 1851 census. It later became the **Milford Haven**, run by Alexander McKay, but it had closed by the 1870s.

Because so many of the properties in Commercial Row have altered and merged in the past 160 years it is difficult to be accurate about where individual inns once stood. However, the **Duke of Wellington** seems to have been at no. 16. It was mentioned in the *Pembrokeshire Herald* in 1854, when the landlord was William Keast, and probably took its name from the wooden three-decker which was launched in the dockyard in 1852. Despite the name of his pub, Keast seems to have been less than sympathetic to the military cause and in 1855 he appeared in court charged with inciting soldiers to mutiny. The Monmouthshire Militia were stationed in Pembroke Dock at the time, and so disaffected were the men that over 150 of them demanded their discharge under the terms of the Militia Act. Many refused to go on guard duty, so that the dockyard was left undefended and there was chaos in the town as the militia-men headed for the town's pubs and brothels rather than the parade ground.

When a military picket arrived outside the Duke of Wellington in search of some of the men who had gone A.W.O.L., licensee Keast refused to admit them. He told a Royal Artillery Lieutenant: 'If I was a private I would shoot you. I might shoot you anyway if you don't take care'. The case was heard before a local court, but responsibility for sentencing was handed over to the Admiralty. Their decision isn't known, but Keast seems to have vanished from the scene shortly after this incident.

A chemist named Charles Andrews then took over, combining his business as a druggist with running the pub from part of the same premises. In 1878 he handed over to D.W. John; as Reynolds recorded: 'A house in Commercial Row named after the Iron Duke was Messrs. D.P. Saer and Mr. John's chemist shop'. The pub closed in 1892.

At no. 15 was the **Bell and Lion** where William and Elizabeth Herbert were the licensees from 1858 to 1868. At some stage the pub was added to the

collection of spirit merchant William B. Price of the Crown Stores and tenants included James Chappell, Fred Lewis and Josh Kenniford from Cosheston who was licensee in 1891. Publicans came and went in a steady procession during the early 20th century until Mrs. Nellie Walton took over in the 1930s. She remained the licensee till her death in January 1953,

The former Bell and Lion in Commercial Row. and it is said that during her day the Bell and Lion used to be popular with Gypsies, who would gather there to smoke their clay pipes. The pub was considered surplus to requirements by local magistrates in May 1953 and forced to close under the redundancy ruling — one of the last pubs in Pembrokeshire to suffer this fate. It is now a private house.

James Dawkins ran one of the town's many **Commercial Inns** in the 1840s and '50s. This was at no. 12 Commercial Row and by 1861 the occupier was Sidney Webb, described as a licensed victualler of 'Pembroke Dock House'. A pioneer photographer, Webb later moved to run the Prince of Wales in Laws Street and the pub in Commercial Row closed with his departure.

Between the Commercial and the Queen Street corner was the **Porter Stores,** run in the 1870s by local brewer William White. In January 1884 he handed over to Fred Lewis, formerly of the Bell and Lion, and the name was altered to the **Royal Exchange**. Lewis was a butcher by trade, with a shop next door to the Royal Exchange, so he sub-let the pub to a couple of tenants including Evan Evans and Bert Toohig. In 1896, Lewis decided he could take on the two businesses himself and he described himself as 'butcher and vict-ualler' in the 1901 census. By 1906 he had left town to take over the Brewery Inn at Cosheston, leaving his son William to run the Commercial Row enter-prises, which he did until his death in 1936. His widow Mary kept the licence going until 1939 when she too died and the pub closed. The town's R.A.F.A. club now occupies the site.

The 1851 census shows three ale-house keepers living in Commercial Row — John Athoe, Jane James and Jane Williams — but there is nothing to indicate the sign of their houses and none of the enterprises seems to have survived long. In addition, J.M. Owen believed that there were once pubs in Commercial Row called the **Weighbridge** and the **Britannia**, but no trace of them has turned up in the records.

Lower Commercial Row was a cluster of half-a-dozen properties at some distance seaward of the rest of Commercial Row, near where the dockyard railway entered the yard. Thomas Phillips ran the **George** beer-house from 1830 to 1852; he also lived in Lower Commercial Row. Susan Thomas was landlady of the George in Commercial Row in 1867 and this may well have been the same place.

The **Red Lion** or Old Red Lion was also in Lower Commercial Row, being one of the chain of pubs under the control of Bush Street spirit merchant W.T. Smith. In 1870 the licence was held by John Fitzpatrick and he was followed by a string of tenants, the only ones to last any time being Charles Leathlean and his widow, Mary. The pub closed in 1893 and the houses in Lower Commercial Row no longer exist, having been demolished by the council in the early 1950s.

Behind Commercial Row are three parallel streets that link busy Albion Square with Queen Street. These were once called Nailers Lane, Front Cottages and Friday Street — later renamed Wellington Street, North Brewery Street and Clarence Street. These were largely residential terraces and appear to have mustered just two public houses between them.

One of these was the often lively **Castle Inn** in Clarence Street. George Luke was the landlord of the Castle in 1835 followed by Thomas Bradley in 1840, a young joiner named Charles Philpin in 1844 and Grace Sewells who was the landlady in the 1850s.

The Castle was the scene of a riot in July 1861 when about 50 soldiers from the town barracks entered the pub and proceeded to smash it up. Every glass, bottle, clock and ornament in the house was smashed, and the damage was estimated at £50. The landlord at the time was William Powell, who ran the Castle with his wife Eleanor. While several of the ringleaders of the riot later appeared in court, the Powells patched up the pub and carried on in business. Soldiers were apparently still tolerated at the Castle, because in 1866 the Powells were fined 15s. for the unusual offence of 'taking a soldier's medal in pledge for beer supplied'. Eleanor Powell ran the pub for a time following the death of her husband in 1870.

John Price, who was licensee in 1878, was fined £2 'for allowing his house to be the habitual resort of known prostitutes', and the reputation of the Castle went so far downhill at this time that when Henry Larkin took over in April 1880 he changed the name to the **Hawthorn** in an effort to wipe the slate clean. However, there were further convictions recorded in 1885 and 1889, and in 1891 the licence was not renewed.

Wellington Street seems never to have had a pub, but there was one in North Brewery Street (now just Brewery Street). This was the **Plough,** which was located about ten doors down from the Albion Square end of the street. It was kept in the early 1860s by a retired police officer named James Vaughan and his wife Ann. but it doesn't seem to have been a success and was closed by 1871.

CHAPTER EIGHT

Pembroke Dock
PEMBROKE ST., MARKET ST., PRINCES ST & MELVILLE ST.

The terraces of workers houses north of the market were built from the early 1830s onwards on land owned by the Admiralty. The eastern side of Pembroke Street was largely in existence at this time, and boasted several fine inns, so that the new building works saw the completion of the west side of the street and the creation of Market Street, Crown Street, later renamed Princes Street, and Queen Street (West), now Cumby Terrace. These terraces ran parallel with Pembroke Street from the lower slopes of the Barrack Hill to the newly-improved Melville Street — an arrow-straight road which ran from the market place to the dockyard gates.

As well as the regular market trade, many hundreds of dockyard workmen passed this way twice every day, so it is no surprise to find plenty of pubs and ale-houses in the area, particularly around the junctions where Market Street and Princes Street met Melville Street. The profits to be made by providing refreshments to the shipyard workers had long been recognised; in the early days of the dockyard an old woman named Ann Jones — 'Nanny Herring' — sold beer and biscuits to the workmen from her thatched cottage near Paterchurch Tower. Sadly, many of the old Market Street and Princes Street pubs are no longer in existence, this area having been devastated by German bombing during the Second World War.

At the bottom of Pembroke Street stands the **White Hart,** one of only two pubs still surviving in the area. The sign on the front proclaims that this fine old Pembroke Dock inn was established in 1820, but it seems to have begun its life as the **Royal William**, perhaps named in honour of William, Duke of Clarence, who visited the new town in 1827, just a few years before his coronation as William IV. In December 1830 the Royal William was advertised as being for sale; it was described as being 'opposite the Market-place' and consisted of cellars, kitchen, brewhouse (with 'superior brewing utensils') and two parlours.

The White Hart has happily reopened after a period of closure, but there has been no such reprieve for the Navy Tavern next door.

Dockyard workers and market traders were among the regular patrons when the pub was in its prime, while a number of the societies that thrived in Victorian Pembroke Dock used to have their headquarters here. In 1845 the Pembroke Dock 'Court' of the Ancient Order of Shepherds — a Friendly Society allied to the Foresters — met for the first time at the Royal William, and in the 1880s the pub was the meeting place of the Pembroke Dock Provident Society, a local Friendly Society with 145 members.

The earliest known licensee was William Painter or Paynter who kept the pub from 1840 to 1852, while his son-in-law Robert Conchar, a Scottish linen draper, was the landlord from 1855 to 1880 by which time the junction became known as 'Conchar's Corner'. Thomas Page took over the pub in April 1880 and immediately renamed it the White Hart, while from 1891, until his death from dropsy in 1901, the landlord was Richard Kingston Flutter. A noted steeplechase jockey in his younger days, Flutter rode winners at courses up and down the country, and once rode Gazelle in the Grand National, but without much luck. From 1906 until his death in 1929 the licensee was William McCracken Gray.

'The White Hart has always been a prominent and notable place', wrote James Meyrick Owen in 1965, 'and it is easy to imagine what a flourishing place it was in the happier days of the town'. Fred Davey was landlord at the outbreak of war and Cecil Woolnough held the licence for some 20 years from 1945. Cinema proprietors Mr. and Mrs. Harold Lancaster were there in the 1970s during which time the White Hart hosted a successful folk club. The White Hart closed for a while in the 1990s, but happily has reopened and is arguably the oldest surviving pub in the town.

Next door, the **Navy Tavern** was once the centre of social life in the dock-yard town before the Victoria Hotel rather usurped its importance. In 1828 a horse-race meeting was held at Pembroke Dock, following which a celebratory dinner was held at the Navy Tavern. The inn was also the meeting place of the St. David's Friendly Benefit Society which had a lodge-room at the tavern. The correspondent of the *Carmarthen Journal* waxed lyrical about a meeting of this friendly society at the Navy in 1830:

> Thus in toasting and singing, the music filling up the interim, was the evening spent in the greatest hilarity and good humour imaginable; and to the credit of the party be it spoken, such a spice of sobriety beamed thro' the day's amusements that nothing could exceed the good order which pervaded the whole, in proof of which it is sufficient to say the tavern was rid of its visitors completely by eleven o'clock.

Walter Weir and his wife kept the pub at the time. He was a stonemason, having been the foreman of the firm which built the market house, and also a freemason; several times Brother Weir played host to masonic get-togethers at the Navy Tavern. Despite this steady trade, Weir often had trouble paying his creditors and he was imprisoned for debt in 1831.

William Thomas kept the pub from 1835 to 1851 followed by his widow Sophia Thomas, who was still there in 1867. The 1870s saw various tenants come and go, while John Thomas was landlord from 1884 to 1901. He was followed by Harold Kennedy, who had previously kept the Red Rose Inn. Kennedy found himself up before the magistrates in 1912, charged with allowing the premises to be used as a brothel. The court heard evidence that soldiers and local women had been caught 'misconducting themselves' in the stables at the back of the inn. Kennedy denied all knowledge of what was going on, and the magistrates rather reluctantly decided to give him the benefit of the doubt and found him not guilty. Even so, he left soon afterwards, because Tommy Twigg took over in 1913. William Egerton was landlord in the 1920s, but when he departed the pub changed hands repeatedly. By 1935 the landlord was Wally O'Sullivan, while in the 1940s the pub was known as 'Tommy Tucker's' after the popular licensee. Vince Watkins was there in the 1950s and from the 1960s to the 1980s the Navy was run by Phil and Peg Humphrey.

As one of the three 'market' pubs — the others being the White Hart and the Market Tavern — the Navy benefited from being allowed to open all day on Fridays. Nevertheless it seems to have become unviable in the late 1980s when it closed its doors for the last time; it remains boarded up — a sad end to an historic pub.

Three doors up from the Navy Tavern was **Price's Brewery**. This was the brewery tap of William Price from 1850 to 1867, having previously been a draper's shop. Price controlled a

A sad end to one of the town's oldest inns, the Navy Tavern in Pembroke Street.

number of pubs in the town and in 1854 one of these was tenanted by a widow named Mary Howell. She ran the pub on the basis that she would receive two shillings on every 18 gallons of beer that she sold, with Price paying for heating and candles. Whichever pub it was, it can't have been very profitable because in the first fortnight she was there she only sold 18 gallons of Price's beer.

Early in 1871 the local press carried reports that the licence of Price's Brewery was being transferred to Robert Andrew, and that the pub would henceforth be called the **Market Tavern**. From 1877 onwards, it was part of a successful business run by grocer, baker and wine and spirit merchant Thomas Rogers. However, in 1889 the owner of this property — an elderly lady named Miss West — became converted to the temperance cause. She decreed that the Market Tavern should no longer serve alcohol and that Mr. Rogers should turn it into a coffee tavern, or possibly a soup kitchen. This didn't suit Rogers at all, but fortunately he already owned another house in the same street,

The R.N.A. club - formerly the Market Tavern.

two doors further up, so he was able to shift the pub, lock, stock and several barrels to the new address.

When Thomas Rogers moved up the street he kept the name Market Tavern and he was still running the pub in 1891, although George Sloggett was there in 1901. The licensee in 1906 was Harry Seaton, while Ernest and Catherine Walker kept the pub from 1910 to 1923 and Mrs. Walker was there on her own until 1932. 'Queenie' Payne — 'a smashing bloke who had a plate in his head', according to one source — kept the pub from 1946 to 1960 when William Wisher took over. Like the Navy Tavern, the Market Tavern closed in the 1980s. It was then taken over by the Royal Naval Association which still runs it as a social club.

Next door to the Market Tavern was once the **Steam Packet Inn**. This was kept by Edward Burrows from 1840 to 1861, but the pub closed in about 1864 and the building became a butcher's shop.

The **Olive Bar** at 31 Pembroke Street was at one time noted for its imposing frontage and still looks a little unusual with its pilastered façade. This was a spirit merchant's shop for many years, and was run as a licensed house called the **Spirit Vaults** in the 1870s. John Thomas was in charge in 1875, but in 1877 the licence passed to Francis and Agnes Goodfellow and then to Rebecca Evans in 1880. Perhaps because the Spirit Vaults had gained a bad name for harbouring prostitutes, the new licensee decided to change the sign and so it became, rather oddly, the Olive Bar. Howard Smith was the landlord in the 1880s and Mrs. Jemima Vallance was there from 1901 to 1913 when she handed over to Thomas Jones of Neath. David James was licensee of this Hancock's house from the early 1930s until 31 December 1945, when the Olive Bar had its licence withdrawn by the magistrates due to its toilet facilities — or, more accurately, its almost complete lack of toilet facilities.

The Olive Bar can be seen on the right of this early postcard view of Pembroke Street.

Although officially in Victoria Terrace, the Clarence Inn and the Victoria Inn stood for many years on facing corners at the top of Pembroke Street like a pair of sentinels guarding one of the main

Pembroke Street from the Barrack Hill, showing the Victoria on the left and the Clarence on the right.

thoroughfares into the town. The **Clarence** was much the older and smaller of the two inns. It is believed to have been named in honour of the launch of the gunship *Clarence* in Pembroke dockyard in 1827 — the launching ceremony being carried out by the Duke of Clarence, later King William IV. The inn was described as 'the principal carriage house in Pembroke Dock' in 1829 when it was served by a regular coach service from Cold Blow, and in 1830 it hosted a dinner to mark the completion of a successful horse-race meeting held at the Redwell race-course on the nearby hill now called the Barrack Hill; Anna Jones was licensee at the time.

By the mid 1830s the Clarence had gained a reputation as Pembroke Dock's most radical inn. Newspapers would arrive here by stagecoach and crowds would gather outside to hear the latest news being read aloud from the front step of the inn. Since this was the meeting place of the local Reform Committee, any newspaper editorial opposed to the various Reform Acts would be roundly jeered; in 1832 a copy of the rabidly Tory *Carmarthen Journal* was publicly burnt, to the delight of the gathering outside the Clarence. The passing of the 1832 Reform Act was the cue for a night of celebration at the inn.

The inn also housed the local freemasons for a time; in 1835 the brethren gathered at their lodge room in the Clarence to celebrate the Festival of St. John and were reportedly well catered for by the licensee, Mrs. Anna Jones. When the enterprising Mrs. Jones opened the rather more opulent Victoria Hotel across the road in 1836, the masons switched their lodge room to the

Crowds would gather outside the Clarence Inn to await the arrival of the mail coach.

new establishment. The Clarence was put up for sale in September 1836, at which time it was described as having 'two good front parlours, a bar, tap-room, four bedrooms, large kitchen and brewhouse, coach-house and six stall stables.' By 1841 Mary Gibby was running the Clarence, while in 1844 her 23-year-old daughter Catherine was the innkeeper.

The following year she handed over to George Thomas Husband who remained landlord for over 20 years. George Husband had a varied career. He had been a farmer in Monkton as a young man before becoming butler to the Owens of Orielton House and Landshipping. In about 1835 he took over the running of the pub and farm known as the Landshipping Inn, now the Stanley Arms, from where he moved to the Clarence. The inn doubled as the town's post office, and Husband acted as postmaster as well as being water bailiff for Milford Haven — prosecuting skippers who dumped their ballast in the harbour. He remained the postmaster at Pembroke Dock for 25 years, moving to the new post office in Meyrick Street in 1869. He eventually died in 1871 aged 72. Reynolds recalled him as: 'Legal adviser, philosopher and friend to many in and around the locality, mine host Mr. George Husband of the Clarence, the town's first Postmaster and last Water Bailiff'.

In 1870 a licence for the Clarence was granted to local brewer William Price, but he died the following year and the licence passed to James Gwyther, a dairyman from Lamphey. He remained there until his death in 1889 after which his widow Caroline took over. William John kept the pub from 1906 to 1914 while Alfred Ham held the licence in 1926 when the Clarence became yet another victim of the redundancy ruling. The bulk of the compensation pay-out of £620 went to Mrs. Alice Morris of Colwyn Bay, the owner of the property. The building was so badly bomb-damaged during the war that it was demolished in 1948, and remains a bomb site to this day.

The **Victoria Hotel** on the opposite corner played an important part in the early social life of Pembroke Dock, being 'a famed house of entertainment'

The Victoria had been converted into a school by the time this photo was taken in the early 1900s.

according to one writer in 1854. It was built as a coaching inn in 1835 at the instigation of Anna Jones of the Clarence. As the *Welshman* newspaper reported in December 1835: 'Few inns in the Principality have greater accommodation than this newly-erected hotel'.

The Victoria was fully operational by March 1836 when Mrs. Jones assured 'those ladies and gentlemen who may honour her with their commands that nothing shall be wanted on her part to render everything comfortable'. The hotel proved ideal for the ceremonial get-togethers of the multitude of societies and associations which existed in the dockyard town at that time. It became the regular meeting place of the local freemasons between 1836 and the 1850s as well as being home to the Loyal Victoria Odd Fellows lodge which was formed in 1837. A large dining room was added in 1846 which proved very popular.

Anna Jones remained landlady of the Victoria until 1853, when dockyard official Samuel Jenkins, who had married Mrs. Jones' eldest daughter Eliza in 1845, took over. A freemason and council bigwig, Alderman Jenkins ran the Victoria as a thriving commercial, family and posting hotel, enlarging the premises in the spring of 1857. A new three-storey extension was built with kitchens and coach-houses on the ground floor, a ballroom and card-room on the first floor and bedrooms on the top floor. From 1872 onwards the county court hearings for South Pembrokeshire were held in a room in this extension, reached via an archway from Pembroke Street and two flights of stairs.

During the time of Mr. Jenkins the hotel enjoyed probably its finest hour, hosting the magnificent banquet that followed the launch of the Japanese corvette *Hi Yei* which was built at Jacob's Pill in Pennar in 1877. However Mr. Jenkins sold up the following year, leaving to take over the running of the town's Bush Hotel, a decision perhaps taken in the light of the dwindling role being played by coaching inns in the new railway age. He sold the Victoria to a schoolmaster who turned it into a preparatory school for boys. The building was refurbished recently and converted into flats.

There appear to have been three other pubs on the west side of the street. The **Duke of York** was at number 14, but it has a confusing history compounded by the fact that there was briefly another Duke of York in nearby Princes Street. John Furlong seems to have kept the Pembroke Street Duke of York from 1840 to 1844 while Ann Furlong was the licensee between 1858 and 1871. James Wade from Milford then kept the pub until 1874, followed by a succession of licensees, none of whom stayed long.

The former Duke of York is now a tattoo parlour. Note the second door, installed at the insistence of the town's magistrates to separate the public bar from the shop which occupied the same building.

The building had been owned by the Admiralty, but the freehold was bought in the 1880s by Mrs. W.T. Smith, a local wine-merchant, for £245. The licensee in the 1880s was John Footman, who also ran a grocery shop in part of the building. This was nearly his undoing, because a passageway connected the shop with the pub — a state of affairs severely frowned upon by the magistrates. They gave him a choice, either block up the passage or lose your licence. Footman called in the builders the following day.

Mrs. Eliza Thorne was the landlady in 1906 and she was followed by George and Sarah Williams who also provided lodgings for sailors. Sarah Ann Jenkins was the next licensee and she was forced to conduct a running battle with the town's magistrates who were determined to close the pub. Twice in three years the magistrates recommended that the Duke of York be closed; twice the redundancy committee failed to act on their recommendation. The reason the magistrates gave for trying to close the pub was that there were simply too many licensed premises in the area. They quoted the following as evidence:

> From this house to the Olive Bar is 27 paces; to the Clarence Inn 123 paces; Market Tavern 66 paces; Navy Tavern 123 paces; White Hart 139 paces. There are six licensed houses in Pembroke Street. There are 23 private houses in the same street.

When Sarah Jenkins moved on, Catherine Shaw took over as tenant of the pub, which was by now a James Williams house. But she wasn't there for long. A third recommendation for closure landed in front of the redundancy committee, and on this occasion it finally agreed that 'having regard to the character and necessities of the neighbourhood the licence in respect of the premises is unnecessary'. Compensation was set at £300 and the pub closed in about 1915. It is now a tattoo parlour with two separate front doors, a legacy of the time when the grocery shop and the pub which shared the building had to have independent entrances.

Three doors down was yet another of the town's **Commercial** inns. The landlord in all but name was Edward Brown, but since he was a joiner in the dockyard and disqualified from running a pub, the licensee in the 1860s was his daughter Mary. It was a popular place, partly because it offered extended credit to dockyard workers on the 'slate'; several times Mary was forced to go to the County Court to force tardy payers to settle their accounts. By 1871 the pub had closed and had become a lodging house; it is now a private house.

On the corner with Melville Street was a property known as **London House**. This was kept as a pub by John Nathan, but in 1849 an advert appeared saying that the premises were to be let, complete with counter, pewter and lamps. The advert said that the place was 'coming in moderate as the present occupier is about leaving Wales'. It was still recorded as a pub in the 1852 trade directory, but with no licensee named, and seems to have become part of Teasdale's drapery business soon afterwards. The building was demolished in 1956 and the Nunnery for the Sacred Hearts of Jesus and Mary built on the site.

The bottom of Market Street was once a real boozer's paradise, with five pubs clustered around the junction with Melville Street. The **Farmers Arms** was near the corner of Market Street and Melville Street, facing the market. According to Mason it had a long room upstairs, reached by an outside stairway, which was 'a favourite place for supper parties (much in vogue then) and for shows'. Richard Williams, who was landlord there from about 1830 until his death, aged 52, in 1841, owned several properties including a grocery shop next door on the corner of Market Street. When Williams died, his widow Mary took over the licence, but by the time of the 1851 census the pub was standing empty.

Elizabeth Griffiths was licensee from 1852 to 1855 and a joiner from Llanstadwell called George Griffiths had charge in 1861. It was said of the Farmers Arms in 1864 that 'John Syme's name is on the sign, but Isaac Lloyd keeps the pub'. Perhaps to sort out this confusion. the pub was given a change of name after being taken over by Cosheston brewer David White in the late 1860s, becoming the **Vine** for a dozen or so years. However the new name didn't really catch on and it was the Farmers' Arms again by the time John Davies took over in 1873. Theophilus Thomas kept the inn from 1901 to 1906, John Henry Morris was behind the bar from 1912 to 1932 and Billy Morris was the landlord at the time the building was destroyed in the Blitz in November 1940. Part of the nunnery mentioned above was later built on the site.

Just round the corner from the Farmers' Arms on the eastern side of Market Street was the **Picton Castle**. George Griffiths from Nash was licensee in 1861 and Jane Fortune was the landlady in 1866. The licence swapped hands a couple more times before the changes in the licensing laws saw the pub close in about 1868 and become a lodging house. The building was another casualty of the Blitz and council houses were built on the site in the early 1950s.

Two doors along was the **Crystal Palace** where George Williams held the licence in the 1850s. Many of the enormous sheds which covered the dockyard slipways were built by the firm which constructed the Crystal Palace in London in 1851, which may be how the name came about. By 1864 it was still known as the Crystal Palace, but was no longer licensed; instead it had deteriorated into one of the town's more notorious brothels. When William Williams, a local shoemaker, complained in court that he had been robbed of 11s. 6d. by a prostitute at the Crystal Palace, the magistrates dismissed the case. 'If you frequent such houses you deserve to be robbed,' they admonished him. Williams was forced to pay 1s. 6d. costs — which he did 'amidst much tittering in the court'.

Another two doors up the hill was the briefly-lived **Cross Keys** where Jane Sutton was licensee in 1844, and next door to this was the **Masons' Arms.** Stonemason Abraham Beed from Angle and his wife Margaret ran this beer-house in the 1850s and '60s, no doubt hoping to capitalise on the influx of troops quartered in the nearby Defensible Barracks. It had become a lodging house by 1871 and the building is still standing in the centre of what remains of the old terrace

On the other side of Market Street, near the bottom and directly opposite the Picton Castle, was the **Ivy Bush** with its popular skittle alley. However, this wasn't the original Ivy Bush which seems to have been elsewhere in the same street. A Mr. and Mrs. Rogers kept this earlier Ivy Bush in 1847 and hosted regular get-togethers of the town's Harmonic Society, while Ann Thomas kept the pub in 1850. In 1910, an article appeared in the *Pembroke Dock and Pembroke Gazette* stating that the first Ivy Bush was:

one of the principal lodging houses and a rendezvous for the Royal Marines. It also possessed a spacious skittle alley. In the early days of the dockyard, money paid to the pensioners was changed at this house, among others. It was a stronghold of the Liberal Party.

Like several other Pembroke Dock pubs, the Ivy Bush issued its own brass tokens or 'checks' which could be used to buy drinks in the house; these were in denominations of threepence and a penny-ha'penny.

Thomas John was the licensee in 1852, with Priscilla Thomas running the pub in 1858. At some stage in the 1850s the Ivy Bush was damaged by a fire which broke out in a bedroom over the skittle ground and caused £70 worth of damage. This may have prompted the move to the new building which was formerly a lodging house, the skittle alley being transferred along with the licence. Martha Rogers from Narberth was licensee in 1861, and her husband George T. Chappell was the landlord from 1871 to 1878. When he died, Martha, by then known as Martha Rogers Chappell, took over again. The Christmas supper at the Ivy Bush was one of the great social occasions in that part of town. In 1860 over 150 people enjoyed a festive meal which was followed by the usual endless round of toasts. 'Songs were in great profusion', noted the *Pembrokeshire Herald* dryly, 'some of which were well rendered'.

In 1889 the pub was offered for sale. At the time it included a bar, smoking-room, back parlour, tap-room and skittle-alley 'with every convenience', including servants' quarters above. William Thomas was the licensee in 1901 and William Gwilliam was the landlord from 1906 to 1910 when the Ivy Bush was declared surplus to requirements and was forced to close by the local magistrates. Badly bombed in the war, the building no longer stands.

The **Prince Albert Spirit Vaults** next door was on the junction of Market Street and Melville Street and possessed a classic street corner entrance. There was a pub on the spot in 1841, kept by Martha Weir, widow of Walter Weir who once ran the Navy Tavern, but it looks to have been short-lived. The Prince Albert seems to have opened in the late 1860s and John Griffiths held a licence here in 1871. James Thomas was the landlord from 1875 to 1878, followed in fairly rapid succession by Richard Dawkins and William Herbert, who briefly changed the name to the **Bunch of Grapes**. When Herbert left to run the Three Tuns he was followed by J.C. Harrison and William Rowlands who was the landlord in 1906. William Hughes and his wife Helen kept the pub in 1914; they built a skittle alley at the back to replace the one lost to enthusiasts by the forced closure of the Ivy Bush. Miss Doris Treharne kept the pub from 1923 to 1926, followed by Mrs. Mary Elizabeth Treharne Evans. The Prince Albert received a direct hit during the

The Prince Albert Spirit Vaults and the Ivy Bush next door (with the lamp outside) were both destroyed by German bombing.
(Picture courtesy of Mr. Philip Carradice.)

air-raid of 12 May 1941, killing Mrs. Evans and three residents — James Allen, Thomas Phillips and Henry Roach.

Princes Street, too, was devastated by the bombing in 1941, especially the raid on the night of 12 May which killed nearly 40 people in the town. Much of the old terracing has now gone, replaced after the war by council housing. On the eastern side of the Princes Street junction with Melville Street stood a pub variously called the **Crown and Cushion**, the **Crown**, and the **Crown Stores**. It was referred to as the Crown when it was run by Thomas and Dorothea Phillips in the late 1820s and early 1830s. They were followed by their son George who was still there in 1851. During his time it became the Crown and Cushion, and since this is a name usually coined to commemorate coronations, the change would appear to date from Victoria's big day in 1837.

William Benjamin Price — 'one of the smartest businessmen in Pembroke Dock' — took over as landlord in the 1850s. The son of William Price, the Pembroke Street brewer, he later became proprietor of the Royal Edinburgh Hotel and carried on a thriving business as a wine, spirit, ale and

*William Benjamin Price of the Crown Stores advertises
his services in 1880.*

porter merchant. He changed the name again, to Crown Stores, and ran it with his wife Margaret until at least 1884.

The Crown was completely destroyed by fire in 1892, when it was described in the press as being one of the oldest inns in the town. A Mr. and Mrs. Mitchell and family were in residence at the time, but fortunately escaped unscathed. The pub was rebuilt, and Jacob 'Jake' Lewis kept it until 1909 when he handed over to James Williams, formerly of the Grey Horse in Tenby, who held the licence until 1916.

W.H. Davies was the landlord in 1923 and he was followed in rapid succession by several other licensees — a symptom of the uncertainty caused by the closure of the dockyard. In 1930 the licence passed from Albert Stitfall to his sister, Deborah Tanner, but when she left in 1932 the pub fell into disrepair. It was given a substantial facelift and reopened by Ralph Rollings in 1935, before he handed over to Mrs. Mildred Gwyther. However the long and somewhat chequered history of the Crown ended when it fell victim to the air raid of 1941.

Three doors up from the Crown was a pub kept in 1852 by a naval man called John Ellard and in 1861 by his widow Jane. No name is given in the census, but it seems to have been known as **Ellards Hotel**. It may later have become the **Caledonia**, described by Slater's trade directory of 1867 as being in Princes Street and being run by T. Collins. And further up on the left, at the top of the original terrace, was the **Duke of York** beer-house, which was run by John Furlong of Stackpole in 1851 and by John Butler in 1861.

Hannah Thomas kept an inn opposite the Duke of York in 1861. This was probably the **North Wales Tavern** which was later run by Edward Burrows, formerly of the Steam Packet in Pembroke Street. Halfway down this western side of the street was the **Bush**, a beer-house kept by Richard Jones in 1855 and by Maria Jones in 1861.

At the bottom, the **Dock Gate** was on the corner of Princes Street and Melville Street, opposite the Crown Stores. It came into being in 1870 when

The Navy Inn is still going strong.

a new licence was granted to Richard Cousens, but the licence passed to his father George Cousens three years later. George had been a baker on the same spot for the past 30 years, and 'Daddy' Cousens as he was known continued to fill the dual role of alehouse keeper and baker until at least 1884 when he was 71. When the pub closed isn't known, but it may have been in the building which still stands on the corner.

Apart from the White Hart, the only other pub in the area still open is the **Navy Inn** on the corner of Cumby Terrace and Melville Street. This was built as a private house by dockyard boatswain Richard Weatherley and stood at the bottom of a terrace originally known as Queen Street (West) or 'Officers Row' because of the number of dockyard officials who lived there. It was converted into a pub in the 1850s and has been much altered down the years. John Jones held the licence in 1858 and David Howells was landlord in the 1860s.

Longest-serving landlord at the Navy Inn was William Hyde who was there from 1874 to 1901. John Henry Morris was the landlord in 1906 before moving to the Farmers Arms and J.D. Jones was landlord in 1913 when the pub was regularly frequented by the crews of torpedo boats stationed in the Haven. Thomas Rooke, formerly of the Plough in Sageston, took over in 1932 but died the following year; his widow Clara continued to run the business through to the war. Michael Nugent took over in 1953 and remains the best-remembered post-war licensee. The Navy was one of the first places in town to offer 'pub food' and a 1979 guidebook accurately decribed the inn as follows: 'Traditional public bar and large, done-up lounge bar; carpets, brass, new Tudor'. And it is still a thriving pub, despite the recent diversion of Irish ferry traffic away from its door.

CHAPTER NINE

Pembroke Dock
PENNAR, BUFFERLAND, PROSPECT PLACE
& LLANREATH

Pennar is a distinct community in its own right, as proudly independent of the rest of Pembroke Dock as Hakin is of Milford Haven or Prendergast is of Haverfordwest. Unlike those other two neighbourhoods, however, Pennar has never been historically associated with riotous drinking, possibly due to the sobering influence of the various chapels in the vicinity.

Many of the workmen who came to Pembroke Dock to establish the dock-yard were nonconformists, and from an early stage they began to look around for somewhere to build meeting houses in which to worship. They found the landowning Meyrick family surprisingly unhelpful in this respect, so turned instead to the Owens of Orielton who owned most of the land on which Pennar now stands. Sir John Owen proved far more accommodating, and in 1818 the Baptists built Bethany chapel at the west end of High Street — the first chapel in the new town — while the Wesleyans opened the Ebenezer chapel a couple of years later in nearby South Row, later Wesley Row.

A number of substantial houses were built in Treowen Road at around this time, and also in Cross Park, although when the Defensible Barracks were built in the mid-1840s numerous properties in the area were acquired by the Board of Ordnance and demolished to give the guns at the fort a clear field of fire in all directions. Many of the displaced residents moved to nearby Bufferland or Prospect Place, while a few streets of workers cottages were constructed at about this time near the shore at Bentlass Ferry. The terraces of Military Road and Owen Street followed in the 1860s, housing workers not just from the Royal Dockyard, but also from the private yard at Jacob's Pill on the Pembroke River.

Pennar continued to be a strong chapel-going area, and Gilgal, which opened in 1862, set its stall out early as an enemy of the drinking man. A resolution passed at a chapel meeting in 1865 declared: 'We do not hold any brother or sister in fellowship who keeps a public house or sells intoxicating drink'. That these weren't idle words was underlined a few months later when one member was excluded from the chapel 'for being engaged in the drink traffic'. And at a temperance meeting held in Pennar in 1862, no fewer than 50 people signed the pledge.

In such an atmosphere of intolerance and sobriety, it wouldn't be surprising to find no pubs at all in Pennar. But there were enough people brave enough to withstand the disapproval of the chapel elders to create a boozy little colony of pubs at the eastern end of Military Road. The **Commercial** at 1 Military Road was kept by Robert Court Griffiths from the early 1870s until 1889 when the licence passed to his widow Mrs. Ann Griffiths, while Thomas Griffiths was in charge by 1901. Brewers James Williams subsequently ran the

The Sherlock Holmes was for many years the Kilwendeg.

pub, but failed to find a tenant with staying power until 1921 when James and Phoebe Turner took over. They were still there in 1934 when Police Sergeant Charlie Bodman, something of a scourge of the town's licensing trade, recommended the pub for closure. The Commercial was duly closed in July of that year with £425 paid out in compensation.

On the same side of the road, the **Sherlock Holmes** at 19 Military Road was for over a century called the **Kilwendeg**, under which sign it took the prize for the pub name with the greatest variety of spellings, being written as 'Cilwendeg', 'Kelwendeague' 'Kilwendy' and even 'Kalwentage'. It was so-called because it was built on land owned by Miss Lloyd of Kilwendeg House on the Cardiganshire border.

There was a regular turnover of licensees in early 1870s, but John Williams from Carew settled things down by becoming the landlord from 1875 until his death in about 1897. He was a Trinity House man, so for much of the time the pub was run by his wife Rebecca, a member of the Rees family who kept the Cardigan Inn at West Williamston. She died in 1912, aged 70, after which her son George and his wife Sarah kept the pub until the Second World War. Billy Gwynne was landlord from 1940 through to the 1960s followed by Brian Colley who kept the 'Kil' for over 20 years. When he retired, the licence passed through a number of hands until 1998 when brewers James Williams sold the house to Michael Kerr. Reasoning that a change of name might bring a change of luck for the rather down-at-heel business, he rechris-tened the pub the Sherlock Holmes, partly to reflect the classic Victorian nature of the property and partly because the post-code was SH! With a new extension and a growing emphasis on food, the pub is happily enjoying a new lease of life.

The **Plough and Harrow** was a pub in Military Road which failed to stay the course.

The Royal Oak in Military Road, shortly before it closed in 2002.

William John held the licence in 1868 but lost it in 1870, apparently under an unofficial 'three strikes and you're out' rule. When John applied to have his licence renewed in September of that year, the magistrates pointed out that he had been fined three times in the past year for serving out of hours and so decided he was unfit to run a pub. A later application to allow a chap called George Nicholas to run the pub was also refused and the Plough and Harrow seems to have closed forthwith. It was a few doors along from the Kilwendeg, probably one of the houses on the corner of the lane.

Recently closed is the corner-cottage **Royal Oak** on the opposite side at 36 Military Road, which was run from 1872 to 1891 by David Nicholas. William Goodridge held the licence in 1901 and Joseph Paulett was the landlord from 1906 to 1913 when he handed over to Tommy Roberts. 'Many will remember Mrs. Roberts and her talented son and musician Boysie Roberts', wrote J.M. Owen in 1969. In 1921 the landlord was Edward McKay and Mrs. Margaret McKay held the licence from 1926 until 1931. Various licensees then came and went before the arrival of David John who was landlord from 1943 to 1956. Ivan Beynon, whose sisters kept the Caledonian, took over and was there throughout the 1960s. It is now a private house.

The **Gloucester Inn** was about nine doors along from the Royal Oak, towards Pennar Park. William Phillips, farmer and haulier, was the only recorded licensee, running the pub as a sideline in the 1870s and '80s.

In Lower Pennar, the **New Swan** was in Ferry Road at the junction with Castle Street. It was the Banner family inn and was a handy watering-hole for workmen trudging between the Royal Dockyard and the rowing boat ferry connecting Pennar and Bentlass. Henry Banner is mentioned in the *Welshman* in 1867 as being the landlord; six years earlier he had been running the 'Old' Swan in Queen Street. He was followed by various other members of his family, notably his daughter Miss Hannah Banner who was the landlady from 1891 to 1914. According to Reynolds:

> The last house to be closed in Pennar was the Swan Inn. Many will remember Miss Banner, the landlady. In the bar for many years was displayed a list of the ladies names who made the colours of the old Pembroke Dock Rifle Volunteers. This house was considered to be the cleanest and best-kept in the locality. The aquatic sports held off Bentlass Ferry will be long remembered, the good lady of the Swan being one of the best hostesses of her day.

Arthur Banner was behind the bar in 1923 while Wilfred 'Whiffy' Edwards was running the New Swan in 1936, the year it was referred for compensation on the grounds that it was 'not required to meet the wants of the neighbourhood'. Thereafter the building stood empty and derelict for many years before being demolished as part of the redevelopment of this area in the early 1970s.

There was once a pub called the **Windsor Castle** on the south side of Cross Park — this could be the beer-house mentioned in a trade directory as being run by Charlotte Griffiths in the early 1850s. By 1861 it was being run by Daniel and Charlotte Jenkins but there are no further sightings in the records. Mr. John Hogg thought that the building which housed the pub was demolished during the last war 'possibly as a result of enemy action'.

In 1864 George Thomas was granted a licence to open a pub in Pennar. The sign of this pub isn't known, but George Thomas, mason, was living at 14 Cross Park at the time of the 1871 census.

The **Cambrian** was described by Mason as 'forming a buttress at the corner of Wesley Row with Phillips' grocery establishment next door' — this being the terrace leading off Treowen Road, parallel with and north of Cross Park. The pub was built in about 1818 on land leased from the Orielton Estate and the freehold was sold to the War Department in 1822. In 1843 the Board of Ordnance began buying out the leases of houses in Wesley Row so that they could be demolished to create a clear field of fire for the guns. Henry Williams and his wife Mary had kept the pub since at least 1830, but they were obliged to move to Lower Prospect Place where the pub continued to prosper under the same sign.

Also in Wesley Row was the **Caledonia** or Caledonian which dated back to the 1820s when James Kelly hosted meetings of the Pembroke Dock Provident Society there. By 1830 Elizabeth Davies was the landlady and she was followed by John Hill. The pub was apparently notable at one time for having as its inn sign a life-sized replica of a kilted Highlander — probably one of the models used in the 1830s and '40s to advertise Scottish Snuff.

The Caledonia was kept in the early 1840s by a widow named Catherine Lawrence, but when the Board of Ordnance kicked her out of Wesley Row she opened the **New Caledonia** in the High Street — the present **Caledonia Inn** — before taking over the Albion in King Street.

There is some suggestion that there was once an ancient farmhouse on the site of the present pub, while according to both Mason and Peters the Caledonia was formerly a private school kept by a druggist named James Barclay. The 1851 census shows Barclay to be still in business as a druggist in High Street with the pub up and running next door, the landlord being David Miller. When Barclay died in 1853, ownership of the Caledonia passed to his daughter Sophia, a schoolmistress from Lower Meyrick Street. Benjamin Davies was landlord in 1861 and James Phillips was in charge from 1867 to 1877. Phoebe Harries took over but gave up the pub a few months later after being fined for serving after hours. Her successor, dressmaker Martha Morgans, held the licence from 1878 to 1887.

Fred Noakes, formerly of the Duke of York, kept the pub between 1888 and January 1925 when William Beynon bought the lease from him. In 1940 a German bomb flattened the fish and chip shop next door, but undeterred by massive damage to the pub and loss of stock, landlord Beynon was soon open again, 'an action much appreciated by the many local patrons of this old established house', as Mr. Bill Richards recalled in his book *Pembrokeshire Under Fire*. Despite this swift return to business, the building was still described as being in a 'bad' condition as late as 1950.

William Beynon died in 1941 after which the pub was run by his widow, Mary Sophia Beynon, until 1962. The Beynon family had purchased the freehold of the pub from the Bush estate in 1960 for £2,000 and it continued to be run by two of Mary's daughters, Fay and Barbara, elderly spinsters who came down hard upon any customer foolish enough to utter even the mildest swear word within their hearing. Since 1980 the 'Cally' has been run by Mrs. Susan Woods who has enlarged the pub and added a beer-garden while happily still preserving the tiny front bar — surely the smallest 'snug' in town.

The building opposite Bethany chapel, on the corner of High Street and Bellevue Terrace, was once known as the **Porter Stores**. Mrs. Peters believed that these premises were once kept by a Mr. Jones and that this was the original meeting place of the Pembroke Dock Lodge of Freemasons, which was formed in 1824. When Mr. Jones and his wife Anna moved to the Clarence Inn down the road, the brotherhood moved with them. Henry White, whose main brewery was at the top of Meyrick Street, also held a licence for the Porter Stores in High Street between 1859 and 1889, describing it as a brewery, malthouse and porter stores. Whether it also had a tap-room is not known. To add to the confusion over these various porter places, there was also a **Porter Brewery** public house at 14 Bellevue Terrace in 1901, kept by Edward Llewellyn; these are probably all the same place, but it is difficult to be certain.

Bufferland grew up between the 1840s and 1860s, but has only ever had one pub — the **Alma** on the western corner of North Street. Local tradition has it that the pub was opened in 1854 by a soldier returning from the Crimea and that it stood in splendid isolation for some years before the rest of the terrace was built. If so, it must have been a beer-house in its early days, because the first full licence was obtained by a sailmaker named Charles Reynolds in 1869. Elizabeth Reynolds was the landlady from 1874 to 1879 when the Alma became one of several pubs to come under the control of local brewer and spirit merchant William B. Price. He installed various tenants throughout the 1880s and early '90s, none of whom stayed long.

The Alma Inn as it looked in 2002.

Mrs. Susan Anderson was licensee between 1897 and 1910, in which year she was fined the hefty sum of £20 for 'permitting drunkenness on licensed premises'. She left soon afterwards and Maurice Williams ran the pub as a tenant from 1910 to 1914. In that year he purchased the Alma and drew up plans for an attractive, new-look pub. 'The age of the building calls for immediate repair', pointed out Mr. Williams in a letter to the council, his plans involving turning the corner-cottage pub into a two-storey building, with three bedrooms upstairs. However the rebuilding never took place, possibly because of the outbreak of war.

Mr. Williams employed various managers to run the pub until 1930 when he once again took the helm himself, remaining in charge until 1943 when Albert Gosling took over. Local builder Cyril Walden became licensee in 1961 and made numerous alterations, finally succeeding in turning the Alma into a two-storey building. Former Glamorgan wicket-keeper Haydn Davies kept the pub for a time and the present licensees, Norman and Geraldine Porter, have been at the Alma since 1983.

Some 20 doors along High Street from the Caledonia, on the same side, was the long-departed **Wheatsheaf**. Levi and Frances John ran this terraced cottage pub from 1861 until Levi's death in 1883, after which the licence was not renewed. The building no longer stands, having been demolished to make way for the building of High Street Close.

133

The Red Rose Inn is still going strong.

Almost opposite was the **Myrtle Tree**, which came into being when a tailor from Milford called William Russan turned his house into a pub in 1871; perhaps the fact that he had eight children to support influenced his decision! It was the town's last out-and-out beer-house when William Thomas ran it from the late 1870s until 1898, in which year he was twice hauled before the magistrates for serving beer on a Sunday. As a result of these offences, 78-year-old Mr. Thomas lost his licence at the next Brewster Session. The Myrtle Tree stands out as a two-storey building among the row of cottages and has recently been subdivided into 61 and 61a High Street.

A dozen houses along, almost at the corner, was where Thomas Harris briefly ran a beer-house in the late 1840s after he retired from being a ship-wright. This may have been called the **Grapes**, which was mentioned by Reynolds as being a former pub in High Street.

Back across the road was the **Britannia Arms.** A map of 1863 shows this to be the last building in the long terrace of cottages on the right as one leaves Pembroke Dock — beyond this were fields. When a road was eventually built southwards to connect High Street with North Street and Albany Street, the Britannia found itself on the corner. The new street took its name from the pub which had been opened in the 1840s by a gardener named Thomas Rees; his widow Mary was still the innkeeper in 1861. It seems that when she died in the 1860s the pub died with her. It is now a private house, much altered, on the west corner of High Street and Britannia Road.

The **Red Rose** at 113 High Street still survives as a comfortable street corner local, having been pleasantly refurbished in recent years. It was opened in the 1860s in a cottage formerly occupied by a shipwright's family and seems to have

The former Cambrian Inn in Prospect Place.

been part of the portfolio of pubs built up by spirit merchant W.B. Price. He installed a sequence of tenants to run it, including Richard Crowe, Catherine Gibby and the inevitable Jesse Chappell. Harold Kennedy was licensee from 1906 to 1909 before moving to take over the Navy Tavern. Joseph Denner was landlord in 1914, while John and Elizabeth Denner continued to run the pub up to the last war. Captain Leslie Stanley, who was licensee in the 1950s and 1960s, remains the best-remembered post-war publican.

From the Red Rose junction it is possible to drop down into Pembroke Dock via Prospect Place, which, as its name suggests, provides a panoramic view of the town and Haven. Originally, and confusingly, the present-day Prospect Place was divided into Prospect Place East and Lower Prospect Place, while the present-day Milton Terrace was divided into Prospect Row and Middle Prospect Place, the names not being changed until 1906.

There may have been as many as three pubs in Milton Terrace at different times, but it is difficult to pin them down. Both John Tapp and James Oliver ran beer-houses in this terrace in the 1850s, and Oliver's was called the **Waterloo Arms**. He gave up the licence in a fit of pique in 1861 after being fined half-a-crown for serving on a Sunday. 'That's the last money you'll get from me', he stormed at the magistrates. 'I'll give up my licence. Sometimes I don't sell a quart of beer in a week'.

James Meyrick Owen suggested in one of his articles that 32 Milton Terrace was once the **Brown Cow,** run by a family named Davies; it has proved impossible to find confirmation of this, although the building certainly looks the part.

A man named William Scott ran a beer-house in Prospect Place (East) from 1858 to 1861. This seems to have been called the **Railway View**, since Reynolds, writing in the 1930s, reported: 'I learn my old friend Mr. William

The Prospect Tavern closed in 2002.

Scott, now 86, has stated there was a licensed house in Prospect Place named the Railway View, now closed, but there was no view of the railway'. Reynolds' elderly friend must surely have been a relative of the beer-house keeper.

The **Cambrian** was located just off Treowen Road until about 1844 when it was moved to a prime position in Prospect Place, being on the corner of the steep hill which linked Milton Terrace with the top of Meyrick Street. Licensees at the time of the move were Henry and Mary Williams, one of whose sons, Cornelius, became a chemist and a noted figure in the town. Mary later ran the pub on her own, while subsequent licensees included Samuel Gregory, Francis Hawkens and Thomas Griffiths who kept the pub from 1901 to 1909 when the licence wasn't renewed. Although now divided into two properties, the building is still called Cambrian House.

The **Prospect Tavern** was in Lower Prospect Place, across the junction and a few doors down from the Cambrian at no. 20. It was run in 1871 by widower James Morgans from Lawrenny, but when he died two years later the licence passed to Martha Morgans. She moved to the Caledonia, to be succeeded by James Lewis in January 1875. It is said that at this time a tunnel ran from the cellars of the Prospect Tavern under the road to Henry White's Pembroke Dock Brewery at the top of Meyrick Street, though whether this was to aid deliveries or to allow after-hours drinkers an escape route isn't recorded.

Lewis handed over to William Emmerson in July 1881, and he was followed by Mrs. Frances Emmerson who was landlady in the years leading up to the First World War. In 1923 the landlord was Thomas Cockeram and from 1928 to 1939 Charlie Knight was in charge. One of the best-remembered landlords was Arthur Skerry, a promising rugby player whose career was cut short by the Second World War. He was licensee from 1948 through to the 1960s, when the pub's back room was a popular evening haunt of senior masters from the local grammar school. Former district councillor Dick Forster was in charge in the 1980s when the pub was extensively renovated, 'making it, in the opinion of many, one of the most comfortable family pubs this side of Kathmandu' according to J.M. Owen.

Having changed hands a few times in recent years, the Prospect finally closed in about 2000, but an interesting relic of the pub can be found in the numismatic collection at Scolton Museum. This is a tavern token or 'check' for a penny ha'penny, issued by one of the early proprietors of the pub and bearing the words 'Prospect Tavern, Prospect Place, Pembe Dock'.

In 1849 a Primitive Methodist Chapel was built at the top of Upper Park Street, close to the steep bank below Prospect Place. This chapel only held about 50 people and the Methodists abandoned it for bigger premises in about 1866. The building was sold to the Dickensian-sounding Samuel Sloggett who infilled the gap between the chapel and Prospect Place to build a pub which he called, aptly enough, the **Temple Bar**. Access to the inn was from Prospect Place, while the old chapel formed the basement of the pub and could be entered from Upper Park Street. Sam Sloggett kept the pub in 1874, followed by his son John Sloggett in 1876 and then William Harries. A young widow named Annie Davies took over the licence briefly in April 1880 before another of the Sloggett tribe, Thomas, took charge in 1882. The pub appears to have closed soon afterwards, although the licence was kept up until 1892. The building later became a private house but burnt down in the early 1960s; the site is now a patch of wasteland.

Now much in demand for the construction of 'executive homes', Llanreath was originally a tiny hamlet of a few houses clustered around a shingle beach. One of these houses was built and occupied by a stonemason named David Price, reputedly one of the first men to arrive from Milford to build the dockyard. This became the **Dolphin** and was apparently popular with the dockyard workmen who rowed back and forth to Milford every day and who beached their boats on the shore nearby. According to Mason's history: 'The beer sold, which was home brewed, was so wisely diluted that no fights were ever known to be the outcome of drinking it. In other words, it did not affect the head'.

The freehold was sold in 1856 by the Orielton estate and the property is shown in the catalogue as 'Dolphin Beer House and Orchard'. It was situated at the lower end of Beach Road and must have closed at an early stage, perhaps the late 1820s when more workers were living in the town and fewer were arriving by boat from Milford.

137

Llanreath grew considerably in the 1840s to become a small village capable of supporting its own chapel and pub, or even two pubs, because J.M. Owen has recorded that there was once a beer-house called the **Royal Standard** hereabouts. Better documented was the **Weary Traveller** in Chapel Row at the top of the steep hill leading up from the beach. It was kept by dockyard labourer Essex Lewis and his wife Ann from 1851 until October 1877 when Richard Beynon took over. He was still landlord in 1892, but the following year he installed James Lewis as tenant/licensee. The arrangement couldn't have worked out because the Weary Traveller closed in 1894. Since then Llanreath has been 'dry', but in 2002 planning permission was given for a new pub to open in an old boathouse near the shore.

CHAPTER TEN

Pembroke Dock

BUSH ST., PARK ST., MEYRICK ST., LEWIS ST., LAWS ST., DIMOND ST & APLEY TERRACE

From Albion Square, a street developed in an easterly direction which became one of the main arteries of the town's grid-iron layout. Originally a lane of shanty homes called Pigs' Parade, this grew in the 1840s and '50s into a busy commercial thoroughfare renamed Bush Street and most of the town's north-south streets intersect it at right angles. For such a long street it wasn't very well served with hostelries even in the hey-day of Pembroke Dock boozing, and only two pubs still remain open along its entire length. Nearly all the pubs and the political clubs, were on the north side of the street, and it seems that the south side and the residential area to the south east of St. John's church was designated a sort of 'mini Temperance Town' with no pubs being allowed to open there.

Benjamin Phillips, formerly of the Clarence in Pembroke, opened the **Prince of Wales** in about 1844 and he was still there in 1852 when he was listed as a 'retailer of beer, Bush Street'. The 1851 census showed him occupying one of only 11 houses which then stood in Bush Street, but the pub must have closed soon afterwards, allowing the present Prince of Wales in Laws Street to adopt the name.

The **Charlton**, on the corner of Bush Street and Upper Park Street, is a happy survival of a classic Pembroke Dock Victorian pub, with a long, gleaming counter where dozens of pints would be lined up each evening ready for the influx of thirsty dockyard workers. The name is connected with the Meyrick family on whose Bush estate the town was built, Charlton being the original surname of Thomas Meyrick who changed his name when he succeeded to the estate in 1858. James Hancock opened the pub at about this time and ran it until his death in the mid 1860s; his widow Mary Hancock kept it going until 1889. William J. Ford took over, while Isaac Harries kept the pub from 1906 to 1914 and in the 1920s the landlord was George Carter.

Two policemen pass the time of day outside the Charlton in this early postcard view.

The Charlton has recently reopened after a period of closure.

Danny Jenkins kept the Charlton from 1933 until his death in 1947, and he was followed by Howard Johns who was there throughout the 1950s; other notable post-war licensees have included former Pembroke Borough footballer Trevor James, and Billy Scourfield. The Charlton has always had the reputation of being a 'drinking-man's pub' and only reluctantly allowed females onto the premises in the 1970s when it was forced to do so by law. The pub has always been full of characters of all ages (many of them to be found crouched over the ancient shove-ha'penny table), making the Charlton something of a throwback to the great days of dockyard beer-drinking. There were fears for its future when it closed in 2001, but happily this fine, red-brick pub reopened in the summer of 2002.

The **Pembrokeshire Arms** was on the west corner of Bush Street and Lower Meyrick Street, directly opposite Bethel, and seems to have led a fairly blameless existence. It was run by Thomas Williamson in 1861 and then by John and Alice Jones in the 1870s and Albert Saxby in the 1880s. Other licensees included Charlotte Brooman, Elizabeth Williams, George Adams, Alfred Rimmington, Daniel James and George Leesing, none of whom stayed long enough to make much impression. The pub was forced to close under the redundancy ruling in 1928, having fought off a similar attempt 10 years earlier. Since the dockyard had not long closed, plunging the town into depression, the licensees were probably not too unhappy at the magistrates' decision. It is now a music shop.

On the eastern corner of Lower Meyrick Street was the **Phoenix**, which was run by Cornelius Williams in the 1870s as part of his druggist shop. He later acquired the Bee Hive in Commercial Row when he took over the chemist's business there, eventually handing over both to his son Arthur Ll. Williams. These two chemist shop pubs were a source of annoyance to other local licensees who were forced to obey all kinds of rules and regulations that didn't seem to apply to Mr. Williams' two establishments. In 1910 the newly-formed Pembroke Dock L.V.A. objected to the licences being renewed, but their objections were over-ruled by the local magistrates who heard that the Phoenix and the Bee Hive were among the best-run drinking establishments in town (they probably drank there themselves), and the Phoenix still held an 'on' licence as recently as 1962.

The **Greyhound** must be one of the few pubs in the country where the beers have been replaced by biers — it is now an undertaker's business! The building is said to have once formed part of the vicarage for St. John's church opposite, but it was subsequently acquired by wine merchant W.T. Smith and used as a wholesale stores in the 1870s. The Smiths owned several pubs in the town, but chose to open and manage the Greyhound themselves — it was run by Mrs. Jane Smith in the 1890s.

In 1909 the pub was taken over by Arthur Cooper who was succeeded by Mr. Val Gibby. When he died in 1926 he was followed by Mr. and Mrs. J. Moorhouse. By the 1930s the Greyhound was owned by Hancock's Brewery and in 1936 Mrs. Amy Harrell took over as tenant, signalling the most successful period in the pub's relatively brief history. This was despite a strange quirk in the licensing laws which meant that that the Greyhound had to close at 9.30 p.m. instead of 10.30 p.m. each evening, the only pub in town so afflicted. This early closing could cause problems when visiting seamen were in

The former Greyhound is now an undertaker's business.

port and Mrs. Harrell had to try to persuade them to drink up and leave an hour earlier than they expected.

The Greyhound remained popular during the early years of the war, with sing-songs round the pub piano helping to maintain morale during the bombing of the town. The pub's large cellar made a convenient air-raid shelter, but fortunately the Greyhound escaped the German bombs. It couldn't escape the licensing authorities, however, and in 1943 Hancock's was ordered to renovate the pub's primitive toilet facilities or face closure. The Brewster Sessions in February 1944 was told that 'the owners of this house have intimated that they are unable to carry out any repairs to the premises'. As a consequence, the Greyhound's licence was withdrawn on 31 December 1945. The pub's lively trade was reflected in the compensation pay-out which was set at £1,000, the bulk of it going to Hancock's. The building is now the premises of local undertaker Mr. John Roberts.

Despite being closed for a few years in the 1990s, the **Bush Tavern** is once more flourishing at 65 Bush Street under licensee Mr. Allan Brookes. It appears to have opened in the 1850s with Charles Gardner as landlord, and it was a substantial pub for its time, being noted for the paintings of Derby winners which adorned the walls. The Army Reserve Pensioners were appar-

The Bush Tavern in 2003.

ently paid here, perhaps receiving some of the tuppenny tokens or 'checks' which Gardner issued himself. His widow Harriet Gardner was the landlady from about 1869 to 1875, while in 1882 a young woman named Laura Russell took over. She was there for just a few months before being fined for serving out of hours — the fact that the customer was her bridegroom-to-be cut little ice with the unromantic magistrates!

Mrs. Howard Smith was licensee in 1901, while in 1913 the licence passed from Mrs. Mary Locke to Frederick Heck. Just three weeks after taking over, he played host to the footballers of Swansea Town A.F.C. who had their luncheon and tea at the pub, in between which they thrashed Pembroke Dock 6-1. Mr. Heck remained the landlord until 1927 and Emily Pettit was

142

there in the early 1930s followed by Edward Thomas. He died in 1943 and Mr. and Mrs. Jack Nicholson ran the pub until 1949 when Eddie Jones became licensee, running the Bush Tavern until well into the 1960s.

Subsequently the licence changed hands fairly regularly (although Chris Austin was there for much of the 1980s) and by the early '90s the pub was closed. It was rescued in 1995 by Mr. Brookes, who carried out a great deal of necessary refurbishment and remodelling, adding a function room and generally giving the old pub a new lease of life.

Standing four-square on the corner of Bush Street and Laws Street, the **Bush Hotel** was originally an 1840s beer-house run by Mary Williams. It was rebuilt as a moderately imposing inn-cum-hotel in the 1850s by the Meyrick family, being the place where the Bush estate held its social functions. William Dawkins was the innkeeper in 1858 and he also hired out horses and gigs from the stables behind the hotel. Edward Crowe was there in 1861, while Henry Phelps George was landlord from 1867 to 1875, followed by his widow Elizabeth who catered for regular get-togethers of the town's various organisations, notably the Pembroke Dockyard Mechanics Amicable Benefit Society. The Bush was damaged by a gas explosion in 1881, in which year Alderman Samuel Jenkins, formerly of the Victoria, became the proprietor. When he died in 1894 his daughter Sarah took over, while Mrs. Jemima Jones was the landlady from 1906 to 1932.

The cover of the sale particulars of the Bush Hotel in 1919.
(Picture courtesy of the Pembrokeshire Records Office.)

According to Reynolds, British Prime Minister Lord Roseberry together with Prince Louis of Battenberg once called at the Bush, but more typical of

143

Telephone: Pembroke Dock 181

BUSH HOTEL

MR. AND MRS. L. H. MANDRY

A.A.   LAWS STREET   R.A.C.

PEMBROKE DOCK

PRIVATE and COMMERCIAL

LUNCHEONS and DINNERS

Terms on Application

*A 1960 advertisement for
the Bush Hotel.*

the clientele were the commercial travellers who arrived in numbers at the nearby station. In 1936 a chap from Tenby named John Leet took over, but Mrs. Joan John was in charge during the war, when the upper floors of the hotel were so badly damaged by the bombing that some of the rooms were not habitable again until 1952.

The Bush continued to operate through to the 1980s, hosting weddings, folk club gatherings and other functions as well as being the headquarters of Pennar Robins A.F.C. in the days when the club played on nearby Bush Camp. But increasingly the Bush began to look its age and struggled to compete with smart, purpose-built places such as the Cleddau Bridge Motel. It closed in about 1990 and has been converted into flats.

Returning to Albion Square, the pubs which once thrived, or floundered, in the streets that cross Bush Street at right angles are worthy of inspection. Brewery Row was the original name given to the west-facing terrace now known as Charlton Place. There was an alehouse here in the 1830s called the **Barley Sheaf** and run by George Wort (formerly of the New Inn at Herbrandston), but it seems to have been short-lived. In 1859 James Watkins was granted a licence to open the **Steam Hammer** in Charlton Place, in the house next door to the now-demolished Albion Bakery on the Bush Street corner. In 1870 the licence was transferred from Watkins to Thomas Nelson Pack, an ironwork erector from Norfolk, who was still the landlord in 1875. The splendidly-named Mary Maria Nelson Pack held the licence in 1881, by which time the Steam Hammer had gained something of a reputation for being a knocking-shop, much frequented by soldiers from the nearby barracks. This notoriety continued to grow, and in March 1893 the new licensee, whose name was Anne Lodwick, was charged with running the pub as a brothel. She was found guilty and fined £5 and the pub licence was immediately suppressed.

The **Royal Marines** in Upper Park Street also had an unsavoury reputation, and in the 1860s it was the haunt of two notorious prostitutes known as Queenstown Ellen and Sally Duff. In the early hours of a December morning in 1872 the whole street was roused by a commotion outside the pub. Hammering on the door was the officer in charge of a military patrol who was accompanied by a local police sergeant. They were searching for a couple of

Bush Street looking west.

private soldiers from the Royal Welsh Fusiliers who had failed to report back to the nearby Defensible Barracks. In the upstairs rooms of the pub they found the errant soldiers enjoying the company of two local women — no doubt the aforementioned ladies of the night. While the soldiers were marched back to barracks to face a military hearing, landlady of the Royal Marines, Mrs. Margaret Thomas, aged 66, was summoned to appear in front of the Borough Petty Sessions charged with 'keeping her house open during prohibited hours and allowing men and women to cohabit therein'. Evidently appalled at such goings-on, the magistrates ordered the immediate closure of the pub and banned the landlady from ever again holding a licence. A stunned Mrs. Thomas, who had kept the Royal Marines since 1841, pleaded with the court to be allowed to sell off the stock which remained in the house. This was refused, with the magistrates adding a rider that the premises, which faced the town cemetery, should never again be licensed.

The Royal Marines was the seventh house on the left going up from the Bush Street junction. Five doors further up was also a pub in 1841, the licensee being named in the census as Martha Smith. This was probably the **Hand and Heart**, an early Park Street pub where Rebecca Jones was the landlady by 1844. The name refers to an ancient symbol of friendship, so this may well have been the meeting place of one of Pembroke Dock's many Friendly Societies.

The **Nelson** was on the other side of Bush Street in Lower Park Street, not far from the junction. George Rogers from Carew and his wife Hannah were the licensees from 1856 to 1864 when they lost their spirit licence due

145

to various misdemeanours. They appear to have re-opened it as a beer-house, optimistically renaming it the **Triumph**, probably after a ship of that name which had been in the dockyard for a re-fit. However a continued disregard for the licensing laws meant that the pub was closed altogether in 1866. (John Davies kept a pub called the **Nelson** in Pembroke Dock in 1835, but there is no clue as to where it was. It does not appear to be the Park Street establishment).

There are no public houses in Meyrick Street today, either above or below the Bush Street junction, but this wasn't always the case. Starting at the top of Upper Meyrick Street and working down the hill, the first of the licensed premises was on the west side, just below Prospect Place. Henry White ran a small brewery there from about 1871, and since it had a tap-room at some stage the **Pembroke Dock Brewery** counts as a pub. In 1909 the licence was allowed to lapse, the police reporting that the premises had become structurally unsound for carrying on the retail part of the business. Reynolds wrote that the Brewery was latterly known as the **Hotel Bristol** although there is no record of this. He also claimed that there was a pub called the **Soldier's Return** on the opposite side of the road, next door to Trinity, but this has also proved impossible to confirm. However the **Hope** was somewhere around here; a young widow named Eliza Scurlock was the innkeeper from 1858 to 1861.

Potter's Electric News reported in 1859 that the licence of the **Nash Brewery** in Meyrick Street was being transferred to George Young, while the 1861 census showed George Young running a pub in Upper Meyrick Street between the British School and Bethel chapel. This had become the

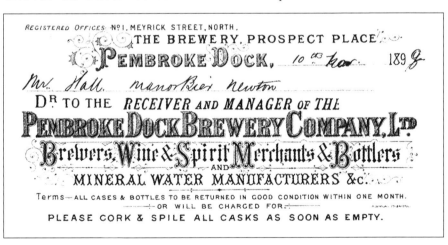

A billhead from the Pembroke Dock Brewery which was located at the top of Meyrick Street.
(Picture courtesy of the Pembrokeshire Records Office.)

Blenheim by 1868, the name being derived from a guardship which was anchored off Hazelbeach for some time.

By 1872 the pub had become the **Cardiff Arms**, under which name it passed from Theo Broom to Elizabeth Williams in 1874. Amazingly, she changed the name yet again, to the **Talbot**, before handing over to Benjamin Williams in 1878. John Griffiths, a retired shipwright from Lawrenny, was in charge in 1881, and he was followed in quick succession by a string of licensees. This high turnover of tenants suggests that the pub was less than profitable and, not surprisingly, it closed in 1893.

Crossing the road and passing the previously-mentioned Phoenix and Pembrokeshire Arms on the Bush Street corners, is Meyrick Street proper. Writing in the 1980s, Owen stated: 'Next door to the present NatWest Bank building in Meyrick Street was the **Prince of Wales**'. Apparently it was one of three pubs of that name in the town, the others being in Bush Street and the present pub in Laws Street. Towards the bottom of the street, also on the west side, was the **Coburg** beer-house, which was run for a few years in the 1850s and 1860s by various members of the Voyle family from Lawrenny.

Across the street was the **Lamb and Flag** — a suitably Christian name for a pub that was one door below the Catholic Church. Mary Evans was the landlady in 1858, but by 1860 it had been taken over by Daniel Dally and had become a den of iniquity. Three times in six months he was fined for running a less than respectable house. 'It seems to be no caution to him as he continues to keep a most disorderly house, both day and night', grumbled the *Pembrokeshire Herald*. 'His house is the resort of prostitutes and disorderly persons'. Dally took the hint and gave up a few weeks later, handing over to John Jones, formerly of the Navy Tavern. The pub was closed before 1872, and according to Mrs. Stuart Peters it became an office for the Great Western Railway company before it was taken over by the post office authorities. When the new post office was built in Dimond Street in the early 1960s the building was sold to the Catholic church next door. It was later demolished by the church and rebuilt in its present form as a presbytery.

William Jones was granted a licence for the **Angel** in Meyrick Street in 1859. This was four doors down from the Lamb and Flag, and William and his wife Letitia ran it as a pub-cum-boarding-house for several years. Other licensees included James Mogford in 1865 and William Bell in 1867, but it had closed by 1871. The building houses a beauty parlour in 2003.

In the early 1850s William Laen opened a chemist and druggist shop towards the bottom of Meyrick Street, and it gained fame as being the first premises in the town to be illuminated by gas. As often happened he opened a bar in part of the chemist shop and from 1872 to 1891 he held the licence of the aptly-named **Pestle and Mortar.** This name was changed to **Imperial** following his death.

The leasehold of the Imperial was sold by auction in February 1904; rather ironically the sale took place at the nearby Temperance Hall. The successful bidder was Mrs. Lilian Heatherley, who was followed a couple of years later by Thomas Williams. Having accommodation for neither people nor horses, the Imperial was always likely to be a target for redundancy, and it was recommended for closure by the local magistrates in 1910. They felt, not without justification, that there were more than enough pubs in the Meyrick Street area:

> The Imperial is 198 paces from the Pembrokeshire Arms, 44 paces from the Queens, 62 paces from the Edinburgh, 138 paces from the Gun Tavern and 104 paces from the Albert Inn ...

ran their report to the redundancy committee. The licence was eventually suppressed in 1914 with the licensee at the time, William Williams, getting £63 of the £560 compensation. Leaseholder T. G. Bowling received £448; the Meyrick estate got the rest. The building later housed a cycle shop for many years and is presently a charity shop.

Lewis Street was built in the the late 1840s and by 1850 boasted two pubs — both on the west side of the street. Shipwright Peter Roberts kept an unnamed beer-house near the top of the street in 1850, while further down towards the Dimond Street junction was the **Salutation**. This was a typical town centre beer-house where Catherine Gibby was the long-serving landlady from 1850 to 1884, having previously held the licence of the town's Clarence

Inn. She was a 59-year-old unmarried mother in 1881 with a 25-year-old daughter named Sarah Jane. Mrs. Elizabeth Tasker was in charge in 1901 and Mackay McLeod was the landlord in 1906. The pub was described as 'fairly clean, but doing little trade' when its was forced to close under the redundancy ruling

The Co-operative Bakery bread-cart stands outside the Bird in Hand in about 1910.
(Picture courtesy of Mr. Philip Carradice.)

in 1909, by which time it was owned by Mrs. M. James. She had recently spent £130 buying the business from McLeod and a further £50 doing the place up, so she was understandably a bit miffed at losing her livelihood. The court awarded her compensation of £200. It is uncertain which of the houses in the terrace was the Salutation but it may well have been the present number 24 which is the only double-fronted house in the row.

Across the road and a bit further down was the **Mariners' Inn** which was kept in 1858 by John Dean, a shipwright from Burton, and in 1861 by his widow Jane. James Mogford and Thomas Rowe both kept the Mariners' for a while, but in 1870 it passed to Joseph Griffiths who immediately changed the name to the alarmingly inappropriate **Alhambra Tavern** before handing over to Thomas Hunt in the autumn of 1871.

Thankfully the name was soon changed again, to the **Bird in Hand** — perhaps a punning reference to the Bush just round the corner. A master tailor from Narberth, one William Morris, changed the sign, running the Bird in Hand from 1874 to 1884 with the help of his wife Elizabeth. From 1906 to 1909 the landlord was John Lewis, who was succeeded by Maria Michael, whose sister ran the Farmers' Arms, and then by John Brown. From 1910 to 1928 the Bird was run by John Williams, formerly of the Commercial in Queen Street; at this time the front of the pub was surmounted by a signboard which ran the width of the building and on top of which was a large image of a hand.

The Bird in Hand in Lewis Street, pictured in 2002.

Alderman Joe Gibby and his wife Esther then took over and they were still there when the pub was devastated by a German bomb in August 1940. Alderman Gibby suffered minor injuries and the pub was described at the next Brewster Sessions as 'having been destroyed by enemy action'. However it was eventually rebuilt and reopened in April 1948, and well-remembered licensees since then have included John 'Jock' Fraser, a Scottish confectioner who was there in the 1950s and '60s, and Tony Le Britton, a singer/guitarist who attracted a musical crowd to the pub in the 1970s. The

Bird has changed hands a few times since, but is still a busy town centre local.

Laws Street was built in the 1840s and '50s, and was named after Edward Laws who was an executor of the will of Thomas Meyrick. Where the street intersected with Dimond Street became one of the busiest junctions in town, and also one of the booziest, with a pub on all four corners.

The red-brick Prince of Wales on the corner of Laws Street.

For a brief spell in the 1990s the **Prince of Wales** was lumbered with the name **Celts**, but happily the earlier sign has been restored to this classic red-brick Victorian corner pub. The inn appears to date from the 1850s when William Goverd, a pilot and victualler, ran it as a beer-house. By 1861 it was known as the **Prince Regent** and was kept by Irishman Peter Delahunt, while by 1868 it was being run by William Jones; it was Jones who changed the name to Prince of Wales and perhaps the pub was rebuilt in its present style at that time.

Joshua Huzzey was landlord from 1872 to 1879 when he handed over to William Henry Gibby. 'Many will remember Mr. Huzzey with his

An Edwardian view of the 'Alex'.

grocer's shop and his Dalmatian dog', wrote Reynolds. Photographer Sydney Webb (previously encountered in Commercial Row) ran the pub in the 1880s, followed by Arthur Morris and James Victor Lee who was the landlord in 1906. The pub then changed hands repeatedly over the next few years, the licensees including William Andrews who lasted just 11 weeks before being fatally poisoned by a tin of mock turtle soup! In the 1920s the pub was run by the Isaac family; Mr. Isaac was a pioneer of the local charabanc service while his wife Elizabeth ran the pub. Following her husband's death, Mrs. Isaac remarried and carried on running the pub as Mrs. Elizabeth Orr. Phyllis West was there in the 1930s and licensees in the 1940s included Mr. and Mrs. Fred Street (he was one of the managers of the local gas-works), and Stan Smith. There have been a number of different tenants in recent years, and that temporary name-change, but the 'Prince' is still going strong.

In 1863 the Prince of Wales, later Edward VII, married Alexandra of Denmark and the **Alexandra Vaults** was named in her honour, standing as it does on the opposite corner from her prince. Although it has been closed from time to time in recent years, the Alex is open in 2003 and looking smarter than it has for some time. William Page kept this substantial pub from 1867 to 1884 and the catering talents of Mrs. and the Misses Page were highly regarded, particularly by the Pembroke Dock Quoiting Club which used the 'Alex' as its headquarters. William was followed by Thomas Page and at this time the Alex was more commonly known as 'Page's Hotel'. John J. Vittle was licensee from 1901 to 1907 and Mrs. Elizabeth Vittle was still there in 1914. In the 1920s the licensees were Mr. and Mrs. W. Egerton, while Les Ebsworth from Amroth took over as manager for James Williams in about 1937, becoming the full-time licensee shortly afterwards. The Alex was severely

ALEXANDRA HOTEL
(L. L. EBSWORTH, PROP.)

RESIDENTIAL & COMMERCIAL FULLY LICENSED
BASS, WORTHINGTON & WATNEYS RED BARREL
ON DRAUGHT

BED AND BREAKFAST - FULL BOARD

DIMOND STREET and WATER STREET,
PEMBROKE DOCK

Have You Visited our Newly
Opened Isolina Cocktail Bar

Telephone : PEM. Dock **109**

A 1960 advertisement for the Alexandra Hotel

The Alexandra Inn as it looked in 2002.

damaged during the air raids on the town, but Mr. Ebsworth oversaw the renovation work and continued to run the pub until well into the 1970s. The licence has changed hands on a fairly regular basis since his retirement.

Opposite the Alex stood the **Star** which had a corner entrance between Water Street and Apley Terrace; the junction is still known as 'Star Corner' in honour of the pub. Martha Allen kept the Star in 1858 and her brother William Allen of Pembroke Ferry was the owner and licensee from 1867 to 1874. When he retired he let the pub to a relative named Samuel Frise, a ship-wright who had briefly kept the Ferry House at Pembroke Ferry. During Frise's time the annual 'Star picnic' became one of the highlights of the social calendar in that part of town, usually involving a boat trip up the river and a picnic on the shore. By 1906 the licensee was Samuel's son, Arthur, one of 13 children.

The next licensee was dockyard policemen Bill West who sublet the Star to a number of tenants before running it himself when the dockyard closed. It was a substantial building by this time, and included a club room where local sports teams would gather for after-match refreshments in the days before clubs had their own bars. In March 1930 the local police objected to the renewal of the Star's licence on the not unreasonable grounds that there were four other licensed premises within 50 yards. The magistrates agreed, withdrew the licence, and licensee West duly received compensation for the loss of his livelihood. The Star was reopened as the highly-popular R.E.O.C.

The Star Inn in the days when Bill West was the licensee.
(Picture courtesy of the Western Telegraph.*)*

club in 1935, but it has recently changed again to become the Star members' club, and since there are still four other licensed premises within 50 yards it has to be said that the magistrates' decision made very little difference to the consumption of alcohol in this part of town!

Apothecary's Hall, a chemist's shop diagonally opposite the Star at 1, Dimond Street, was also licensed to sell alcohol, and for a while in the 1880s Mr. J.H. Bowling seems to have run one room within the premises as a public house. (He also advertised 'Teeth carefully extracted!'). The presence of this pub meant that the crossroads had a boozer on every corner, much to the disgust of Mr. W.E. Seccombe who, in 1887, became the first teetotal mayor of the Borough. A stern advocate of total abstinence, he fought hard to reduce the number of pubs in the two towns and reserved his deepest dislike for the street corner locals, of which there were any number in Pembroke Dock. 'These corners are really nothing more than loafers' corners, and the greatest abominations are carried on there!' he once thundered, no doubt with the Star Corner in mind.

Further up the street, on the same side as the Prince of Wales, was the **George and Dragon**, kept in the early 1850s by Jeffrey Yardbury. This became the **Three Crowns** when Sarah Scurlock took over; she held the licence from 1858 to 1874, followed by Mrs. Jane Price who was there until 1884. William Peters, known as 'Peters the horse jockey', held the licence in 1889 and Mrs. Ann Peters was licensee in 1901.

John Brown was charged with watering down the whisky in 1908 and soon departed, to be followed by William Collins, who was there during the First World War. Alf and Susannah Bowen were in charge by 1924, Mr. Bowen being regarded as the man who introduced the game of darts to Pembroke Dock. He was an ex-boxer and a friend of Jimmy Wilde, who often visited the pub.

Described as 'one of the most popular and cosy inns of pre-war Pembroke Dock', the Three Crowns was severely damaged by the devastating German air raid during the night of 12 May 1941 which killed pub

The Three Crowns was once on the other side of the road.

historian Harry Reynolds who lived next door. Miraculously Mr. and Mrs. Bowen were brought out alive the following morning from the rubble of the wrecked building. Both were injured, but nothing daunted they subsequently reopened the Three Crowns in its present building on the opposite side of the street. Sadly, Mr. Bowen died in 1945 as a result of the injuries he had received in the bombing. Mrs. Bowen soldiered on for a few years, but the pub was closed in the early 1950s due to her increasingly poor health.

Former Milford councillor Kenneth Wade reopened the business in about 1952, and after a couple of changes of licensee it fell into experienced hands. 'The new premises of the Three Crowns are now owned by well known and popular Mr. Jack Nicholson who has re-established these premises as an attractive and flourishing establishment', wrote J.M. Owen in 1965. The Nicholsons were well established in the town's licensing trade, having kept the Conservative Club, the Queen's and the Bush Tavern at various times. Their son Eddie later ran the Three Crowns, as did Mr. Allan Brookes — during whose time the pub sign was changed to **Brooksie's**. He was there for 16 years, and added to the pub's popularity by building the first skittle alley to be seen in the town for many years. When he left to run the Bush Tavern in the 1990s the sign reverted to the Three Crowns.

The **Adelphi** once stood on the corner of Gwyther Street and Apley Terrace. A disreputable and rowdy 1860s drinking den, it was run by a chap called Moses Oram and his wife Jane. Mr. Oram lost his licence in September 1864 after local magistrates were told that the pub was 'a harbouring place for bad women'. As one angry neighbour told the court: 'It is not safe for my wife and family to go out on account of the drunken men and women frequenting this house. There is fighting and dancing and dreadful language is used...' The

The only known illustration of the Railway Hotel which was destroyed by fire during the First World War.
(Picture courtesy of Mr. John Hogg.)

154

Adelphi was subsequently rebuilt as the rather more respectable **Railway Hotel**, which had a classic street corner entrance with the pub name emblazoned on the wall above.

Sarah Davies was the landlady from 1867 to 1871, evidently as the tenant of Bush Street wine and spirits merchant William Smith. She was succeeded by a Scot named Walter Borrowman who seems to have been a bit of a sporting gent, always ready to challenge someone to a game of quoits in the meadow beside the railway station, especially if there was a wager to be won. In June that year he refereed a running match on the nearby Garrison cricket-field between two of his more corpulent customers who both tipped the scales at around 19 stones. The race, which was for a stake of five guineas, was eventually won by a Mr. Sloggett. The licence passed from the cheery Mr. Borrowman to James Harlow, while Henry Elliott was landlord from 1874 to 1884. George John Page kept the hotel in the 1890s (when the only known photograph of the pub was taken) and he was followed by Mrs. Mary Page in 1901.

Samuel McCulloch was the landlord on the fateful night in October 1914 when the Railway was burnt down. It being war-time, a sentry was on duty guarding the station just across the road. At about 1.30 a.m. he noticed smoke pouring out of the inn and quickly raised the alarm. The pub barman escaped by jumping from an upstairs window, while the only other occupant of the building, Mr. McCulloch, was rescued by ladder. Despite the arrival of a steam fire engine and a detachment of soldiers from Llanion Barracks, the building was completely gutted with damage estimated at £1,200. The site remained wasteland for over 40 years before a doctors' surgery was eventually built there.

The **Three Tuns** near the railway station was another victim of the German air raids of May 1941, but was rebuilt and reopened some years later. Ann Scurlock was the landlady between 1868 and 1875, followed by Maria Phillips. William Herbert was

The Three Tuns in 2002.

155

landlord from 1891 to 1901, having moved from the Prince Albert, and Mrs. Ann Herbert was the landlady in 1906. William and Margaret Canton held the licence from 1912 to 1939, and after her husband's death Mrs. Canton ran the pub on her own. She was followed by the couple's daughter Mrs. Iris Woolnough and her husband 'Tiffie'.

The present owners, Mr. and Mrs. Alan Lloyd have been at the Tuns since the 1970s, and they have done much to open up and modernise the interior of this typical Pembroke Dock terraced pub.

The **Station** at Pembroke Dock is exactly that — the old Pembroke Dock railway station building. This was cleverly converted into a pub in the 1990s by Pembroke micro-brewer David Lightley and has become well known for its music nights and its annual beer festival.

When Queen Street was extended eastwards, from the junction with Meyrick Street, it was originally called New Road; later, however, it became Dimond Street in honour of London solicitor Charles Palmer Dimond who, like Edward Laws, was an executor of the will of Thomas Meyrick who died in 1837. The town's Temperance Hall, now the Pater Hall, was built there in 1847, but its disapproving presence didn't stop a number of pubs opening up along the street. Indeed, the **Burton Brewery** at 22 Dimond Street was right next door to the Temperance Hall.

John Llewhellin was the licensee from 1858 until his death in 1875; 'Brother Llewhellin' was a freemason who occasionally hosted masonic shindigs at his establishment. Following the death of licensee William Rodney in 1878, his widow Mary Rodney ran the pub. She was succeeded by John Meyrick in 1881, while by 1891 his widow Charlotte Meyrick was landlady. Her son-in-law William Morgan took over in 1896, but he too died at a rela-

The Station in 2003.

tively early age, so that his widow, Mrs. Charlotte Morgan, had to take on the pub herself, running it from 1898 to 1908. A few months later this James Williams house was forced to close under the redundancy ruling during the 'pub purge' of 1909. The brewery received £630 in compensation, with nothing going to tenant John Jones who had only been there a few weeks. The building later became a butcher's shop and was demolished in 1961; the town's post office now stands on the site.

Across the road was the **Albert** which stood at 11 Dimond Street and which was run from 1868 to 1893 by Mrs. Ann Llewellyn, a widow who was apparently 'greatly esteemed'. David Jas. Joseph kept the pub from 1896 to 1908, followed by Lettice Joseph. She was still there in November 1917 when the pub was ordered to close by the local magistrates who softened the blow with a compensation payment of £500. For a while the Albert was the offices of the *West Wales Guardian* before being demolished to make way for Woolworth stores.

Of the other pubs in Dimond Street, the **Army and Navy** was the most notorious, largely because of the antics of landlord William Roberts. Before moving to Pembroke Dock from Merthyr, Roberts had once been fined £10 for beating up three policemen, and in Pembroke Dock he was soon up to his old tricks once again. When a constable visited the pub late one night in 1864 he discovered seven men drinking, but before he could take any action he was promptly chased out of the house and down the street by the irate publican. This was the last straw for the authorities and the pub was closed later the same year.

Dimond Street from an early postcard.

157

There may have been three other pubs in Dimond Street at various times. Jane Scale kept the **Farmers' Arms** in 'New Road' in 1858 (but as there were lots of new roads being built in Pembroke Dock at the time it might not have been in Dimond Street at all). A reference in a newspaper of 1864 placed the **Blue Bell** beer-shop in Dimond Street, next to a toy-shop, while Abel Griffiths was granted a licence for the **Montague** in 1866. He was still there in 1870, but both pub and landlord had vanished by the time of the 1871 census.

CHAPTER ELEVEN

Pembroke Dock
WATER ST., LLANION, WATERLOO
& PEMBROKE FERRY

From the boozy Star Corner junction, the road leading down towards Llanion is called Water Street. At one time, part of this road skirted the shore of the Haven and was known as Shore Street, and there was even a small quay where the Criterion roundabout now stands. However gradual reclamation of a muddy tidal inlet has seen the roadway retreat further and further inland and the old name has long been abandoned. There were a few watering holes in Water Street, and just down from the Alexandra was the **Waverly**, a small hotel which opened around the beginning of the 20th century but was soon converted into the Belle Vue Dairy.

On the opposite side, about a dozen houses below the Star, stood the **Porter House** run in the 1870s by brewer and spirit dealer William White — one of several establishments in the town where it was possible to drink in the tap-room of the brewery.

The **Quay Head** stood at the junction of Water Street and King William Street and was opened by Frederick Maggs in 1870, having previously been the premises of Copeman and Lacy, army contractors. It doesn't appear to have lasted for more than a couple of years and may have occupied the building known as Shore House.

A little further along, the **Dumfries** was also on the right. This was a substantial pub-cum-hotel built on reclaimed marshland by Scottish travelling drapers, of whom an inordinate number found their way to Pembroke Dock. The first tenant was serial licensee Jesse Chappell who was there in 1874, and the hotel also employed a full-time billiards marker who 'lived in'. It later became notorious as a haunt of prostitutes and led something of a chequered existence with various tenants coming and going. At one time the Dumfries was owned by John Borrowman, a draper with premises in

Meyrick Street, but when he died in 1897 the inn was bought for £650 by Richard Culley from Cardiff.

The Dumfries was often in trouble with the law and was closed under the redundancy ruling in 1912 when the licensee was Samuel Farrant who had been there since 1909. The owners demanded £1,650 in compensation; they received £635. The building later became the premises of the Pembroke Dock Steam Laundry, but it no longer stands, having been badly bomb-damaged during the war and later demolished, to be replaced by the present police station.

German bombs also put paid to the **Criterion** on the corner of Water Street — a building with a long and varied history. According to Mrs. Stuart Peters, writing in 1905:

> The place now known as the Criterion, and earlier as the Bombay Hotel, was originally a malt-house with a dwelling-house and outbuildings attached. This malt-house was kept by a man named Edward Smith, and, being roomy, it was occasionally used by itinerant ministers for preaching purposes.

Edward Smith or Smyth was in business as a maltster in the 1820s and '30s, but by the 1850s the malt-house was being operated by his son-in-law Alexander Skinner who lived in the house next door. The building in those days was known as 'The Round House', but in about 1860 it was converted

The battlemented Criterion Inn was destroyed by German bombs during the last war.

into the **Bombay**, a rather odd-looking pub/hotel complete with fake battlements — perhaps an attempt to recreate the 'Raj' look in Pembroke Dock. Margaret Phillips from Solva held the licence in 1861, while the ubiquitous Jesse Chappell was the landlord in 1868. He must have run a lively establishment because the local magistrates were soon tut-tutting about 'music and dancing being carried on there, with a crowd of boys about the door'. Landlord of the Bombay in 1875 was Thomas Berry, who also found himself in trouble with the authorities on a regular basis, followed by Ellen Berry. She left in 1883, and it was the new landlord, Benjamin Price, who changed the name to Criterion. By 1891 Margaret Price was in charge and the landlord in 1901 was Isaac James.

Shortly afterwards the licence passed to John Charles Lister, aged 70, who ran the pub for the next 15 years. A remarkable character, Charlie Lister was a widely-travelled Cockney who claimed to have known both Dickens and Garibaldi. A boilermaker by trade, he had served in various ships including the *Great Eastern* before settling in Pembroke Dock where he worked in the dockyard before taking over the Criterion. It was said he knew the works of Shakespeare intimately and could quote almost any part of the Bible, and when he died aged 99 in 1935 he was the oldest freemason in the county. John Pritchard was landlord from 1927 to 1932, and the last occupant was Mrs. Annie Gill; when the pub was wrecked by the bomb-blast she moved to run the Queen's Hotel. The junction of London Road and Water Street where the pub once stood is still called Criterion Corner.

Edward Smyth also owned a very early Pembroke Dock pub called the **Shipwrights Arms**, which appears to have been run at one time by Richard Davies and then from about 1817 onwards by John Oriel, a brother to the George Oriel (junior) who kept the Union Tavern in Pembroke. The Shipwrights was described in 1827 as being 'in the direct road from Pembroke Dock to Pembroke town', and may later have been known as the **Ship**, but where it stood remains a mystery.

A patch of grass at the bottom of Tremeyrick Street is all that marks the site of the **Pier Hotel** which received a direct hit from a German parachute mine on the night of 12 May 1941 — the same blast which devastated the Criterion. The proprietor, Mr. Rhys Morris from Solva, his daughter Eileen Morris aged 15 and Elizabeth Williams, 32, all died in the ruins. Stanley Herman Buxton, 27, was severely injured and died the same day at Llanion Barracks. He was a platoon commander in the Home Guard.

A three-storey building with a balcony on the first floor, the Pier Hotel was probably built for James Huzzey, a ferryman, farmer and publican who ran the Ferry House inn at Pembroke Ferry for many years. He certainly

A German parachute mine destroyed the Pier Hotel.

owned the hotel in 1858 when it was described as a 'commercial, family and posting inn' and he offered horses and gigs for hire. He was followed by his daughter Ellen who kept the hotel from the 1860s through to 1884. 'Many old prints of toll-gate scenes etc by Herring (senior) were to be seen in the place in Miss Huzzey's time', reported Reynolds. Philip Jenkins took over the hotel in the 1890s and changed the name to the **Three Lamps,** but it reverted to its old title when he left in 1898. Arthur Seaton was the landlord in 1906 followed by Mrs. Rose Leigh from 1912 to 1927 and then Jack Newman.

Writing in the *West Wales Guardian* in 1965, J.M. Owen recalled:

> One remembers the comfortable premises known as the Pier Hotel which, alas, was the subject of special attention by the Hun and which was totally destroyed and never rebuilt. This hotel was much frequented by military personnel, including, it is said, Lord Kitchener when a subaltern serving at Llanion Barracks. We remember the use of part of these premises as a gymnasium where Bill Johnson, Ocky Davies and other ambitious pugilists practised the noble art. At the rear of these premises many a young soldier will remember the shop wherein faggots and peas and fish and chips were superbly provided by Sam Frisc, the old Pembroke Dock Welsh League goalkeeper.

In 1859 William Bristow, a Norfolk man, opened a pub in Bachelor's Row. This was a terrace of two-storey houses leading up the hill to the barracks from the Pier Hotel and facing westward — hence the name of the pub, the **Setting Sun.** The terrace had been built in the 1840s by a couple of local bachelors, but the name was later changed to Tremeyrick Street. No doubt Bristow was hoping to make a handsome profit from the vast number of soldiers being accommodated in the hut encampment which had just been built opposite his home. However he may have miscalculated; in January 1859 over 50 inhabitants of the huts signed the pledge after hearing a lecture by Mr. Robert Nisbet of Solva. The Setting Sun at no. 14 only

162

Soldiers on parade outside Llanion Barracks which were completed in about 1906. The presence of a large garrison meant plenty of trade — and sometimes plenty of trouble — for the town's pubs.

lasted a dozen years and there is no hint now that the building was once a pub.

One of the old barracks buildings was opened as a pub in the 1980s, but despite a promising start the **Guardroom** didn't stay the course and closed a few years later.

Down at Hobbs Point was the **Royal**, which was opened in 1838 to coincide with the launch of the new mail packet service to Ireland from the pier. The great and the good all turned up to a house warming party in August 1838 to welcome landlady Sarah Williams, formerly of the Mariners, Haverfordwest — and since the royal mail coaches all terminated here, she duly became the town's post-mistress as well. When Sarah Williams left the Royal in 1847 it was taken over by John Llewhellin of Haverfordwest, but the inn lost all its trade a couple of years later when the Irish packet service was controversially discontinued. The mail coaches stopped coming, the post office was transferred to the Clarence in Pembroke Street, and Llewhellin moved into town to open another Royal in Queen Street — later the Royal Edinburgh. The now redundant inn at Hobbs Point was handed over to the coastguard service.

The specially constructed road to Hobbs Point was called the London Mail Coach Road (now just London Road) and it became the main route into Pembroke Dock, avoiding the need to go via Pembroke. Several inns were opened along its length, and one of the earliest was the **Castle** which was run by John and Mary Dunn in the 1840s and early 1850s. This building was

163

close to the Round House and seems to have been later incorporated into the construction of the Bombay Hotel.

Mason, in his book on the history of Pembroke Dock, stated:

> Mr. W. Murray built the house adjoining the Round House on the east side which was opened as a public house under the name of **Coach and Horses**, where accommodation for man and beast could be obtained. After cessation of the mail coach traffic in in 1848, it was turned into a private dwelling house.

There is no sign of this pub in any of the records, however, although a William Murray is known to have leased a plot of land in London Road in 1838 on which to build 'a stone dwelling-house'.

In September 1860, George Collins was given permission to turn his billiard hall a couple of doors further along London Road into a public house, and being a proud Bristolian he called it the **Bristol Arms**. However it became the **South Wales Inn** when it was acquired by the White family of Cosheston Brewery in the 1860s (they had an annoying habit of changing the name of houses when they took them over). For 10 years it was run by various, often disreputable, tenants before it gained respectability as the Chappell family hotel. Between them, James Chappell, Mrs. Susan Chappell and their daughter Miss Sarah Chappell held the licence from 1877 to 1931.

The Welshman's Arms, pictured in 2002, was once the Railway Inn.

Edward Evans and Fred Sine both kept the inn during the 1930s, when the hotel's billiard room was still a popular feature, while William Rudd had not long taken over when the bomb which destroyed the Pier Hotel also damaged the South Wales beyond repair.

The 1861 census showed John Arlow of Monkton living in a detached house on the south side of London Road. This became the **Railway Inn,** and as buildings grew up around it over the next decade, so the pub eventually found itself in the middle of Llanion Terrace. The town station, which opened in 1864, was nearby, and a rail spur to the pier alongside Hobbs Point passed alongside the back of the inn, so it was certainly well named. Mr. Arlow remained landlord for over 20 years, but by 1891 the licensee was William Morris, while Miss Charlotte Page was landlady in the years leading up to the First World War. Former Royal Navy officer Mr. John L. Jones, 'Jones the Railway', was the long-serving and much-respected landlord from 1932 through to the 1960s when he was one of the oldest licensees in the town. With Pembroke Borough A.F.C.'s pitch just down the road, the Railway was always a popular place on a Saturday during the team's Welsh League years. Since the 1960s the pub has undergone two name changes, being known as the **Kerry** for some 20 years before changing again in the 1990s to its present name — the **Welshman's Arms.**

Passing the old turnpike gate, the London Mail Coach Road met the turnpike road from Pembroke to Pembroke Ferry at a place known as Waterloo. The name is said to be derived from the fact that General Sir Thomas Picton passed this way *en route* to a hero's death at the famous battle. The **Commercial House** stood on the junction at Waterloo, and as the final pub before leaving town, it enjoyed several nick-names in its time, including 'The Last Step' and also 'Greenland'. This latter name had nothing to do with the fact that the pub was a long way away from

The First and Last was once one of the town's numerous Commercial Inns.

anywhere else; the landlady at one time was called Greenland. One tradition observed at the Commercial for many years was the annual election of the 'Mayor of Waterloo'. The last person to hold that notable honour is thought to have been a Mr. Tommy Waite, but when these elections ceased is unknown.

Landlord of the Commercial House in 1872 was James Phillips who handed over to Martha Greenland in 1877. The pub appears as the **Waterloo** in the 1881 census, but by the time John Clement took over in 1889 it was again known as the Commercial, and no doubt attracted its quota of the growing number of commercial travellers arriving in the town. Miss Edith Picken was landlady in 1906, John Davies was landlord in 1914 and from 1923 to 1936 the pub was 'spotlessly maintained by Mr. George Foreman, a retired Sergeant Major in the old mould' according to one account. He was followed by Jack Wood from Tenby and ex-Royal Navy man Jack Horrigan before the pub was taken over in 1961 by Herman Westenborg (who was invariably called 'George'). It still remains in the same family today, being run by his grandson Richard Maynard, and was the last of the county's Commercials to change its name to something more colourful, becoming the **First and Last** in 1991.

The old turnpike road from Pembroke to Pembroke Ferry was once an attractive, leafy lane, passing Llanion House and skirting the shore of Cosheston Pill. Richard Fenton, who passed this way in 1810, thought it an area of outstanding beauty; he would be surprised to see the busy roadways, factory units and housing which now dominate the area; not to mention the bridge which nowadays spans the Haven,

Long before the bridge was built, the horse-ferry at Pembroke Ferry was the most important river-crossing in the county and there must have been a cottage alehouse here for several centuries, indeed, the ferryman was usually the innkeeper as well. As with many such crossings, the Pembroke ferry rights were held by the Crown, on whose behalf it was administered for many years by the Owens of Orielton House. It wasn't always a smooth passage. Richard Rose quotes one early tourist in 1791 as stating:

> If a traveller with a Carriage and any Horses that he values wishes to go from here to Haverfordwest I would advise him not to go by the Pembroke Ferry as the boat is a very inconvenient one & it is most probable that either his Carriage or his Horses will be materially hurt in getting them into and out of the boat ...

There were two ale-houses on the Pembroke side of the ferry crossing at the end of the 18th century. One was run by Elizabeth Patton in 1784 and by William Allen between 1795 and 1810; since he appears to have been a

Trinity House pilot it comes as no surprise to learn that it was called the **Pilot**. This pub seems to have closed in the 1820s.

The other was run by William Nicholls between 1784 and 1804, and subsequently by his widow Sarah. Nicholls was described at various times as a 'wine merchant' and 'vitler' and seems to have been a businessman of some standing. His granddaughter Elizabeth married Roger Eynon of Boulston in 1810 and they appear to have taken over the running of the public house side of the business. The sign of this pub is not known.

For many years, members of the extended Huzzey family from Barnlake owned property and ran pubs on both sides of the river, as well as holding the ferry franchise at various times. James Huzzey took out a 60-year lease on the Right of Ferry from the Owens of Orielton in 1820, and this included the tenancy of the **Ferry House** public house. Over the course of the next 10 years Huzzey did his best to stop rival ferrymen from operating the Neyland to Front Street route further downstream, claiming to have exclusive ferry rights on the Haven. However he eventually lost an acrimonious test case at Haverfordwest assizes, much to the delight of the boatmen of Neyland and Llanstadwell. He also sued William Allen of the Pilot for assault in 1821, so there was obviously a certain amount of neighbourly ill-feeling down at the Ferry.

A traveller who passed through Pembroke Ferry in 1823, is reported by Thomas Lloyd as noting:

> The Ferry over Milford was very dangerous, the wind blowing up from the sea very hard and the waves, rolling very heavy, made this voyage although short the worst we had. We were some time fastening the chaise and getting the horses on board to be properly secure. While this was doing I went into the Ferry house and had a glass of brandy and water, not feeling very well.

PEMBROKE FERRY AND PUBLIC HOUSE,

With Right of Ferry, Stable, Brew House, Barn, Gig House, Piggery, Boat House, Culm House, Cottages, Gardens, and the following Lands, viz.

No. on Plan.	Description.		Cultivation.		Quantity. A. R. P.
115	Three Cottages and Garden	....	......	....	0 1 12
115a	....	....	Garden	....	0 1 4
115b	....	....	Pasture	....	0 3 12
392	Ferry House and Right of Ferry	....	......	....	0 0 16
393	Cottage and Garden..,	....	......	....	0 0 15
			TOTAL ACRES		1 2 19

The whole is let to JAMES HUZZEY; No. 115a and 115b, as Yearly Tenant, at £3. 1s. 5d. per Annum; No. 115, on Agreement for Lease dated 26th July, 1853, for 61 Years, from 25th March, 1853, at £4. 16s.; No. 392, with Right of Ferry, as Yearly Tenant, at £85. per Annum; No. 393, on Lease for 60 Years, from 29th September, 1820, at £1. 1s. per Annum and for a portion of Land not shewn on the Plan, forming part of 5A. 3R., held by the Vendors of the heirs of Meyrick as Yearly Tenant, at £2. 10s. per Annum; making a Total Annual Rent of £96. 8s. 6d.

And the Tithe Rent Charge of 4s. which is paid by Tenant in addition to his rent.

Sale particulars of the Ferry House from the 1850s.

167

The Ferry Inn stands in the shadow of the Cleddau Bridge.

Despite being much taken by 'the very pretty young woman' who served him, the traveller was none too impressed with what he found.

> When I went into the house I observed in the room two dogs, three pigs and three children, the young woman and a servant girl, and whilst drinking my liquor in comes the landlord and the first words he uttered were 'Peggy, why don't you turn the pigs out of the parlour to give the gentleman room to sit down'. Now the parlour I think scarcely had a chair or anything of use in it, so I told him I should soon be off, therefore it did not signify and I also had other thoughts in my head to prevent me caring about the room. So having paid for my cigar I went on board of a small boat, the chaise and horses being on board the horse boat.

A trade directory for 1830 has John Huzzey, brother of James, as licensee of the **Watermans' Arms** in Pembroke Dock. This may have been an alternative name for the Ferry House (which does not appear in the directory) and it may be that John ran the pub for a few years while James and another brother, Peter, operated the ferry. It is recorded that in 1832 Sir John Owen let the ferry rights to James Huzzey of the Ferry House Inn for an annual rent of £200 — a substantial sum. Fares in those days were one halfpenny for a foot passenger and one penny for a man and a horse. For carts and carriages the levy was a hefty one shilling per wheel.

James Huzzey was still overseeing the ferry in 1850 when he was forced to cut his prices to compete with the *Cambrian* steamer which had just started a service between Hobbs Point and Neyland. By this time he was in his 60s and was acting as innkeeper of the Ferry House and also farming on a small scale; it was left to Peter Huzzey to row passengers across to Burton. The Orielton estate sale particulars of 1858 show that the annual rent for the ferry rights had now dropped to £85, indicating how much trade had been lost to the Pembroke Dock to Neyland route.

No doubt sensing which way the wind was blowing, James Huzzey built the Pier Hotel in London Road and may have decided to close the Ferry House as an inn; the 1861 census described him as a 'farmer', and when he retired in 1861 his property sale at Pembroke Ferry included various harvested crops together with a dozen bacon pigs, but no mention of any brewing or innkeeping equipment.

If the pub was indeed closed for a few years, it was reopened by Samuel Frise (later of the Star Inn). He was granted a full licence for the Ferry House in 1867, while from later that year until 1883 the licensee was John Belt. He was a son of the John Belt who ran the Waterman's in Pembroke, and his wife Margaret was a daughter of the William Allen who previously ran the Pilot, so he was well connected to the trade. In September 1875 Belt was collared for serving after hours and compounded the crime by trying to bribe the police officer to overlook the misdemeanour. He was described in the 1881 census as 'shipwright, ferryman and publican', while Reynolds observed: 'Many will remember Mr. Huzzey and Mr. Belt where the devotees of wild duck shooting and ship and yacht building gathered'.

Stephen Mathias took over the pub, and possibly the ferry, in 1883. The landlord in the 1890s was Charles Allen and from 1906 until his death in 1923 it was Howell Pugh. His widow Mrs. Louisa Pugh remained the land-lady until 1934 when John Kitts took over. He is thought to have been the last to hold the ferry rights, since the Pembroke Ferry — Burton Ferry route was discontinued in the 1930s (the horse-ferry having been taken out of service in 1890). Post-war licensees have included William Dance, who was there throughout the 1950s, Billy Rourke and Commander Monroe. The inn remains popular with locals and 'yachties' and has an interesting collection of photographs recalling the building, and dramatic collapse of the Cleddau Bridge.

Also at Pembroke Ferry was the **Plough** which seems to have been more or less next door to the Ferry Inn and was owned by James Huzzey, a son of the former ferryman. The Plough appears to have been opened by Stephen Mathias who was there in 1867, while George Rees, a Trinity House man, held the licence between 1870 and 1873 despite objections from the police that his occupation kept him away from the inn for lengthy periods. Two of the Huzzeys, Margaret and Elizabeth, then ran the pub themselves for a few years, while a widow from Dale named Mrs. Martha Woodbine was there in the early 1880s. Margaret Stamford was licensee from 1886 to 1891, in which year the licence of the pub was for some reason not renewed.

CHAPTER TWELVE

Eastwards from Pembroke

COSHESTON, LAMPHEY, FRESHWATER EAST, JAMESTON, MANORBIER, ST. FLORENCE, LYDSTEP, PENALLY & THE RIDGEWAY

The earliest known pubs within the parish of Cosheston were near the shore at Jenkins Point, from where a ferryboat crossed to Lawrenny Ferry. There were busy shipyards and plenty of pubs on both sides of the water at one time and two ale-houses stood on the Cosheston shore in 1784, one run by John Cousins and the other by John Canton. The Cousins family kept the **Brig**, while the Cantons were shipbuilders on both sides of the river, so their pub was called the **Ship**. Thomas Canton kept the pub from 1812 to 1822 and David Canton was licensee from 1823 to 1828. The growth of Pembroke Dock as a shipbuilding centre killed off many of the smaller shipyards on the river, and when the yards closed, so did the ale-houses that supplied the workers with their daily sustenance.

Perhaps one of these early ale-houses was later re-opened as the **Dock Inn**, which stood directly opposite Lawrenny Ferry and appears on the Ordnance Survey map of 1867. This was in the much-modernised house which still stands by the shore.

In Cosheston village itself was the **Carpenters Arms.** This stood to the west of the crossroads and, naturally enough, was built by a carpenter. James Leach was a skilled craftsman and foreman of the rebuilding works at Lawrenny Castle, and in the 1850s he built himself a house on Lawrenny estate land in Cosheston. He may have opened it as a beer-house before obtaining a full public house licence in 1865 and he continued to hold the licence until 1891.

In 1895 the freehold changed hands for £240, the property being bought by John Goodrich; however the Leach family remained as tenants, Miss Jane Leach being the landlady from 1906 to 1914. The landlady from 1923 to

The former Carpenters Arms in Cosheston.

1946 was Mrs. Harriet Phillips, after which it passed to her daughter Molly and her husband Ernest Martin, a former captain in the army, who modernised the place a little. Following the death of Mr. Martin in the early '60s, Mrs. Martin carried on running the pub with the help of her daughter Mary. Not exactly brim full of facilities — though always spotless — the pub is remembered as having a tiny front bar with a counter in one corner, a couple of barrels of beer and a small supply of spirits which was kept under the stairs. The dart-board area was partially fenced off by a screen of chicken-wire to prevent customers being speared by rebounding arrows. The pub, which was a good, old-fashioned village local, closed in the early 1970s as Mrs. Martin's health deteriorated; it is said also that she didn't care overmuch for the new decimal currency. Moves to reopen the pub in 1980s were defeated following objections over car-parking.

The attractive Grade II listed building which now houses the **Cosheston Brewery Inn** was once used as a dower house by the Roch family of Paskeston Hall. Although an older house may once have stood on the site, the present building appears to date from the early 1840s and may well incorporate work by James Leach. In the 1850s the property was taken over by David White who built a malthouse and brewery at the back, so that by 1867 it was described as 'a valuable brewery in full work'. The Whites had several tied houses in south Pembrokeshire and built up a thriving business in the days before the big breweries began to monopolise the industry. David's son John White, brewer, maltster and farmer, ran the brewery in the 1880s before leaving the village; he later ran the Kimberley pub in Milford Haven.

In 1889 the business was up for sale. The inventory included a dwelling house, offices, brewhouse and malthouse and two small meadows. The new owners evidently had no interest in continuing the brewing side of the business and instead turned the house into a pub, Anthony Thorn moving from Pembroke Dock to be the first licensee. Another Pembroke Dock man, Frederick Lewis from Commercial Row, was the landlord in 1906 and G.C.F. Harris was the landlord from 1923 until his death in 1929. John Brace took over, leaving in 1935 when he handed over to Walter Heaven, who ran the place from 1936 to 1943. Harold Poate was mine host before moving to the

The Brewery Inn at Cosheston as it looked in 2002.

Milton Brewery in 1953, while the longest-serving post-war licensee was Georgie Phillips. Current licensee Mr. Keith Bell has made a few internal changes to the inn, including the creation of a new restaurant called, rather incongruously, The Druid.

Hill House, a 'gentleman's residence' on Cosheston crossroads was turned into a pub in the late 1970s to replace the defunct Carpenters Arms, but despite a promising and lively start — especially when ex-footballer Len Prior was in charge — it ran into difficulties and closed after about 15 years. **Nash Rectory**, on the main road between The Fingerpost and Slade Cross, enjoyed a similarly brief lifespan — although this was always more of a restaurant than an out-and-out pub.

In medieval times Lamphey was the favourite residence of several of the bishops of St. David's, who built a palatial fortified mansion there, complete with deer park, fishponds, and a brewery. The ruins of this bishop's palace lie alongside the Georgian manor house (now an hotel) which succeeded it. One of the local squires, who lived at the manor, is said to have been opposed to having a pub on his estate, and for many years Lamphey was 'dry', the thirsty locals having to make the trek to the Railway in Pembroke or the Grotto Club in Freshwater East.

Lamphey had its own malt-house in the 1840s run by John Jones and this had developed into a brewery by the 1850s under the management of William Morgan. Tradition has it that the bakery house in the middle of the village was once a coaching inn called the **Venison**, but this must have closed at an early date for the first recorded pub in the village was the **New Inn**, where the landlord from 1795 to 1823 was Jeremiah Thomas. Lettice Thomas held the licence in 1824 but Lewis Child had taken over the running of the pub by the following year and was still there in 1828. It was evidently closed by 1838, as in that year a portion of the Portclew estate was up for sale, including a cottage and garden in Lamphey 'formerly called the New Inn'.

The **Black Horse** is recorded as being kept by William Powell in 1835, while Mary Powell was a publican in the village in 1841. Busiest time of the year for the pub would have been around the Lamphey hiring fair in September. In 1834 it was said that

> the afternoon was enlivened by horse and pony races, running in sacks, grinning through horse collars and other rustic amusements. A pig with its tail shaved and greased caused great diversion to the merry group, owing to the great difficulty of holding it.

Another Lamphey pub was the **Plough**, where the landlord from 1822 to 1841 was a farm steward named George Macken. Following his death it was taken over by his widow Margaret Macken, but when she died the lease of the inn was put up for auction. The inventory included a house, offices, yards and garden, 'five very superior Milch Cows, one Pony and two Pigs'. An advertisement for the sale declared:

> There is a considerable retail business in Ale and Porter carried on at the Plough Inn, and it might be greatly increased as no other licensed house is likely to be established in the parish. Alternatively, the Plough may be, with little expense, converted into a comfortable private residence.

And this seems to have been its fate, although the whereabouts of these early Lamphey pubs is something of a mystery.

When the railway reached the village in 1863, an enterprising carpenter named William Hall tried opening the **Railway Inn** near the station, but it closed in about 1869 and the village remained 'dry' for the next 100 years.

This changed when the **Dial Inn** was opened in 1967, being converted into an inn from a private house by local antique dealer Mr. Wally Howells.

The interior of the Dial Inn shortly after it was opened by Mr. Wally Howells.

A view of the Dial Inn in 2002.

The old house, which was known as Dial House because of its sundial, had plenty of charm and character which Mr. Howells was careful to preserve.

> Wherever one looks in the olde worlde Dial Inn there are interesting antiques, and on the edge of the adjoining car park there is an antique shop from which items can be purchased,

reported a guide book at the time. The Dial has been much extended since Mr. Howells' day, with the addition of a games room and the building of squash courts in the car park, and despite several changes of licensee it has remained one of the most popular 'eating out' pubs in the south of the county.

Nearby Freshwater East was once just a dune-backed beach with a scattering of cottages and farms on either side. But early in the 20th century it became *de rigeur* for Pembroke and Pembroke Dock businessmen to own a holiday chalet among the dunes and soon a small shanty village of beach huts with twee names had taken shape. In time, more solid houses were built overlooking the bay, and eventually the village acquired its own licensed premises. The **Grotto** was built as a private house in 1912, but soon after the Second World War it was acquired by Pembroke bookmaker Mr. Bill Johnson who turned it into a members' social club. This had the great advantage of Sunday opening, but the disadvantage of being unable to cater for the casual holiday

175

The Freshwater Inn, formerly the Grotto.

trade. As a result, Mr. Johnson's daughter Trudie and her husband Mr. Ernie Huxtable successfully applied for a full on-licence in about 1970. They ran the Grotto as a public house for several years before handing on to Mr. Ken Wordley. Since his departure the pub has changed hands a couple of times and has also been rechristened the **Freshwater Inn**.

Post-war holiday development saw caravan sites begin to sprawl along the valley behind the beach. To cater for these holidaymakers, George and Collette Bethwaite opened the Golden Sands Restaurant and the Freshwater East Club in about 1968. As with the Grotto, however, only members and diners were allowed a drink. Accordingly, the Bethwaites applied for a full on licence for the premises, while privately believing it would be a 'miracle' if they obtained one, given the mass of planning and licensing restrictions then in force. When permission was unexpectedly granted, the Bethwaites duly called the pub the **Miracle Inn** and it quickly established itself as one of the county's most popular night-spots. Alongside the inn was a dance-hall which was packed at weekends as locals and holidaymakers enjoyed regular live music from local bands and big names like Billy Fury, Russ Abbott, the Merseybeats and Hot Chocolate.

The hey-day of the Miracle Inn was fairly short-lived; its popularity began to wane after the Bethwaites left in 1975 to open the Welcome Inn at Castlemartin and it eventually closed. A prefabricated timber building, the

Miracle was something of a landmark on the roadside, but it failed to survive the recent redevelopment of the area and was demolished.

Jameston, a small farming village within the parish of Manorbier, once boasted a lively fair on St. James' Day. This fair, held on Jameston Green, always attracted large crowds, who danced to the music of travelling fiddle-players and generally made merry — it is said that every cottage in the village became an unofficial ale-house for the day.

George Robinson ran a pub called the **New Inn** in Manorbier parish between 1810 and 1828; this was probably in Jameston. Ann Buckney certainly kept the New Inn, Jameston, in 1841 and when she died in 1850 the licence passed to her nephew Evan Thomas, despite grumbles from one magistrate that 'an ale-house is a great evil in a parish'. By 1861 George Llewellin was the innkeeper and he also farmed the land which went with the pub.

In 1863 the railway from Tenby to Pembroke was built, passing near Jameston with a halt at Beaver's Hill. The name New Inn no longer appears in the records after this date; instead we find the **Railway Inn**, so-called even though it was in the middle of the village and a long way from the halt. Local grocer John Shears kept the pub in 1867 and in 1871 it was kept by William Williams and his wife Martha. A mariner from Bristol named Thomas Nicholas ran the pub in 1881, while in 1889 the licence passed to Henry Meyrick who was still the licensee in 1914. James Davies was the landlord

Rabbit-catchers outside the Swan Lake in the days when
it was still the Railway Inn.
(Picture courtesy of Mr. and Mrs. Cyril Cole.)

177

The Swan Lake Inn, Jameston, photographed in 2002.

in 1923 and Arthur Gay was there in 1931. Harold Williams, who took over in 1934, changed the name of the pub not once, but twice. He first changed it to the **Ship** — an even less appropriate name than the Railway — before rechristening it the **Swan Lake**, in April 1935, less than a year later.

Although the Lamphey to Lydstep road once passed the front door of the pub, it was later re-routed to pass behind it, thus causing some confusion. A visitor to Jameston in 1935 wrote as follows:

> There is one pub, but no-one strange to the place would think there was a pub in the village. It did business for many years under the sign of the 'Railway Inn' although the railway is a league or so away. Why the tavern has its rear abutting the road I can't say. Maybe the designer considered the bulk of customers would come over the fields...

Pembroke building contractor George Argent and his wife Gwenllian came into possession of the pub in 1940 and they ran it for several years with the help of various managers. When they moved to Tenby in the mid 1950s, Mr. and Mrs. Larry Loughlin moved in as tenants. The Swan Lake was extensively altered in the late 1960s by new owner Ted Klein who opened up two large lounges (one had been a cowshed at one time) and also turned the semi-private parlour into a public bar. The Swan Lake has been run by the Gill family for the past 14 years.

There were a couple of other ale-houses in the village as well. Plough Cottage was once an ale-house called the **Plough** run by former quarryman

George Badham and his wife Mary from the 1850s to the 1880s. Mary Badham held the licence on her own for a few years, but when she died in the 1890s the pub died with her. A couple of doors along is Elm House; tradition has it that this was once the **Black Horse** although no record of a pub of that name has come to light.

The former Plough Inn at Jameston.

A terrace of houses and cottages once stood opposite the Plough, but this was pulled down in the early 1960s and replaced with council bungalows. Two of the vanished buildings are thought to have housed pubs at some stage, one of them unknown, the other probably being the **Royal William**. This beer-house was mentioned in 1858, while in 1861 John Nicholas and his wife Margrit were described as 'beer and porter sellers' of the Royal William.

In September 1870 John Beynon of **Buttiland** farm near Manorbier Station was granted a public house licence. He farmed some 100 acres while his wife Martha ran the pub — evidently hoping to pick up trade from the train passengers. But it wasn't a success and they soon went back to farming.

Manorbier village stands at the head of a valley leading down to an attractive sandy cove, guarded since Norman times by a magnificent castle. Now popular with summer visitors and surfers, the sheltered beach was once the focus of a highly profitable smuggling operation run by a gang of Cornishmen who operated under the front of a local farm. The 'farmhands' went by such graphic nicknames as Jack Tar, Blue Boy, Jack Strong and The Long 'Un, and under cover of darkness they landed vast quantities of brandy, rum and gin on Manorbier beach, as well as tea, tobacco and silks. If the Cornishmen were the ringleaders, the local country-folk were willing helpers, lighting warning beacons on the headlands if revenue men were about or scrambling through the surf to unload the contraband. It is claimed that as many as 80 people would assemble on the sands to off-load a cargo of brandy, and by tradition one of the kegs would be broached on the beach for all the helpers to drink their fill.

Such was the volume of illicit goods coming ashore at Manorbier that the smugglers began to run out of places to store it. So with a breathtaking piece of audacity they actually rented the ruins of Manorbier Castle to be used as a storehouse. 'Of late years the castle has been appropriated to smuggling on a most daring scale', wrote one visitor, 'the person concerned having filled the subterranean apartments and towers with spirits'.

Eventually, in about 1804, a party of revenue men led by Lord Cawdor of Stackpole Court, acting on a tip-off, raided the castle and discovered over 300 kegs of spirits stashed in secret hiding places. The Cornish smugglers beat a hasty retreat and Manorbier settled back down to being a quiet farming village. The opening of the nearby artillery range and a growing tourist industry have meant a few changes, but the village still retains much of its timeless charm.

There was an ale-house in Manorbier in 1784, kept by John Davies, while by 1795 there were two ale-house keepers in the parish — David Morris and Simon Hughes. This had increased to three by 1810, with Hughes being joined by Joseph Jermyn and George Robinson (of Jameston). What Jermyn's inn was called isn't known, but it may have been a forerunner of the pub on the Ridgeway kept some years later by John Jermyn.

Simon Hughes was a shoemaker, so naturally enough his ale-house was called the **Boot and Shoe.** He still held the licence in 1828 but by the time of the 1841 census he was simply described as a shoemaker, aged 80. In 1853, the lease of a house 'formerly called the Boot and Shoe and now known as the **Lion**' was assigned to John Hughes, another shoemaker, who was still the landlord in 1870. His daughter and son-in-law Margaret and William Matthews took over that year and ran the pub until 1882, while Mrs. Matthews was still there in 1906. In 1916 the property passed to Agnes Gay and her husband Fred, a retired civil servant whose brother ran the pub in Jameston.

Attempts by the police to have the licence taken away in 1930 on the usual grounds of redundancy failed, the magistrates being of the opinion that the pub served a useful purpose in catering for the growing number of tourists visiting Manorbier. Despite this reprieve, the owners made no application to renew the licence in 1931. The building is now a small block of flats known as Lion House.

It is said that farmers from round about would always meet up in the Lion while the people of the village itself used to drink next door in the **Castle Inn.** In September 1848, a licence for the sale of beer was granted to Francis Twigg and he remained landlord of the Castle until the 1870s when he was followed by Tom Twigg, evidently a younger brother. Tom Twigg was a 'famous crabber' who, so it was said, 'knew practically every hole where crustaceans could be found between Manorbier and Skrinkle'. His daughter Ann Twigg was the landlady from 1891 to 1910, running the pub with the

An early view of the Castle Inn, Manorbier (partly hidden by bushes) and the Lion Inn next door.

The Castle Inn, Manorbier, pictured in 2002.

help of her sister Jane and also taking in laundry. The owner of the pub at this time was Mr. R.G. Ferrier of Orange Hall, Pembroke.

The long-serving landlord from 1914 until his death in 1954 was William Morse, while Mrs. Agnes Morse was there until Alfred Brooke took over in 1962. Ken Lewis was the licensee in the late 1960s and '70s followed by Mr. and Mrs. Alan Tyrell and Anthony and Gwen Maytum who took over in 1987 and whose family still run this attractive village local.

In 1861, a tailor named John Saise applied to Pembroke magistrates for permission to open a pub in Manorbier, and because he was 'strongly recommended by a great many respectable and influential inhabitants of the village' the licence was granted. The **Old Castle** was kept by Saise and his wife Elizabeth through to the 1890s, the name perhaps referring to the promontory fort on nearby Old Castle Head. The building is now known as Cross House and faces the entrance to Manorbier Castle.

The growth in tourism saw a couple of pubs being opened in the village in recent years, although both were relatively short-lived. The **Glyders** guest house in the middle of the village became a pub for a ten year period in the 1980s and '90s, while the oddly-named **Pirate's Lantern** had a slightly longer lease of life. This was the Glan-y-Mor guest house before it was converted into a pub in the 1960s by the owners, Mr. and Mrs. Buck Riley, who leased it to a succession of tenants. It soon became popular, especially in the summer months, but was closed in the early 1990s and reverted to being a private dwelling.

The Old Castle, Manorbier, is now a private house.

As the centre of a thriving agricultural community, the attractive medieval village of St. Florence has always been well supplied with pubs. The village boasted a weekly market in the 17th century and B.G. Charles has uncovered references to the 'Newe Inne' in St. Florence parish dating back to 1609. This **New Inn** wasn't the present village pub, but the farmhouse out at Minerton Cross which still bears the name. Morgan Ferrier is known to have run an ale-house in the parish between 1784 and 1798 — probably the New Inn — while a chap called James Williams was the landlord of the New Inn at Minerton from 1810 to 1828. George Bowen had taken over by the time of the 1841 census which simply described him as a farmer with no suggestion that it was still a pub.

In St. Florence village itself was the **Ball** which survived for a good many years. It may have been a drovers' pub at one time, since the old drovers' trail to Sageston via East Jordanston and Summerton started at the side of the pub (it later became a footpath). William Davies was the licensee from 1810 to 1828 and a widow named Elizabeth Hardy was there in 1841. Carpenter William Morris, who previously lived next door, ran the pub from 1850 until his death in 1877. His widow, Mrs. Elizabeth Morris, carried on until her death, aged 91, in 1897; she was assisted by her carpenter sons, James and Maurice, but they gave up the licence after her death. It is thought that the Ball later became Grove Farmhouse.

In July 1841, the coming-of-age of local squire Nicholas John Dunn was celebrated in St. Florence with peals of church bells and cannon fire. The *Welshman* reported:

> The houses of Mr. George Shears of the **Three Horseshoes** and Mr. Shears of the **Sun** were brilliantly illuminated and the merry song and exhilarating glass were not forgotten on the occasion.

At first glance this appears to be a mistake, since George Shears was the long-serving landlord of the Sun from 1822 to 1861, by which time he was 82. But in fact there were several people called George Shears in the village at the time and another gentleman of the same name — perhaps a blacksmith — could well have run the now-forgotten Three Horseshoes.

There is a local tradition that the Sun dates from as far back as 1717 and that it was once part of a village brewery enterprise. In later years it was the registered office of the St. Florence Friendly Society which dated from 1832, and in 1845, 60 members of the society gathered at the Sun, where 'a good and substantial dinner' was provided by George Shears. 'The company broke up at an early hour, each returning to his home in a decent and orderly manner', reported the *Pembrokeshire Herald* somewhat unconvincingly. The pub was rebuilt in 1847, in its present attractive style, by John Thomas, mason, of Tenby who charged £63. George's widow Ann Shears remained as

The Sun, St. Florence, as it looked in 2002.

landlady until her death in 1879 at the age of 95 when the pub passed to her daughter, another Ann Shears, a sprightly young thing of 69. Her sister Martha Shears held the licence in 1895; she was nearly 70 at the time and also ran a bakery at the pub. From 1914 to 1948 the licence was held by Mrs. Leah Skone and she was followed in the 1950s and early '60s by her son Neville Skone. When he retired the pub changed hands on a regular basis, but it is now back in 'local hands', being run by Mr. Tommy Roberts.

The present **New Inn** in the village was opened by Thomas and Mary Ann Morris in about 1875 and they ran it into the 1880s; Thomas was a carpenter and appears to have been one of the Morris family from the Ball Inn. Charles Burn, a Navy pensioner, had taken over by 1891, Mrs. Jane

Ann Burn kept the pub from 1906 to 1910 and James Burn was licensee in 1914. The New Inn was put up for auction that year, together with an adjoining black-smith's shop; highest bidders were wine merchants James Williams of Narberth who bought the property for £210. They installed Thomas Gough as licensee and he remained until his death in 1932; he was sexton of the church and a parish councillor to boot.

The New Inn in the days when
Harold Butler was licensee.
(Picture courtesy of Mr. Roger Davies.)

His widow Jane took over and was still running the pub and its tiny tin-roofed grocery shop in 1948 when she handed over to Mr. Harold Butler. A local smallholder, parish councillor and notable character, Mr. Butler then ran the pub in idiosyncratic fashion until his death in 1978. As the village history book *St. Florence Past and Present* noted: 'During the day the pub doors were not locked. If Harold was feeding his pigs and hens or helping his mother, a notice invited visitors to serve themselves!' Customers were expected to place their money in the old crisp tin which served as a till.

The pub hardly changed in appearance up to the time of Mr. Butler's death, and it was a regular meeting place for villagers and farm-workers who always used the tiny back bar — 'outsiders' usually being shown into the rather more spacious front bar. The Thursday night domino match was also a long established tradition. Kelvin and Christine Hurlow, who took over the pub in 1983 and ran it for some 16 years, made a number of necessary changes and improvements, but the New Inn remains very much a traditional cottage inn.

The New Inn, St. Florence, pictured in 2002.

The **Parsonage Inn** is a relatively recent pub, the old Parsonage Farm being converted in the 1980s into a popular 'family pub' with an emphasis on food, games and sporting activities.

The village of Lydstep began life as a few farms and cottages high above the shingle beach of Lydstep Haven, a regular landing place for smugglers. Sea quarries were later established at the southern end of the beach, with limestone being exported to the West Country ports. To cater for the thirsty quarrymen and sailors, plus a trickle of early tourists, a pub was opened in the village and a former labourer named John Twigg held the licence of the **Quarry** from 1851 until his death in 1878. The pub then passed to Irishman Andrew Nicholl, and he was still there in 1901 by which time it was known as the Quarry Hotel.

Towards the end of the 19th century, Lydstep House and much of the village was purchased by John Wynford Philipps, later Viscount St David's. He extended the house, landscaped the grounds and built new lodges and cottages in the village to house his servants and staff — each property roofed in bright red pantiles. His wife, Lady Nora, was committed to a number of causes, one of which was temperance, and it seems that she was instrumental in the closure of the village pub some time before 1906. In 1912 it was reported:

> The village now has an up to date post, telegraph and telephone office, a tavern for the sale of non-intoxicants only and a restaurant for the weary traveller to refresh himself from the cup that cheers but does not inebriate.

All these businesses seem to have been located in what was previously the Quarry Hotel.

The village was subsequently without a pub until July 1974 when the old inn was reopened as the **Lydstep Tavern** — a response to the fact that by now Lydstep Haven had become a popular caravan camp. It has since been extended and modernised.

The Lydstep Tavern which has reopened on the site of the old Quarry Inn.

The Ridgeway is one of Pembrokeshire's most ancient routeways, having been used by man since prehistoric times. Haunted by ghosts and frequented by footpads it could also be a lonely and nerve-racking place for pilgrims and other travellers making their way from Pembroke to Tenby. Ale-houses on this route were also few and far between, and information about them is equally sketchy. However, there is a long-standing tradition that the **Rising Sun** half-way along the Ridgeway was once an inn. It certainly looks the part and has a classic name, but for the past 160 years or so it has been solely a farm.

A newspaper report in the summer of 1862 referred to an inn called the **Travellers' Rest** somewhere along the Ridgeway and in Jameston parish. The landlord was John Jermyn, but since he was a carpenter in the dockyard, it was left to his wife Jane to run the pub. On the south side of the Ridgeway, just to the east of the lane leading down to Manorbier Newton, is an ancient ivy-covered ruin. Locals refer to the building as **Jenny Kibble's Pub**, possibly the old Travellers' Rest.

At the Tenby end of the Ridgeway, where the road divides and drops steeply to Penally, was the **Wheelabout**. It went by this name in 1841 when a carpenter named John Davies lived there, although whether it was a pub in those days isn't known. However Thomas Evans was running it as a pub called the Wheelabout Arms in the 1860s and he was still the landlord in 1875. When he died his widow Mary took over, later remarrying to become Mrs. Mary Richards, and she was still there in 1891. Her daughter Mary Ann Evans had taken over by 1901, and it seems likely that this was the Mrs. Mary Ann Morgan who was the licensee from 1906 to 1914. The pub seems to have been closed by the 1920s and the building stood empty and increasingly derelict for some years before being rebuilt by the Harriet Davis Seaside Holiday Trust for Disabled Children.

Pleasantly situated overlooking Tenby golf course and the sea, Penally enjoyed a reputation as a fashionable place to live in the 19th century and the village still boasts a number of well-preserved Georgian houses and Victorian villas. The coming of the railway in the early 1860s and the establishment and growth of the nearby artillery camp had a big effect on life in the village. Three pubs opened in the village in the 1860s, although off-duty soldiers tended to seek their entertainment amid the Tenby flesh-pots rather than in the quiet backwater of Penally.

Two of the pubs are still open on opposite sides of the winding main street. The **Cross Inn** was formerly a pair of cottages in the possession of the landowning Cooke family. They were converted into an attractive inn which was run by Lewis Phillips from Martletwy between 1867 and 1884. It was then kept for several years by Mike Hackett, a founder member of Penally parish council, while Mrs. Mary Jane Hackett was the landlady from 1906 to 1924.

The Cross Inn, Penally, was once two cottages.

187

The Cross Inn as it looks today.

Frederick Rose then ran the Cross for some years before it passed to his son Ted in 1945. Ron Welch took over the licence in the 1960s and kept the pub for about 20 years.

Across the road is the **Crown Inn**, for which Thomas Davies obtained a full licence at Castlemartin licensing sessions in September 1868. John Minton was landlord in 1874 and in 1875 the pub was described as being let on a yearly tenancy at £20 per annum and doing a good trade by being so close to the barracks. Scotsman John Booth kept the pub from 1878 to 1906 and, like Mike Hackett, was a founder member of the parish council. Sarah Chapple was landlady from 1909 to 1914, Frank Davis was the landlord in the 1920s, while the 1930s and early 1940s saw half a-dozen changes of licensee.

In 1948 things settled down when the Crown was taken over by Fred and Elsie Thomas from Milford Haven. They made a number of alterations and by the time their son Malcolm took over in the 1960s the inn boasted 12 bedrooms. Both the Crown and the Cross have changed hands frequently in the past 20 years, but both remain popular with villagers and holidaymakers alike.

When the railway station was established at Penally, a dozen trains a day would stop here on their way between Tenby and Pembroke. A **Railway Inn** was duly opened in the village, just up the hill from the station and opposite the Cross Inn. Henry James was the landlord from 1867 to 1880, running the

The Crown Inn, Penally, photographed in 2002.

pub with his wife Elizabeth. It was an occasionally stormy relationship; in 1879 Mr. James was fined 40 shillings for being drunk in his own pub, chasing his wife into the street and throwing a chair at her. Not surprisingly the magistrates came to the conclusion that he was unfit to run a pub, refused to renew the licence the following year and closed the place down. It was later run as a general store.

The late 17th-century farmhouse known as Holloway Farm was converted into an inn and restaurant in the 1970s and given the name of **Paddock Inn**. Unlike several similar places which opened at this time to cash in on the tourist boom and have since fallen by the wayside, the Paddock has stayed the course and is particularly busy in the summer months.

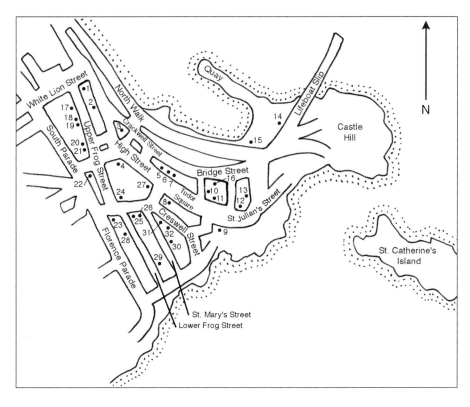

1	White Lion	17	Coach and Horses
2	Cobourg	18	Prince of Wales
3	Sun	19	Prince of Wales (Railway Tavern)
4	Lamb	20	Normandie (Commercial)
5	Ship and Castle	21	Union
6	Grey Horse	22	Blue Ball
7	Vine	23	Bush
8	Green Dragon	24	Five Arches (George - Butcher's Arms)
9	Globe	25	Bee Hive
10	Wheatsheaf (Lifeboat)	26	Three Mariners
11	Buccaneer	27	Ring of Bells
12	Prince of Wales	28	Star
13	Hope and Anchor	29	Crown
14	Albion	30	Shipwrights' Arms
15	Fisherman's Arms	31	Ship under Weigh
16	Prince's Head	32	Horse and Groom

Map showing the location of some of Tenby's more notable pubs

CHAPTER THIRTEEN

Tenby

HIGH STREET, TUDOR SQUARE, ST. JULIAN STREET & THE HARBOUR

Tenby's recently acquired popularity as a venue for stag and hen parties is just the latest chapter in the resort's long history of boozing. As far back as 1604, 55 inhabitants of the town appeared before the mayor Devereux Barrett and a Common Jury charged with illegally selling ale, for which they were fined between 3d. and 2s. apiece. And in 1627, Samuel Ward of Ipswich published a sermon called *The Life of Faith in Death* in which the evils of strong drink figured prominently. Wrote Ward:

> At Tenby in Pembrokeshire a drunkard, being exceedingly drunke, broke himself all to pieces off an high and steepe rock in a most fearful manner, and yet the occasion and circumstances of his fall so ridiculous, as I think not fit to relate, lest in so serious a judgement I should move laughter to the reader.

Anthony Thomas, who wrote a number of newspaper articles about Tenby's old pubs in the 1930s, thought that the town could claim to possess 'a larger number of licensed houses than any other town in the county for its size, and has for generations won for itself notoriety in this respect'. He claimed that there were 26 licensed houses in the town in 1801 for a population of 844 and that 'every other house was a pub'.

Certainly, at one time the narrow streets winding down to the harbour must have contained a healthy (or unhealthy?) number of taverns and alehouses and there would have been many more clustered around St. Mary's Church — perhaps the descendants of pre-Reformation pilgrim inns where pious travellers waited to cross to Caldey Island. However Thomas seems to have been exaggerating somewhat, since an 1811 trade directory reveals just five 'victuallers' as well as three innkeepers and two hoteliers in the town, while by 1830 there were three inns and eight public houses for 2,100 inhab-itants — hardly in the same league as beer-swilling Pembroke Dock. By 1850 the population had risen to 3,200 and there were four inns, 11 public houses and a dozen beer-houses. This total of 27 remained surprisingly constant down the years; there were about 26 licensed premises in the town in 1874 and 27 in 1910. Not all were the same places, of course, but as one hostelry closed so another seems to have appeared to take its place.

Tenby had a strong anti-drink movement in the late 19th and early 20th centuries, with temperance hotels, coffee bars and even a temperance brass band to trumpet the cause. However, it was noted that when the Good Templars staged a mock 'Trial of King Alcohol' in the Assembly Rooms in 1885 the audience was fairly sparse. Even so, with strong backing from the local chapels, the temperance campaigners continually agitated for the closure of the town's pubs; in 1912 the town's Free Church Council objected to the renewal of the licences for the George (now the Five Arches), the Coach and Horses, the Crown and the Prince's Head, for no other reason than to reduce the number of pubs in town. No doubt recognising the need for places of refreshment in a holiday resort, the magistrates tended to ignore these demands, although the Prince's Head, the Jasperley and the Albion did eventually lose their licences.

By 1926 there were just 20 licensed premises in the town — several of which were out-and-out hotels. A list of the licences renewed in February of that year reads as follows: Hilton, Royal Lion, Commercial, Sun, Shipwrights, White Hart, Prince of Wales, Gilbey's Stores, Evergreen, Wheatsheaf, Lamb, Cobourg, Three Mariners, George, Bush, Royal Gatehouse, Hope and Anchor, Coach and Horses, Crown and Imperial. Cases of drunkenness in the town were still fairly common and in 1925 there were 22 people arrested for being inebriated. Most of these were holidaymakers, prompting town mayor Mr. T.P. Hughes to hope that Tenby people were getting themselves arrested for drunkenness while on holiday elsewhere 'so that the figures might be averaged up'. He was only half joking.

Tenby's rise to prominence as a fashionable watering place had begun in the second half of the 18th century. Previously the town had enjoyed considerable prosperity under the Normans when it was a great herring port and famed for its Flemish weavers. From the Middle Ages through to Elizabethan times the town's merchants grew wealthy from their sea-trading enterprises, importing wine and salt and exporting coal and cloth from the town quay. But trade declined in the 17th and 18th centuries following the opening of a market in Narberth, and Tenby fell into such decay that large numbers of pigs cheerfully roamed the ruined streets of the walled town.

The man chiefly responsible for kick-starting Tenby's recovery was an apothecary from Haverfordwest called Jones. He regularly prescribed fresh air and sea-bathing as a sovereign cure for most ailments, and eventually he took over the lease of a disused fishermen's chapel near the harbour which he converted into a bath house for the use of his patients. It proved so successful that he expanded his enterprise over the following years, while a sprinkling of marine villas began to appear on the cliffs to cater for the 'bathing season' visitors. These visitors tended to be from the upper end of the social scale, and by 1788 Tenby was known as 'the summer retreat of the gentry in Wales'.

In the early 1800s the wealthy nabob Sir William Paxton began to take an interest in the town, and he was largely responsible for completing the task of turning 'an obscure sea-port into a considerable public place where the influx of company is at all times very great'. Paxton built a new bath house on the quay with warm, cold and vapour baths, and he also made it easier for people to reach the town via a stage coach link to the Windsor Castle inn at Cold Blow, which he also owned.

The visit of Nelson and the Hamiltons in 1802 helped put Tenby even more firmly on the map, and people began to arrive at the town in increasing numbers. Many took houses for the week or month; otherwise the accommodation in the town was sparse. The 1811 directory lists just two hotels — run by William Jenkins and Thomas Shaw — and three reasonable inns. The latter were the White Lion, the Blue Ball in Frog Street (where Nelson visited) and the Anchor Tavern, soon to be rebuilt as the Cobourg. Elsewhere the White Hart, the Globe and the long-established King's Arms offered fairly basic lodgings for man and horse, while the smattering of rough and ready beer-houses down by the harbour catered for the 'petty shop-keepers, mariners and labouring part of the community', rather than the fashionable visitors.

Soon terraces of fine houses began to spring up along the cliff-tops, some of them boarding houses and purpose-built hotels. Several of the better-positioned inns, such as the White Lion and the Cobourg, reinvented themselves as hotels while some of the smaller, seedier drinking places were swallowed up in the building boom. Later, as the town expanded, so new inns and ale houses began to appear to meet the needs of a growing population of tradesmen and labourers as well as an itinerant army of commercial travellers.

In 1837 a gasometer was a erected and the town became 'brilliantly lighted with gas', thus adding to the attractions of the booming resort. As a trade directory for 1840 noted: 'There are an assembly room, billiard rooms, good libraries, comfortable lodging houses and respectable inns, with every suitable convenience to be met with in this very desirable watering-place'. Throughout the summer the beaches were covered with bathing machines, many of them owned by local innkeepers who rented them out for 9d. each. By the late 1840s, steam packet fares from Bristol were relatively cheap and this brought many more visitors flocking to the town; the steamboats could carry hundreds of visitors, while the stagecoaches dealt in dozens. On one occasion in 1850 the *Osprey* landed 200 passengers at Tenby quay, 'having some names in high degree among them' as a newspaper correspondent smugly reported.

Gradually the railway crept closer and closer. In the early 1850s a coach link was established between Tenby and Carmarthen railway station; by 1856, Narberth Road (now Clynderwen) was the Tenby halt. There was always bitter rivalry between the Tenby coachmen who met the trains and competed fiercely to claim the passengers for their respective inns.

The railway finally reached the town itself in 1863, although the line only ran between Pembroke and Tenby. It was later extended to Pembroke Dock, from where travellers could cross the ferry to New Milford (Neyland) and thus link up with the GWR main line. Later still came the rail link to Whitland which was much more convenient and brought more and more excursionists pouring into the town, while at the same time supplying the kiss of death to the old stagecoach days. Indeed one local coach driver by the name of John Bramble is said to have become so depressed at the prospect of losing his livelihood that he hanged himself in a Tenby stable.

The finest and most fashionable of the old Tenby coaching inns was the **White Lion**. Situated at the top of High Street and commanding a magnificent view across Carmarthen Bay it is now the **Royal Lion**, one of the town's most popular hotels. It was built more or less on the site of the town's massive North Gate, where the road from Carmarthen entered the old walled town. Since that gate was pulled down in 1781, the inn may date from shortly after that time. When William Matthews visited the town in 1786, he described the

A billhead from the White Lion, Tenby in the 1860s when Fred Bowers was proprietor.
(Picture courtesy of the Pembrokeshire Records Office.)

White Lion as: 'A small inn, situated in the first street, having an open and pleasant prospect of the harbour'. He found it to be 'an agreeable house of entertainment for a common traveller like myself, prepared to be satisfied with a simple style of obliging accommodation'.

The *Cambrian Directory* of 1800 described the White Lion as the best inn to be found in Tenby, while in August 1805 the *Cambrian* newspaper noted:

194

The Theatre at Tenby opened on Saturday last under the management of Mr. Lee from Drury Lane who has fitted up the house in a superior style of neatness. The Assemblies at the White Lion have also commenced and are respectably attended every Wednesday evening.

The inn was kept from 1810 to 1816 by John Hales. He was followed by Thomas Faulkner who departed in 1830 to open the modestly-named **Faulkner's Hotel** next door and was succeeded by William Roberts. When Roberts moved to the Golden Lion in Pembroke in 1839 he was replaced by James Mitchell and it appears that the White Lion and Faulkner's were combined at this stage, because the building was called 'The White Lion and Faulkner's Hotel' by April 1841. During this period a coach left the inn daily in the summer months bound for Brecon via Carmarthen and Llandovery.

When Mr. Mitchell moved out in 1845, his departure was marked by a massive clear-out sale. He was succeeded by William Bowers, formerly of the Red Cow in St. Clears, who was also involved in the running of the Picton Inn at Llanddowror. He was a coach and carriage operator as well as an innkeeper, and very soon the service from the White Lion was greatly improved with a new coach, 'The Hit-and-Miss', running three days a week to Pembroke Dock, three days a week to Carmarthen and on Sundays to Penally Church. This was later replaced by 'The Summer and Winter Express', which ran every day to Pembroke Dock, and by a direct coach to Llandovery which met the 'Paul Pry' coach from London via Gloucester. Mr. Bowers rapidly became the leading carriage operator in the area, and it was a common sight to see his string of coach-horses being exercised on the South Beach.

Tenby High Street boasts of its sea views

He also made a number of alterations to the inn, it being reported in 1846 that he was determined 'that its architectural attractions shall be in keeping with its well-known culinary arrangements'. In 1853, as the railway age dawned, a new fast coach service was inaugurated between Tenby and Carmarthen Station. The following year Mr. Bowers was busy enlarging the establishment again, building 13 extra bedrooms, all with sea views, partly to cater for the new railway trade and partly in response to the building of a splendid new hotel across the road — nowadays the **Royal Gatehouse Hotel**. Also in 1854 Mr. Bowers became so fed up with the White Lion corner being used as a 'lounging place

The Royal Lion was formerly the White Lion coaching inn.

for idlers' that he tipped a bucket of foul water over them from an upstairs window. Naturally the idlers responded with a volley of stones which smashed every pane of glass in the window.

William Bowers died in 1860, to be succeeded by his son Fred. In 1862, Fred's 29-year-old brother Sam took part in a 'Lion to Lion' challenge when he was bet £10 he could not walk from the Lion in Tenby to the Lion in Pembroke in under two hours. He did it with six minutes to spare. Fred Bowers was a noted horse-breeder and rider to hounds; ironically he died in 1881 after being badly bitten on the arm by one of his horses.

Mrs. Maria S. Bowers then became licensee and she was still in charge in 1891 by which time the premises were described as a 'family and commercial hotel', having far outgrown the original coaching inn. It is now an out-and-out hotel, although it does have a public bar, the **Stage Door** which fronts onto Frog Street.

The **Anchor Tavern** in High Street was kept by George Hughes in 1811 but the old inn was demolished in about 1815 to make way for a much larger inn and hotel, also run by Hughes, which he called the **Cobourg** and which

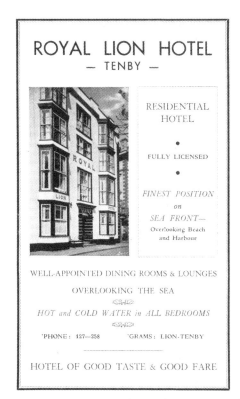

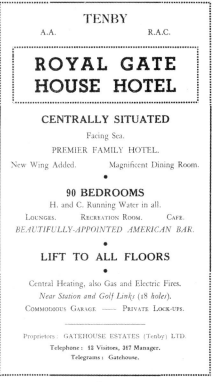

The Royal Gatehouse faces the Royal Lion and competes
in these 1947 advertisments.

remained in the same family for several generations. It was opened in June 1816 and boasted 'every requisite convenience for the accommodation of Visitors in the Bathing Season and Travellers in General' according to an advertisement in the *Carmarthen Journal*. And where the Anchor had tended to turn its back on the sea, being more accessible from Frog Street, the Cobourg was built squarely on the cliff-top to take advantage of the magnificent views.

George Hughes died in 1821, but he lived long enough to see the Cobourg established as one of Tenby's more fashionable inns. Mrs. Elizabeth Hughes, George's widow, took over the running of the establishment and presided over numerous society events such as the 'splendid ball and supper' which was held there in 1823. In October 1832 the 'Mayor's Feast' to celebrate the appointment of Thomas Sleeman as mayor of Tenby was held at the Cobourg. It must have been quite a night. Local artist Charles Norris had a stand-up row with MP Sir John Owen in which 'high language' was used. Meanwhile a chemist named William Walkington came to blows with James Hughes and both found themselves up before the magistrate the

Delightfully situated facing the sea with a Private Lawn on the Cliff. Noted for the excellency of its Cuisine and Service. Hot and Cold Running Water in all Bedrooms. Large Private Garage adjoining.

The Cobourg Hotel Tenby

Established over a Century.

Fully Licensed.

Officially appointed R.A.C. and A.A.

Telephone No. 9.   Telegrams : " Cobourg Tenby."

Proprietress : Mrs. G. J. HUGHES.

following morning — the magistrate being none other than the mayor, Thomas Sleeman. James Hughes, who was the son of Elizabeth Hughes, the licensee of the Cobourg, was bound over to keep the peace.

Mrs. Hughes remained in charge at the inn until her death in 1835, aged 74. James duly took over from his mother and was still the licensee in 1854. He also became a noted agriculturalist and rider to hounds. The Cobourg advertised 'barouches, flies and post-horses' in its livery stable and like the White Lion offered a regular shuttle-service to the nearest rail-head by means of a 'well-appointed four-horse coach'.

'That most amiable landlady' Maria Hughes, James' widow, held the licence between 1861 and 1881, during which time Lewis Carroll and the Prime Minister Earl Russell both stayed at the inn. In deference to the uncertain summer weather, the Cobourg advertised 'soup supplied for all the family' at this time.

The Cobourg in the days when it was a popular hotel.

Maria's son John Hughes succeeded her as innkeeper until his death, from a severe attack of gout, in 1889 at the early age of 45. Captain of the Tenby Volunteer Fire Brigade and secretary of the Steeplechase Committee, Hughes had been well known in agricultural circles and his funeral was one of the largest in Tenby for many years. The Cobourg passed to his widow Joyce and she was still running the business in 1920 by which time it had become a fully-fledged hotel rather than an inn. The building was converted into shops and flats in the early 1980s.

A newspaper article which appeared in 1926 noted that the **Sun** had been established 125 earlier. John Eynon was the landlord in 1835, and he may have been there much longer, since the name of John Eynon, victualler, appears in an 1811 directory. By 1851 the Sun was being kept by a 23-year-old plumber and glazier from Brighton named George Stone, who was destined to make quite a mark on the town's licensing trade. He soon built up

The Sun and the Lamb face one another in this 1970s view.

the business at the Sun, and in 1857 he was advertising 'Salt's Celebrated India Pale and Burton Ales, Schweppes Soda Water and Lemonade', and offering to make deliveries anywhere in town. A fire at the pub in 1857 caused £36 worth of damage to fixtures and fittings, but nothing daunted Stone continued to expand his enterprise. He took over the running of the Lamb Inn, virtually opposite, and he also bought several plots of land near the new railway station, on one of which he built the Hilton Arms tavern and refreshment rooms.

But his business seems to have grown too big, too quickly. In 1867 he went bankrupt and in March the following year all of his properties went under the hammer at the Cobourg. Stone disappeared from the scene for a while (but not forever) and the Sun changed hands a few times in the 1870s. 'The house is in the best position in town for the purposes of trade', ran an advertisement in 1879, 'being opposite the town hall and market'. The person who bought the pub and ran it successfully until 1920 was licensed victualler and council alderman George Childs. As well as running the pub, he was also a wine and spirit merchant and agent for a number of breweries, so that part of the business became an off-licence known as the Sun Stores. He seems to have made a point of sampling his product, because in July 1900 a local newspaper reported that he was being treated for gout at the spa resort of Llandrindod Wells. He returned to become town mayor and to create the De Valence gardens on a former tennis court; his son George E. Childs later built the original De Valence Pavilion on the site.

By coincidence, in 1909 the Sun was again badly damaged by a fire which gutted the bar and destroyed the whole of the stock.

Cecil Gwyther, who ran the Sun and the Sun Stores in the 1920s and '30s, was 'well known for many miles around as a wholesale and retail wine and spirit mechant and bottler'; he also owned the Shipwrights' Arms and the Hope and Anchor in the town. When the freehold of

The Sun Inn, pictured in 2003 after the old name had been restored.

the Sun was sold in 1933, the pub was advertised as containing a bar, a bottle and jug department (partitioned off), a smoke room, urinal and cellar. Percy Bale was the landlord in the 1940s, former Cardiff police officer Harry Wood was licensee in the 1950s, and Victor Thomas — 'Thomas the chimney-sweep' — was there for much of the 1950s and '60s. In about 1995 the pub became known for some reason as the **No Name Bar**, but happily had reverted to the Sun by the summer of 2002.

A butcher named John Andrews was landlord of the **Lamb** from 1840 until the mid 1850s when another butcher named John Adams took over. However, he died suddenly in 1860, the sale of goods which followed his death including feather beds, bagatelle boards and a 120 gallon copper boiler. Benjamin Johnson took over the licence. The original access to the Lamb seems to have been half-way down Nicholas Lane, but at some stage the pub expanded to take over a former greengrocery business fronting High Street. The entrepreneurial George Stone of the Sun, who took over the running of the Lamb in the late 1860s, may have been behind the expansion, and the move may well have hastened his bankruptcy.

Sales at the Lamb in the 1930s.

Mr. W.M. Collins bought the freehold at the bankruptcy sale in 1868, installing Martha Davies and later James Griffiths as tenants. When Mr. Collins, put the place up for sale in 1878 it was bought by

The Lamb Inn as it looked in 2003.

Griffiths for £2,030 and he was still running the pub during the First World War. Edward Evans was the proprietor from 1924 to 1938; he was also secretary of the local L.V.A. John Litherland, formerly of the White Hart, took over in 1943 and ran this James Williams house until about 1965, since when the best remembered licensee has been Billy Davies.

Daniel Richards was landlord of the **Royal Oak** in 1835 and William Thomas held the licence in the early 1850s. The entry for William Thomas, innkeeper, in the 1851 census comes between the Sun and the Lamb, so it must have been hereabouts. Possibly it became Gilbey's Stores, next door to the Lamb, which was one of the town's longest-established wine and spirit stores, having opened in 1870. It was kept for many years by the family of Ben Davies who took over from Messrs. Merriam in 1897.

The **Jasperley** was a wine and spirit stores in High Street opened and run in Victorian times by George White. Mayor of the town on four occasions he was descended from an ancient Pembrokeshire family, one of whose number, John White, was reputed to have helped the young Henry Tudor (later Henry VII) and his uncle Jasper Tudor to escape to Britanny in 1471. The Jasperley wine stores were later owned by Messrs. Clarke and Williams, and in 1912 Mr. H.H. Clarke was granted a pub licence for the building. The Jasperley Arms' main entrance was on High Street, with the 'jug and bottle' department having an entrance off Crackwell Street. The pub was rather surprisingly closed by the local magistrates after just ten years with compensation of £80 being paid out. The building now houses Boots the Chemist.

In 1723, the mayor of Tenby, Thomas Athoe, was hanged for the brutal murder of his nephew at a place called Holloway Water between Tenby and Penally. One of the witnesses at his trial was an ostler from the **Ship and Castle**, described as 'an inn opposite to the north transept of Tenby Church'.

It was the ostler's evidence — that Athoe had inquired closely about the route his nephew intended taking — that helped to convict and hang both the mayor and his son who was also involved in the late-night ambush and murder.

John Reynolds was landlord of the Ship and Castle between 1830 and 1835 followed by William Cale in 1844. In October 1853, Francis Smith, joiner and landlord of the Ship and Castle, was sentenced to six months' hard labour for beating his wife — the first local conviction under the new Act for the Protection of Females. Anthony Thomas stated that the pub was demolished shortly after this date, and an article in the *Tenby Observer* in 1857 seems to support this, as it refers to building work in progress:

> There is a curious old fireplace on the Ship and Castle premises opposite the church. It is ten feet long by about five broad — almost a small room — with the chimney over the centre. This portion of the house is probably as old as the 14th century.

Three old Tenby pubs once occupied the site of these three buildings - the Ship and Castle, the Grey Horse and the Vine.

The Ship and Castle was rebuilt as North Cliff House which is now the main part of Woolworths, although the store also takes in the former **Grey Horse** next door. This pub had opened in St. George's Street in the 1850s, but at some stage in the early 1860s landlord Thomas Griffiths moved the business to the High Street and by 1868 he was advertising the fact that he was licensed to let post horses and carriages. James Griffiths was landlord from 1871 to 1875, while in 1882 the licence was held by two sisters from Greenwich, Sarah and Lavinia Williams, who were both in their 40s. Sadly, Sarah liked a drop herself, and after several times being fined for being 'drunk and riotous' she was eventually confined in a lunatic asylum. Lavinia then applied to hold the licence on her own, but this was refused by the local magistrates.

In July 1883 the freehold of the Grey Horse was put up for auction at the nearby Cobourg, when it was described as a double-licensed inn, opposite the

*Tenby Liberal Club stood on
the site of the Grey Horse.
It is now part of Woolworths.*
(Picture courtesy of the Western Telegraph.)

church, 'with back premises extending to Crackwell Street and overlooking the harbour'. Thomas Howells was landlord from 1891 to 1895, but over the next 15 years the pub changed hands half-a-dozen times. In July 1911 'the freehold public house known as the Grey Horse' was offered for sale by auction. Local auctioneer Mr. F.B. Mason knocked it down for £475 to a Tenby contractor named William Davies. It later emerged that he had bought the premises on behalf of Tenby Liberal Association who wanted a new club in the town. The Grey Horse was duly closed and rebuilt as the new Liberal Club, complete with a half-timbered upper storey and a balcony from which public meetings could be addressed. This façade remains largely unaltered, but the interior has been gutted to accommodate the needs of Woolworths.

Next door down was the **Vine** which seems to have been opened in the late 1840s by Cornishman Thomas Webb. William and Elizabeth Roach ran the pub and the adjoining bakery business in the 1850s and '60s, while in 1867 the Vine was advertised as being to let, along with its billiard room and an adjoining cottage. The new landlord was George Noot, and in September that year he came close to losing his licence when the local magistrates discovered that the pub had a back door leading on to Quay Hill. Back doors were frowned upon by the local constabulary who had noticed that after-hours drinkers had an annoying habit of slipping out the back way while they were banging with their truncheons on the front door. Only when the back door was nailed up to the magistrates' satisfaction was the licence granted.

The Vine was damaged by fire in October 1877, when one hopes the nailed-up back door didn't pose any problems to escapees or fire-fighters.

The landlady at the time was Mrs. Eliza Gunter. The pub was put up for sale by auction in April 1879 when it was described as being 'situate in the centre of the town, having frontages and public bars in High Street, Tudor Square and Crackwell Street and commanding magnificent sea views'. A Londoner called John Whitfield seems to have been the successful bidder, later rather grandly referring to it as the Vine Hotel. When the Vine closed isn't known, but the building now houses Lloyd's Bank.

The **Swan** inn was also hereabouts, and it may even have been an earlier name for the Vine. Jane Rees was licensee of the Swan in 1844.

John Rogers ran a wine and spirit shop in the High Street/Tudor Square area in the 1850s and part of the premises was used as a pub known as **The Grapes**. The business was taken over by George White in about 1860, and he subsequently moved it to Jasperley House.

Three other pubs are believed to have existed in High Street — the **Bull**, the **Rose and Crown** and the **Mermaid** — but all that is known about them is that John Harris kept the Bull in 1788 and that George Poole ran the Mermaid in the early 1830s.

The High Street leads down into Tudor Square which in turn funnels traffic into St. Julian Street. At one time Tudor Square was divided into two narrow streets by a row of buildings down the centre. The thoroughfare on the right going down to the harbour was Market Street and there was a well-established pub at the top end. This was the **Green Dragon**, which was recorded as an inn in 1840 when it was being run by John and Elizabeth Thomas. However it may have been opened well before this time, since Elizabeth's father was Hugh Pelly, a harbour pilot who also appears as a 'victualler' in the trade directories as far back as 1811. Elizabeth Thomas ran the pub on her own in the 1850s, followed by Thomas Thomas, during whose time the front wall of the pub collapsed into the street while a new window was being installed; fortunately no one was injured.

John Lewis held the licence from 1867 until the mid 1870s, followed by

Liverpool-born James Nicholas and Emmanuel Charles Kelly. For some reason the Green Dragon had closed by 1890 and had become a shop and dwelling house. It later became Rodney's Café and is now the right-hand third of the NatWest Bank.

One of the town's early inns was the **Globe** which stood at the bottom of Market Street. It was described as 'a capital inn in full business with five very extensive stalled stables and three large coachhouses' when it

205

came on the market in 1815. The purchaser was Sir William Paxton who demolished the old inn and built himself a fine town house on the site. He also removed the old market cross which stood outside the Globe and from which John Wesley had once preached (it got in the way of his carriage). The building is now the Tenby House Hotel.

Around here was the **Oyster Barrel** (sometimes **Hat and Oyster Barrel**) which was possibly an early 18th century tavern, or possibly not. Anthony Thomas, writing in the *Tenby Observer* in 1936, explained:

> To many old natives this inn seemed an enigma, and was frequently bandied about as an object of sarcasm. I was reminded recently of a well-known and highly-respected boatman who was never happier than when he was engaged in an argument with his chums. No matter what the question at issue was, nor whether he had the best or worst of it, his last thrust at his opponent was, 'Well, you can't tell me where the Oyster Barrel was!'

One person who knew, or at least claimed he did, was T.W. Hordley whose reminiscences of Victorian Tenby were published privately in the 1930s. He placed the Oyster Barrel next door to Tenby House, but admitted that it had long ceased to be a pub when he knew it.

Opposite the Tenby House Hotel is the **Lifeboat Tavern** on the junction of Quay Hill and St. Julian Street. It was formerly the **Wheatsheaf** or **Wheatensheaf** and seems to have been opened in the 1840s by maltster John Smith who held the licence well into the 1870s. Smith took a keen interest in

---

LOT 5.

THE FULLY-LICENSED PREMISES

KNOWN AS

The Wheatsheaf Inn,

Occupying a prominent position in

TUDOR SQUARE,

In the centre of the Town of Tenby.

The Premises which are of Two Storeys contain :

ON THE UPPER FLOOR—SITTING ROOM, THREE BED ROOMS, and a BOX ROOM.

ON THE GROUND FLOOR—BAR, KITCHEN, Wash-house, Beer Store, and Coal-house with

Garden at rear.

Let, including a Loft in the Tenement, No. 3, Bridge Street, to the Swansea United Breweries, Limited, on the terms of a Lease for 21 years from the 24th June, 1901, at the low Rent of **£35 per annum.** Landlords proportion of Compensation Fund Charge paid in 1909, £1 14s. 9d.

The Wheatsheaf goes under the hammer in 1910.
(Picture courtesy of the Pembrokeshire Records Office.)

old Tenby hostelries, and in 1890 he drew up a lengthy list of them which was published in the *Tenby Observer* and has proved invaluable (and sometimes frustrating) to local historians ever since.

T.W. Hordley recorded that the old Wheatsheaf was pulled down at some stage, and a more modern pub built on the site. In 1881 the licence passed from Emily Grigg to her new husband John Stacey. Mrs. Sarah Truman was landlady in 1891 while Griffith Edmonds left the pub in 1901 after being convicted of drunkenness on his own premises; Harry Seaton took over. Thomas Harries was the landlord in the 1920s. The pub appears to have been closed for a period in the early 1940s when it was a Hancock's house, the local magistrates being far from happy about the sanitary arrangements. When this was sorted out to their satisfaction, the tenancy was taken over by Edgar Newman, formerly of the Amroth Arms, who ran the pub until the mid-'50s when Arthur Williams took charge.

Ted Blythin pulls a pint in the Lifeboat.
(Picture courtesy of the Western Telegraph.)

The name of the pub was changed in the mid 1960s, the new name reflecting the fact that this was the regular haunt of the town's lifeboatmen. Aptly enough it was kept in the 1970s and '80s by Ted Blythin, a member of the lifeboat management committee, and his wife Mary. There have been a number of internal alterations to the pub in recent years, but it still maintains a strong nautical flavour.

The Lifeboat stands at the entrance to St. Julian Street. As Tenby historian Arthur Leach noted: 'All the

The Lifeboat Tavern - previously the Wheatsheaf.

traffic from the harbour passed down this way — fishermen, boatmen engaged in trading with Bristol and foreign ports, passengers to and from Bristol by the steamboat service'. Not surprisingly there were several ancient hostelries along here, although the **Buccaneer** a couple of doors down from the Lifeboat is a relatively new pub. In a previous life it was the Tudor Coffee Tavern and Temperance Hotel, and earlier still it had been a boot and shoe shop. It remained the Tudor Hotel until 1969 when Robin and Joan Scanlon took over and renamed it the Buccaneer Hotel and Restaurant. It became a pub in 1981 and the Scanlons remained there until 1997 when they handed over to the present joint licensees, Doug Walters and Mike Evans.

The Buccaneer was once a temperance hotel.

Thomas Philipps Williams was the landlord of the **Prince of Wales** from 1849 to 1852. Anthony Thomas, writing in the 1930s, thought that the pub 'probably takes us back to the early years of the 18th century' and offered as evidence the building's 'old arched cellars and doorways, thick walls, massive oak beams and well-worn stone steps leading to the cellars'. If so, it must have been under a different name, because the Prince of Wales, which stood on the lower corner of St. Julian Street and Serjeant's Lane, seems to have taken its sign from Victoria's eldest son, Edward, who was born in 1841. Thomas added:

> There was issued by the last proprietor of this inn a brass token, the size of a halfpenny. The inscription engraved upon it reads on one side 'Prince of Wales, St. Julian Street'; on the reverse side 'T.P. Williams'. These tokens were much used at election times when free drinks were the vogue. They were issued not only for the candidates' benefit, but also for that of the inn.

The Prince of Wales seems to have been fairly short-lived, as was the **Bottle** somewhere in St. Julian Street; Lewis Rees was landlord in 1835.

Below the Prince of Wales, opposite Rock Terrace, was the **Brig** which was mentioned in the town council minutes in 1808. The Tenby Union Society, formed in 1812, met 'at the sign of the Brig' for its annual get-together in 1829. After bravely parading through the streets with 'gilded oak leaves in their hats and wands in their hands' the members sat down at the Brig for a meal. The Tenby Female Society — evidently the distaff side of the Tenby Union — also held meetings and occasional dances at 'the sign of the Brig'.

From 1830 to 1845 the Brig was kept by John Davies when it was the regular venue for the auction of coasting vessels including the brig *Mary Ann* in 1836, the brigantine *Apollo* in 1839 and the smack *Disney of Tenby* in 1845. George and Hannah Rogers who were there in the early 1850s were the last recorded licensees, although Anthony Thomas thought that the last tenant was a Mrs. Griffiths, better known as 'Peggy the Brig'.

John Smith's list of pubs in the *Tenby Observer* included the **Jolly Sailor** which was described as being at 'Green Gardens (now the site of Lexden Terrace)'. Anthony Thomas was more specific, placing the pub at 'No. 7, Rock Terrace', but it doesn't seem to appear in any of the records.

Moving down St. Julian Street, the old fisherman's pub the **Hope and Anchor** is still going strong, despite an occasionally chequered past. Thomas James seems to have opened it as a beer-house in the early 1830s and he ran it until his death ten years later when his widow Anne became licensee. Edwin Rowland was the landlord in the 1850s before Anne James, by then in

The Hope and Anchor has undergone several transformations in its time.

her 70s, took over once again. She was known as Nanny James and the pub became a favourite resort of Tenby fishermen who would gather here to celebrate a successful haul of fish. The greatest of these celebrations took place in 1860 following an amazing catch of bream off Monkstone Point, said to be the heaviest catch of fish ever landed by a seine boat at Tenby. 'We were drunk for a week afterwards', remembered one of the fishermen, Tommy Parcell, many years later. 'The Hope and Anchor was drank dry. We hired a hurdy-gurdy player and we had no end of a time the week we had the big catch of bream'.

T.W. Hordley, writing in 1934, recalled that in his youth 'four very old houses, including the old public house the Hope and Anchor' were demolished. There is a suggestion that when this happened the pub moved to take over the building previously occupied by the Brig. It is also believed that at one time the pub stood where the adjacent beer garden is now, but that it burned down and the licence was transferred to the building next door. However, so much construction and reconstruction has taken place along this terrace, and so sketchy are the records, that it is difficult to be certain about anything in this area.

Thomas Cashmore held the licence between 1867 and 1884 and advertised 'the celebrated Odumdoroo ale' at 10d. a quart. Miss Annie Williams from Houghton was the licensee in the 1890s and John Pope was the tenant from 1901 until 1907 when he bought the pub at auction for £580. On his death in 1925, the licence was transferred to his widow Hannah. Fred Sawyer, who ran the pub in the 1950s and '60s, was one of the longer-serving post-war licensees, and it was during his time that the pub doubled in size following the take-over of a neighbouring ironmonger's shop. More recently the pub has been run by Gordon Milton in the 1970s and early '80s, and then by Tony and Jane Smith for a further 15 years.

There is a reference in the *Carmarthen Journal* in 1815 to Ann Williams of the **Nelson Tavern** in Tenby. This may or may not have been the **Nelson** pub which was recalled by T.W. Hordley as follows: 'There was at the end of Cambrian House a small, one-storey building which was a public house called the Nelson. This was situated where Dr. Bryant's engine house now stands'. Mentioned in 1852, this Nelson was kept by Edwin Rowland (formerly of the Hope and Anchor) from 1861 to 1867.

The **Mermaid** was once a noted haunt of Tenby fishermen, but in May 1819, an advertisement appeared in the *Carmarthen Journal* to the following effect: 'In Tenby. To be let by auction. An unfurnished house, situated on the Quay, late the sign of the Mermaid, consisting of a parlour, kitchen, bar, cellar and brewing kitchen, with five bedrooms'. It is believed that this pub stood at the seaward end of what is now Lexden Terrace, above the Mermaid Cave, and that its ruins are still visible to this day. According to John Smith there was at one time an inn called the **Bristol Arms** somewhere on Castle Hill.

The **Albion** on the Quay was recorded in 1849. Adjoining Paxton's Bath House, this imposing, split-level inn was much frequented in Victorian times by fishermen and by the passengers and crews of steamers that used the nearby harbour. The inn had two separate bars each with its own entrance — the Upper Albion and the Lower Albion — no doubt designed to keep the fashionable guests away from the local riff-raff. In later years the local trawlermen would congregate in one bar while the crews of the visiting Brixham fishing smacks would drink in the other, thus reducing the opportunity for furniture-smashing punch-ups.

A line-up of fishermen outside the upper entrance to the Albion.
(Picture courtesy of the Western Telegraph.)

In the 1860s, the Albion was at the centre of what came to be known as 'the carpet bag plot'. A passenger arriving on the Bristol steamer handed over his carpet bag to one of the men who regularly gathered on the quay to offer their services as porters. The wealthy-looking visitor gave instructions that the bag should be taken to the Albion where he had arranged a room, but it never arrived. Later the bag was found in the sea, rifled of the large quantity of money it had contained. Police enquiries met a 'conspiracy of silence' and the culprits were never found, although the sudden improvement in lifestyle of a number of Tenby's shadier characters marked them down for life as the chief suspects in the robbery.

For some reason the Albion had a fairly high turnover of licensees. Charles Garrett kept the inn in the 1850s and George Gibby was there in 1867. He was followed by Mrs. Diane de Lisle who was the longest surviving licensee, running the Albion from 1871 to 1884. More landlords came and went, and it was a Buckleys house when Charles Richard Nursey was mine host

The former Albion, photographed from Tenby Harbour.

211

The harbour and the Old Town.

between 1906 and 1910. From 1914 to 1923 the licensee was Thomas Jones, but the Albion closed on 29 June 1924, and it finally lost its licence in February 1929. The building was renovated in 1994 by the Harriet Davis Seaside Holiday Trust for Disabled Children.

The **Fisherman's Arms** was on the opposite side of the Quay, and Anthony Thomas provided an evocative description of this character-filled inn.

> This was a noted inn on the Sluice side of the Harbour, immediately opposite the steps leading up to the old and derelict stores. It was patronised chiefly by the old fishermen who were domiciled in the vicinity, their boats moored along the road before the sluice was formed from the harbour. Habitues of this old inn may have included such veterans whose names have been handed down to us — Davy Price, the oyster king; Daddy Force, whose voyage from Tenby to the Isle of Man in a Tenby boat made his name famous in local history; Joby Jones, a notable blind fisherman who in his early years took an active part in the smuggling escapades along the coast; John Ray, Peter Cook, Toby Nash, Tom Bowen and a host of other lesser lights in the town's history. Here they met to formulate their plans and air their grievances.

Thomas Cadwallader, one of the famous Tenby 'Cads', kept the Fisherman's from 1840 to 1844 after which Jane Cadwallader ran the inn for a couple of years in the early 1850s.

No doubt the Fisherman's Arms played a full part in the annual election of the 'Lord Mayor of Penniless Cove'. Like most of these mock mayor-

The sign bracket is still visible on the wall of the old Prince's Head.

making ceremonies, this involved the consumption of copious amounts of alcohol and any number of drunken speeches by the candidates. The victorious 'mayor' would then parade the streets of the town to celebrate his election; in 1864 he was 'disguised by a hideous mask, decked with evergreens and borne on the shoulders of his faithful but rather groggy supporters' according to one witness.

It is said that a tunnel from the cellar of the **Prince's Head** in Bridge Street used to run down to the harbour below and was much used by smugglers. Although relatively unimposing, this may have been one of Tenby's oldest pubs; a court was told in 1912 that it was between 150 and 200 years old. James Gould was the 'tenant at will' of the Prince's Head between 1827 and 1844, while Edward Bartley kept the pub in 1850 followed by Richard and Rebecca Morgan. Thomas Williams was landlord between 1867 and 1874; former landlord of the Nelson, Edwin Rowland, was there in the 1880s and his daughter, Mrs. Anne Eliza Villiers, was the landlady in the 1890s. At this time the bar and smoking room of the Prince's Head were extremely popular with Tenby trawlermen, while its six bedrooms were often appropriated by the Shipwrecked Mariners' Society to accommodate unfortunate seamen whose vessels had come to grief on the Pembrokeshire coast. It was a rough and ready house, 'not likely to tempt visitors to Tenby' according to one report.

George Guy was the landlord from March 1901 until 1913, in which year the pub closed. A former pilot at Barry Docks, Mr. Guy ran the fishing smack *Atalanta* out of Tenby harbour while his wife looked after the pub business, but when she died in 1910 things went rapidly downhill. Trade fell away, the fishing boat had to be sold to pay creditors, and Mr. Guy was eventually made bankrupt. In the meantime the local magistrates had voted to take away the pub's licence under the redundancy ruling. No doubt the compensation payment of £90 was welcome to Mr. Guy, while a further £410 went to Miss R.A. Morgan, the owner of the property. It has since become a private house, but the bracket which once held the pub sign still projects from the building.

According to John Smith there was once a pub on Quay Hill called the **Sloop**, while the **King's Head** was a short-lived pub in Crackwell Street, being run in 1840 by Thomas Griffiths.

CHAPTER FOURTEEN

Tenby

UPPER & LOWER FROG STREET, ST. GEORGE'S STREET, ST. MARY'S STREET & CRESSWELL STREET

The first licensee whose name appears in the Tenby Court Rolls was John Instones who, in 1605, was granted a licence 'to kepe a comon ale house and to use comon sellings of ale and beere within the saide town of Tenby'. There were various conditions attached to the granting of this licence, Instones being warned not to allow children and servants to 'tipple' in his house, to prevent all forms of gambling and to inform the constables 'if any vagabonds or suspicious persons come to his house'. Throwing-out time was 'nine of the clock at night'.

In those days it was the ale-house keeper who was licensed, rather than his premises, so we don't know the sign of Instone's ale-house. Perhaps it was in the ancient thoroughfare of Frog Street which runs parallel to the south-western wall of the Norman town. Upper Frog Street remains the more commercial part of this busy little street, its seaward side being mainly given over to the covered market and to the redeveloped stable-yards of the larger properties in High Street. The southern side has always been where the hostelries were located, occupying the area between the street and the town wall; sometimes they didn't even have a street frontage, being reached through narrow passageways from Frog Street.

Beginning at the White Lion Street end of Frog Street, the first of these inns was possibly the **Black Horse**. John Williams was a publican in Tenby between 1821 and 1827, in which year he was briefly imprisoned for debt. He appears to have survived, because Pigot's *Directory* for 1830 shows him running the Black Horse. He seems to have renamed it the **Coach and Horses** and he was the landlord there from 1840, the first time the name appears in the records, until his death in 1861 at the age of 75.

Margaret Cousins was landlady from 1871 to 1885 and she paid the local council £15 *per annum* rent (the pub is still owned by the Tenby

Corporation). She was followed by Eli Curtis, while Charles Davies held the licence in 1901. The pub defeated an attempt by the Free Churches of Tenby to have it closed under the redundancy ruling in 1912 and William Priest held the reins from 1914 to 1925. Ethel Wickham was licensee throughout the 1930s followed by Leslie Stock in the 1940s and '50s.

The Coach and Horses is still going strong.

The pub survived a fire in the 1950s which destroyed furniture and charred some of the ancient beams, and it also survived a visit from Dylan Thomas. The poet called at the pub in 1953 after giving a reading to the local arts club of excepts from his recently completed play for voices *Under Milk Wood*. The story goes that Thomas became so drunk that when he finally staggered out of the pub he left his only copy of the play manuscript on a seat in the bar; landlord Stock had to post it back to him in time for the lecture tour of America during which, sadly, he died of alcohol abuse. The pub has changed hands on a fairly regular basis since the 1950s, but is still a thriving concern.

The **Prince of Wales** was opened in the late 1850s in a three-storey building separated from the Coach and Horses by a couple of stable yards. The first licensees were John and Elizabeth Williams who had previously run the nearby Commercial Inn, and who seem to have had no connection with the John Williams of the Coach and Horses. William Williams was licensee in 1867, advertising London and Bath porter and home-brewed ale. Various licensees came and went in the 1870s, and in 1878 a party was held at the pub to mark the departure of Mr. and Mrs. Harry Grigg who were heading off to the Rutzen Arms in Narberth. Peter Kennedy was there in 1884 and the freehold of the pub was offered for sale the following year; it had 17 rooms at the time and was bought by a Mr. Hughes of Treorchy.

John Davies from Meidrim and his wife Elizabeth ran the inn between 1895 and 1923. 'John the Prince' was a noted local character, being the first life member of the town's bowling club and an enthusiastic supporter of the Welsh language. A devout Eisteddfod-goer, he would regularly serenade his

216

1947 advert for the Prince of Wales.

The former Railway Inn now houses the Prince of Wales, while the old Prince of Wales was in the building on the right.

customers with the old Welsh ballad 'Y Mochyn Du'. When Tenby branch of the R.A.O.B. was formed in about 1900 it met at the Prince of Wales.

From 1924 until his death in June 1948, the licensee was Bert Allen, while James Titterton ran the pub in the 1950s and early '60s. It was subsequently bought by Messrs. Hilling and Allen who converted the upper floors into flats and opened an electrical shop on the ground floor.

The building next door down was once the **Railway Tavern**. The railway did not reach Tenby until the 1860s, so it is a little odd to find a pub with this name in the town as early as 1849. Builder and auctioneer George Harries opened the pub and remained the landlord into the 1870s after which the building became an iron-mongers run by W. Belt and later Edwin Lloyd. An ancient right of way had always existed at this point, linking Frog Street with the Parade through a doorway in the town wall. In the 1970s this passageway was utilised to create a shopping arcade on the site of the former ironmongers, and a restaurant called 'La Parisienne' was opened half-way along the arcade. When this was taken over by Peter Brown in the late 1980s, he converted the restaurant into a pub, giving it the name **Prince of Wales** in memory of the former inn next door.

Two doors further down, the **Commercial** seems to have been opened by Samuel Rushton who was landlord of this town centre inn from 1835 to 1852, followed by John and Elizabeth Williams. In the early 1860s the landlord was Thomas Cousens, a Tenby-born veteran of two early voyages of Arctic explo-

217

ration. The second of these was aboard the *Enterprise* which sailed north in 1850 in an attempt to find both the missing explorer Sir John Franklin and also the elusive north-west passage. After a harrowing five year voyage, the *Enterprise* returned having failed to accomplish either mission and Cousens wisely settled down to run an inn. However, his health never recovered from the deprivations of the icebound voyages and he died in 1864, still in his thirties. Scotsman Ralph Gordon ran the Commercial from 1867 to 1884.

In the 1880s the Commercial was the registered office of a local Friendly Society formed in 1836 which went by the rather splendid name of 'The Society of Gentlemen, Tradesmen and Inhabitants'. The inn had become a thriving hotel, popular with travelling salesmen and tourists, when it was purchased for £1,100 in 1890 by Mr. George Clarke of Clareston Road, Tenby. The landlord thereafter was Robert Clarke who sold the Commercial in 1896 to William McCracken Gray; it was described at the time as 'a favourite middle-class hotel'.

The Commercial was again on the market in 1902 when Gray moved to the White Hart in Pembroke Dock. It had seven bedrooms plus a large parlour and smoking rooms on the ground floor, together with 'an excellent bar, 40 feet long'. The advert continued:

> At the rear is good stabling for three horses, a bottling house and a large blacksmith's shop with large doors opening on to the South Parade. There is a separate approach also to the bar and hotel from this favourite thoroughfare along which runs the ancient walls of Tenby, a portion of which forms the western boundary of the Commercial hotel property.

In 1906 the landlord was John Brunt. The Commercial was run by a Mrs. Galvin in 1921 and by Albert Salter, chairman of the town L.V.A., from 1925 to 1949. It had become the **Normandie Hotel** by 1956; the fact that the licensee's name was Bernard Albert Emile Vincent Blaizot gives a pretty good clue where the new name came from. M. Blaizot had previously been *chef de cuisine* at the Old King's Arms in Pembroke. The Normandie remains a popular town centre hostelry.

Two doors down from the Commercial was the **Union Tavern,** kept by William Cadwallader from 1840 to 1858. An enthusiastic bootlegger in his younger days, 'Will Cad' claimed to have been a member of the notorious Cornish-led smuggling gang which operated out of Manorbier. He also seems to have run another pub at an earlier date, because he was described as 'innkeeper of Tenby' at the baptism of his son Thomas in 1816. (It's a fair bet that a proportion of the spirits he sold in those days had been landed in a lonely cove under cover of darkness).

The extensive tribe of Tenby Cadwalladers also handled legitimate goods, and its members operated a string of country carts and wagons before diversifying into Bath chairs and Sedan chairs as well as hiring out saddle-horses, ponies, donkey-carts and horse-drawn bathing machines to visitors. 'Will Cad' seems to have left the licensing trade for a while to become a baker and flour dealer, but he was back behind the bar in 1840, having opened the Union where he also involved himself in the transport business, specialising in the hire of small, closed carriages for conveying people to and from balls. In 1860 it was reported in the *Pembrokeshire Herald* that the 'long room' at the Union Tavern was being used as a drill hall by the Tenby Volunteer Artillery Corps so that training could continue throughout the year. By this time the pub was being run by Martha Cadwallader, but it closed a few years later.

A plaque on the wall of the building two doors down records that this was the site of the **Blue Ball**, a centre of the town's social life in the latter half of the 18th century. It even possessed a small theatre, although this was 'no bigger than a bulky bathing machine' according to one disgruntled visitor. As early as 1773 this theatre played host to a performance by a conjurer and lecturer by the name of Le Sieur Rea, and it was to the Blue Ball theatre that Lord Nelson and the Hamiltons repaired in 1802 to watch a performance of the play 'The Mock Doctor'. Emma Hamilton wore a 'white cotton Indian dress, red morocco waistband fastened with a diamond buckle, red morocco slippers and diamond buckles', and it was reported that the Hero of the Nile 'devoted to her the greater part of the evening'. Sage Harris kept the Ball in 1811, but it would seem that the positional advantages enjoyed by the White Lion and the Cobourg pushed the Blue Ball further and further down the social scale until it fell off altogether some time after 1813.

The **Globe**, which was also located in this vicinity, had links with the town's Globe Theatre which stood between Frog Street and the town wall; it appears to have opened shortly after the closure of the old Globe in Market Street. William Rees kept the Globe in 1830, but in November of that year an advertisement appeared in the *Carmarthen Journal* offering the lease of the inn. 'The premises, which are extensive, are in excellent repair, replete with every convenience and are in full business', stated the advert, adding, intriguingly, 'An unfortunate domestic occurrence is the sole cause of the occupiers discontinuing a concern which was flourishing far beyond the most sanguine expectations'. William Davies ran the pub from 1835 to 1841 with his wife Elizabeth who subsequently held the licence from 1844 until her death in 1856. It later became a blacksmith's shop and by the 1930s, when Anthony Thomas was writing, a shop run by Alfred Nicholls occupied the site of the old Globe. (Since the Blue Ball and the Globe seem to have occupied similar territory between the town wall and Frog Street, and since both boasted fairly primitive theatres, it seems that the Blue Ball may have been rebuilt as the

The five arches about 1910.

Globe; it wasn't unknown for inns named 'Ball' to be renamed 'Globe' in deference to the delicate female sensibilities of the time ...).

From 1835 to 1840 the **Shoe and Boot** in Upper Frog Street was kept by Francis Noott, or 'Noott the Boot' as he was probably called; it was near the corner with St. George's Street. And in 1849 a dwelling house in Frog Street 'formerly called the **Three Horseshoes**' was put up for sale. The occupier was a Mr. Adams, but there is no indication when it stopped being a pub, if indeed it ever was one.

Dividing Frog Street in two is St. George's Street, formerly Jail Street,

The Bush in the days of William McGrath.
(Picture courtesy of Mr. Roger Davies.)

another ancient thoroughfare which runs from the Five Arches gateway towards Tudor Square, eventually becoming Church Street as it takes the bend around the magnificent parish church of St. Mary's. There must have been numerous inns and ale houses huddled into this area in medieval times, and no doubt some of the long-demolished buildings which once backed on to the churchyard were lively hostelries in their day. This was also the fairly rowdy hub of the town's social life in

220

The Bush as it looked in 2002.

the Victorian era as well, with plenty of pubs and beer-houses both along the street and in the narrow lanes leading down to the Paragon.

Tucked inside the historic Five Arches gateway to the old walled town is the **Bush**. It appears to date from about 1860, having formerly been a blacksmith's shop, and Stephen Davies was the first licensee, running the pub until 1872. Former town police superintendent Thomas Thomas was the landlord between 1881 and 1891, while William McGrath ran the pub in the early part of the 20th century followed by Mrs. Sarah McGrath in the 1920s. Wilfred Vaulk was the best known and longest serving of the post-war licensees of the 'Hole in the Wall' as the Bush was often known, and many people can still remember 'Wiffie' Vaulks' pet fox which would occasionally make an appearance in the narrow public bar. Of the subsequent licensees, Peter Brown — now of the Prince of Wales — was one of the longer serving.

The **King's Arms** in Tenby was referred to in the Mompesson accounts of 1617 and 1620. (See Old King's Arms, Pembroke for details). This may have been the inn which was recorded in St. George's Street two centuries later. In April 1834 the *Welshman* newspaper reported the death of Mrs. Elizabeth Leonard at the remarkable age of 102. Even more remarkable was the claim that she was still landlady of the King's Arms at the time of her death. She had kept the pub for 50 years, and it was reported that 'she enjoyed uninterrupted good health until within a short period of her death'. However, Ann Leonard is given as licensee in an 1830 trade directory, so perhaps Elizabeth had taken a back seat by then. From 1835 to 1844 the pub was run by William Davies, but it had closed by 1851 and its exact whereabouts in the street are unknown.

The pub which still stands on the corner of St. George's Street and Upper Frog Street began life as the **Butchers Arms**, changed to the **George** in about 1890, enjoyed a brief spell as **Bennett's Wine Cellar** in the 1950s, became the George again in 1960 and is now the **Five Arches Tavern**. Lewis Adams was a butcher in Frog Street in 1830, and by 1835 he had built the Butchers

Arms on a site shown in Charles Norris' sketches of 1812 to be occupied by derelict medieval buildings. He remained the landlord until 1854, while Jane Adams was in charge between 1858 and 1861.

Anthony Thomas records that during this time, the Butchers Arms 'won for itself notoriety exceeding that of any other inn in this town'. According to Thomas, the pub was 'the rendezvous of the common folk who gathered there to discuss their business or settle their grievances, which frequently terminated in a street fight'. Despite

An early postcard view of The Five Arches Tavern in the days when it was known as the George. The South Wales Hotel can be seen beyond the George.
(Picture courtesy of Tenby Museum and Art Gallery.)

this unsavoury reputation, the Butchers was a meeting place for the local lodge of the True Ivorites Friendly Society between 1854 and 1875 and was 'celebrated for the excellence of its home-brewed ales'.

The interior of The Five Arches Tavern in about 1957 when it was known as Bennett's Wine Cellar.
(Picture courtesy of Mr. John Lyons, Templeton.)

Former Income Tax collector William Smith kept the pub between 1866 and 1880 followed by his brother James. George Richards then took over and he is credited with changing the name to the George. Richards was evidently a bit of a sportsman, and on one occasion he put up a £5 prize for anyone who could run from the pub to Pembroke and back in under three hours. A local man named John Richards covered the 20 miles in two hours 58 minutes to claim the prize. He then had to be carried home exhausted.

The street corner outside the George continued to be something of a battlefield through the 1890s, especially when soldiers from Penally Camp and local fishermen came together. On one such occasion, drunken soldiers from the Duke of Cornwall's Light Infantry fought a running battle with a large gang of equally drunken Tenby trawlermen, the fight raging along Frog Street and White Lion Street and into Warren Street with the local police 'unwilling or unable to put down the row'. Bayonets were drawn, stones were hurled and there were serious injuries on both sides. The town was subsequently placed out of bounds to the entire regiment.

(History repeated itself in 1954 when the licensees of Tenby all put their names to a letter to the Commander in Chief, Western Command, begging him to place Tenby out of bounds to all troops at army camps in the area. This followed a night of fighting and rioting in the town by men of the Lancashire Territorials.)

It was an ex-Army man named George Croft who succeeded George Richards in 1897, while Francis Collins was landlord in 1906. The pub had become a James Williams house by this time and the brewery seems to have had problems finding a suitable tenant. John Reid from Camrose lasted just a few months in 1907; apparently he was drunk most of that time. Other tenants came and went very rapidly, although Thomas Davies remained as landlord from 1916 to 1923, his wife Myra running the pub while he was away at the war. Perhaps as a result of all this chopping and changing the pub was

closed for a period in the 1920s and '30s, although the licence was kept up in the name of Janet Sandercock. The George was run as a grocery shop at this time, and part of the premises remained a grocery business as recently as the last war.

The Five Arches Tavern has undergone numerous name changes. The camera fixed to the corner of the building is a sign of the times in this 2002 photo.

Between 1940 and 1950 the licence was held by George Kinmonth, but the

223

following year the building was taken over by George Bennett and Co., wine and spirit merchants of Fishguard. They refurbished the old pub and called it Bennett's Wine Cellar, under which name it was run for 10 years by Mollie Odlum before it reverted to being the George in 1960 when Alfred Brooks took over the licence. Iain Ferguson, who ran the pub from the late '60s to 2000, effected yet another name change in the 1970s when it became the Five Arches Tavern.

Next door was the **Dolphin** where Thomas Evans was the innkeeper between 1852 and 1861. It later became the **South Wales Hotel**, run by Ann Hawkins, before becoming a temperance hotel.

Directly opposite the Five Arches Tavern, on the corner of St. George's Street and Lower Frog Street, stood the **Bee Hive**. Newman Glover, formerly the coachman at the Cobourg, was the landlord in the early 1870s. On one occasion he was charged with 'suffering persons of notoriously bad character to be on his premises' after the police discovered two local prostitutes drinking in the bar. The case was eventually dismissed but Mr. Glover soon flew the Hive, and James John was the landlord from 1873 to 1891. In 1901, it was reported that 'a large freehold house in Frog Street, formerly known as the Bee Hive Inn, was knocked down to Mr. J. Warlow cheap at £295'.

The **Three Mariners** in St. George's Street is now a lively open-plan karaoke bar, rather different in style from 1830 when William Force held the licence. This was presumably the famous Tenby fisherman, more usually known as 'Daddy' Force, who had been

The Three Mariners pictured in 2002.

going to sea since the age of eight and who, 'like most sea-dogs of the old school was very good at spinning a yarn' as his obituary noted when he died at the age of 91 in 1870.

From 1840 to 1851 Thomas Evans was landlord of the Mariners, and when he left to open the rival Dolphin across the road the rather wayward William Jenkins took over the licence. He was fined £1 in 1865 for allowing prostitutes to gather in the pub, fined again for being drunk and disorerly in 1869, and fined a third time in 1877 for allowing drunkenness on the premises. A few weeks after this third offence he gave up the licence which passed to the redoubtable George Stone, formerly of the Sun Inn and once more back in business after his bankruptcy. His daughter Elizabeth Stone was licensee in 1879, but the reputation of the pub hadn't improved and she was charged with allowing 'dissolute women' to be on the premises. George's wife Mrs. Martha Stone held the licence from 1884 to 1890.

From 1891 to 1914 the licensee was Mrs. Annie Hoffman, another-daughter of George and Martha, and from 1914 until her death in 1928 the landlady was Mrs. Annie Stone. Actually, these two Annies were one and the same person, since she had married Carl Hoffman, a Bavarian watch-maker. He had taken out British citizenship and had prudently abandoned his German name at the start of the First World War, adopting his wife's maiden name. However, this wasn't enough for some people in Tenby, and in 1915 Mr. Lawford Evans of Malvern House got up a petition, signed by 60 people, objecting to Annie Stone being licensee of the Mariners, or any pub come to that. Mr. Evans made it clear he did not object to Annie herself, 'a dear, good lady, the best of mothers and best of businesswomen'. But he felt it wasn't in the country's interest for a pub to be kept by the wife of a German national. The town's magistrates took a different view and ignored Mr. Evans and his petition. When Annie Stone died in 1928 the licence passed to Miss Annie Lewis who was still there in 1937, while Arthur Williams was licensee in the 1940s and '50s. There has been a steady turn-over of licensees in recent years, and the pub itself has under-gone numerous internal changes to cater for the demands of its (mainly young) clientele.

The original **Grey Horse** seems to have been located in this part of St. George's Street. Thomas Griffiths opened the pub in the early 1850s and in 1853 he was fined 1s. for serving after hours and another shilling for allowing gambling in the bar. In the early 1860s he moved the pub to new premises in the High Street.

Just round the corner in Church Street was the **Ring of Bells**, an apt name for a pub backing onto St. Mary's churchyard. William Prout was the land-lord from 1840 to 1858 and the pub appears to have been located in the second building from the end of the present row facing the square, nowadays a bread shop.

Three narrow streets run from St. George's Street down to the clifftop parade known as the Paragon. The first of these, Lower Frog Street, is a continuation of Upper Frog Street and is known to have contained two pubs.

The second building down on the right next to the old police station was the **Star** kept by William Roch in 1835 and by stonemason Thomas Rogers from Minwear between 1844 and about 1880. In August 1884 the Star was converted into a private members' club. This was a direct result of the Welsh Sunday Closing Act of 1881 which saw a number of pubs being reborn as social clubs 'whose members had little in common apart from a thirst on Sundays' according to Brian Glover in *Prince of Ales*. The Star Club had 150 members and was described by its manager Henry John in 1885 as a 'properly constituted workingmen's club'. However, it was a source of great annoyance to the local constabulary who found themselves unable to stem the tide of Sunday drinking. But the Star Club didn't trouble the authorities for too long and by 1891 it seems to have closed, with the building being split into accommodation for three families. The Star Café was located here after the last war.

Another Sunday drinking club in Tenby was the Victoria, one of a string of similar clubs set up throughout South Wales by former billiards marker

James Tilly with the thinly disguised purpose of flouting the Sunday Closing Act. This was also in Lower Frog Street and, like the Star, was fairly short-lived.

The **Crown** is still open at the bottom of Lower Frog Street. In 1867 the landlord was William Tudor and by the 1870s this inn had become popular with local stable-lads who used to gather there to drink and play cards into the early hours. This earned the easy-going landlord H.B. Medcalfe a ticking-off from the local justices for

The Crown Inn in Lower Frog Street.

226

'encouraging boys to acquire such bad habits as intemperance, gambling, card-playing and other kindred vices'. George Clarke kept the pub in 1884 and Tynesider John Lodwick and his wife Alice were there in 1891. In that year, Mr. Lodwick denied a charge of being open after hours, his unusual defence being that the Coast Brigade gunners, who were lounging around the pub at midnight, were only waiting for the tide to go out so that they could walk back to their fort on St. Catherine's Island. Perhaps still smarting from the fine he received, Mr. Lodwick handed over to John Roberts the following year.

William Neate was landlord from 1901 to 1907 while former coastguard Morris Price ran the pub from 1909 to 1914. The Crown survived an attempt by the Free Churches of Tenby to have it closed in 1912 under the redundancy ruling and Mr. John Novarra was the licensee in the 1920s. Alfred Clarke refurbished the place in 1929 and stayed until 1940 when he was replaced by Thomas Kinmonth. However, in 1948 Mr. Kinmonth gave up the

pub and bought a sweet shop in the Mumbles 'having grown to dislike the drink business on moral grounds'. One of the longer serving post-war licensees was Ernest Jefferson, for a time the secretary of the local L.V.A.

Running parallel to Lower Frog Street is St. Mary's Street. The **Shipwrights Arms** opened here in the 1840s and earned a reputation as an unobtrusive side-street drinking den, hardly recognisable as a pub. It was once said of the Shipwrights: 'If you go down the street in which it is situated, you can hardly tell it is a public house at all. Only by scanning very closely can you tell it is a public house by

The Shipwrights' Arms is now a private house. the name'. James Rossiter ran this beer-house in the 1850s, and a widow named Mrs. Martha Rossiter held the licence between 1867 and 1885. Horace and Annie Briddon were there in 1892, Mrs. Elizabeth Clarke was the landlady from 1906 to 1911 and she was followed by a widow named Mrs. Hetty Nursey in 1914.

During that year the Shipwrights was the subject of a bitter attack by local temperance leader and Congregational minister, the Rev. J. Lloyd Williams. He felt that because the Shipwrights was tucked away from public view, it had become a magnet for drinkers. 'It is a house which people can go into without being easily seen, and as such it is a temptation to younger men', thundered the minister. 'And I have seen the lives of many young men ruined through drink'. He demanded that Tenby magistrates refuse to renew the licence. The justices were unimpressed, however and allowed Mrs. Nursey to carry on serving. A sale catalogue dated 1933 stated that the Shipwrights had four bedrooms on the first floor, while the ground floor comprised a bar, smoke-room, snug and scullery. Alfred Evans was the licensee at the time, and following his death in the 1950s the Shipwrights was taken over by James Edwards; it finally closed in the early 1970s to become a private house.

John Way ran a pub in St. Mary's Street from 1840 to 1844. This could have been the **Bear** or the **Talbot**, both of which were in that street according to John Smith, although neither name appears in the records.

The next street along is Cresswell Street which has no pubs nowadays but was a lively place of entertainment in the 1850s with billiard rooms and several ale houses. One of these was the **Ship under Weigh** which seem to have been located in the second house on the right going towards the sea. William Squires held the licence from 1844 to 1850, followed by his widow Jane, but no-one seems to have settled at the pub for any length of time. Last recorded licensees were James and Elizabeth Rogers who took over in early 1877 and were still there in 1881; the pub must have closed shortly afterwards.

Next door was the **Horse and Groom** beer-house where George Bowen was landlord from 1844 to 1858; he also ran a livery stable, which accounts for the name of the pub. Edwin Davies was the licensee in 1867, but the pub doesn't seem to have survived the Wine and Beer-house Act of 1869. The **Lord Raglan**, mentioned in a court case in 1868, was also in Cresswell Street, according to John Smith's list. And towards the bottom of the street on the left was the **Fountain,** the brewery tap of brewer and maltster James Davies in the 1850s.

There was another pub at the bottom of Cresswell Street in 1875 — the **British Workman** — but this doesn't really count as it was a pub with no beer, having been opened as a coffee tavern by the local temperance people. It was described as a place where 'the labouring men of Tenby' could go when they needed 'a seat and a fire without the necessity of drinking beer'.

CHAPTER FIFTEEN

Tenby
OUTSIDE THE WALLS

In medieval times, the only part of Tenby that stood outside the town walls was the North Town, nowadays known as the Norton. This was the area outside the great North Gate, a small suburb which grew up alongside the Carmarthen Road and which no doubt once featured inns that could accommodate benighted travellers who arrived after the gate was closed. The earliest inn to be mentioned in this area was the **Three Cups**, referred to in the Cawdor papers of 1765 and also listed by John Smith but about which nothing is known.

Writing in 1934, Mr. T.W. Hordley recalled that in his youth nearly all the traffic into the town travelled along the Norton.

> Saturday was the busiest day. Butchers and farmers in their spring carts came in great numbers to attend the market. The most interesting visitors, however, were the shoemakers from Narberth. About a dozen of them with their trunks mounted on two wheels and a donkey in the shaft would leave the town, trotting along the Norton in processional order, the driver in each case sitting on the trunk.

By the 19th century the Norton possessed a fair sprinkling of hostelries, the most imposing being the **White Hart** at the junction of the Norton and St. John's Hill, formerly Windpipe Lane. In 1813 this was the scene of the auction of the French lugger *L'Union* which had been captured as a prize by Lieut. T. Scriven of the schooner *Arrow* and which lay in the harbour below. Also up for auction was the tempting cargo of *L'Union* — 92 casks of French claret and 90 casks of cider.

Thomas Morse was the new licensee in 1833 and he was still there in 1841 before being succeeded by his widow Mary. Thomas Hughes was landlord in 1850 and he also acted as a 'carrier', driving the market waggon to Narberth a couple of times a week. His widow Ann held the licence from 1851 to 1854. William Harding was landlord in 1858, and like the two previous male licensees he died in harness, leaving his widow Mary to carry on the business. Since the White Hart was never as fashionable as the White Lion or Cobourg, she tended to cater for a more local trade. James Davies was landlord from 1875 to 1891 and the licensee from 1900 to 1905 was Richard Smith.

Miriam Georgina Evans kept the pub/hotel in 1906 followed by Philip Dalling during whose tenure police drew attention to a 'nuisance' occurring on St. John's Hill. To get to the urinals at the back of the pub, drinkers faced a 45 yard walk from the

The White Hart in about 1906.
(Picture courtesy of the Albany Hotel.)

public bar, out through the front door, down the hill and round into the stable yard at the back. Some men obviously couldn't be bothered to make the whole journey, hence the complaint.

John Litherland held the licence from 1927 to 1943 when he moved to the Lamb and Philip Beesley was there in the 1960s. The White Hart was originally just the corner property, but it has gradually expanded in recent years to swallow up two adjacent premises along the Norton and one on St. John's Hill. It is now known as the **Albany Hotel**, but the public bar with its street corner entrance has changed little since the days of the White Hart.

'Phone :
Tenby 154

Telegrams :
" WhiteHart," Tenby

WHITE HART HOTEL
TENBY

Highly Recommended for Catering and General Comfort

ELECTRIC LIGHT

Hot and Cold Water in all Bedrooms

Situated about 100 Yards from North Beach

FULLY LICENSED

TARIFF ON APPLICATION
H. W. BROOMFIELD Propr.

In 1947 it was still essential to inform potential visitors that the hotel had electric light.

230

The old White Hart is now the Albany Hotel.

The other licensed houses in the area seem to have been much humbler affairs, and several must have been swept aside in the redevelopment of the town into a fashionable resort. These early ale houses, which catered for quarrymen, stable-lads and the like, included the **Masons Arms**, which was first mentioned in 1815 and which appears to have been located several doors below the White Hart. It was run as a beer house by stonemason Thomas Smith between 1830 and 1835. Another mason, Thomas Thomas (Tom the Fox) and his wife Mary were in charge from 1844 until 1861, but the pub seems to have closed following Mary's death in 1865.

In 1839, joiner and borough surveyor Evan Lewis kept an ale house called the **New Inn** on the Norton; he lived a few doors above the White Hart, but the pub was a short-lived venture. The **Ship Aground** was also on the Norton; William Rees held the licence from 1841 to 1844.

According to John Smith's list, there were three other ale houses on the Norton at one time — the **Square and Compass,** the **Brown Cow,** and the oddly-named **I.B.D.** No other reference to these pubs has come to light, although one may have been the ale-house run by John Thomas, shoemaker and beer seller, in 1840.

Near the bottom of St. John's Hill, the **Evergreen** stands in the shadow of the massive seven-arch railway viaduct. It was the building of this viaduct in the mid-1860s which probably brought the pub into being, licensee Jane Williams spotting the opportunity of selling vast quantities of beer to the navvies working on the construction.

From 1874 to 1881 the licensee was William Francis, the licence passing shortly afterwards to his daughter and son-in-law, Emma and John Brinn. In the 1890s, John Brinn was leasing the Evergreen for £10 a year, but when the freehold came up for auction in 1898, he bought the pub for £300. William Brinn was behind the bar in 1920, but the Evergreen subsequently became a James Williams house and Percy Wright held the licence from 1927 to 1960. James Brooking was the tenant in the 1960s followed by Ray Wilding and Bobby Cooke. The Evergreen remains a popular local, and the regulars include the ghost of a woman which floats past from time to time.

The **Hilton Arms** was built in 1867 by George Stone of the Sun Inn on what was then the Pill Field but which was soon to become busy Warren Street, the main route to the railway station. Describing it as the 'Hilton Arms and refreshment room, railway station', Stone installed his father, George senior, as

The Evergreen has its own resident ghost.

tenant. When George junior went bankrupt shortly afterwards, the Hilton was sold.

The licence passed to John Woodman in October 1877 and he took the Hilton firmly down-market, to the extent that it was described in the local press as being 'a notorious and badly-conducted house'. Evidently it was much frequented by soldiers from Penally Camp who were usually guaranteed a late drink, often in the company of ladies of questionable virtue. In the summer of 1879, Woodman was fined £2 plus costs for refusing to admit two police officers who wanted to inspect the premises, and he seems to have left town soon afterwards.

Town councillor Benjamin George Gifford is recorded as being the licensee from 1884 to 1898 and in that year the Hilton was again placed on the market, the advert stating that it was 'the only public house within a radius of 300 yards'. After a fierce bidding war between rival breweries the Hilton was bought by Swansea United Breweries for £1,900; they installed Arthur Seaton as land-

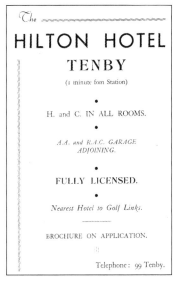

The

HILTON HOTEL
TENBY
(1 minute fom Station)

•

H. and C. IN ALL ROOMS.

•

A.A. and R.A.C. GARAGE ADJOINING.

•

FULLY LICENSED.

•

Nearest Hotel to Golf Links.

BROCHURE ON APPLICATION.

Telephone : 99 Tenby.

Hotels were making a comeback after the war as this 1947 advert shows.

The Hilton Arms has now been converted into flats.

lord. The original pub had ten bedrooms, but it was extended in 1900 by the acquisition of the premises next door which turned it into a fair-sized pub-cum-hotel, handy for the station. Frank Byfield held the licence in the 1920s, while Florence Pentland was the longest-serving licensee, running the Hilton for over 30 years from 1931. The pub closed in the summer of 2002 and has been converted into holiday flats.

The fact that the Hilton was the only pub within a radius of 300 yards was partly due to the class divide which was a feature of Victorian Tenby. On the one hand there existed the fashionable and affluent section of society, living in their marine villas, hiring yachts, playing cricket and attending balls and steeplechases. On the other hand there was a scruffy underclass of fishermen, labourers and beggars who rather lowered the tone of the place. As one correspondent to the local press put it:

> It is a great pity that so fair a place as Tenby should be cursed with such an evil-minded, foul-languaged rabble as now exist, a class of roughs who defile the district with obscene language and malicious, filthy talk too loathsome to be tolerated, deceiving innocent people by their vile and idle reports, using the most filthy language in the streets and generally corrupting the morals of the place.

The ale-house was the natural haunt of the 'foul-mouthed rabble', so those who saw themselves as the guardians of the town's morals did their best to close down the pubs that already existed, and also made sure that no new ones were opened in the smart estates being built outside the walls. This was particularly true of the area between Trafalgar Road and the cliffs above the south beach — regarded as prime building land. There must have been a pub in this area at one time, since George Thomas was a beer-seller in Chimney Park in 1840. (This was the original name of Trafalgar Road, the name being changed to honour local naval hero, Captain Hugh Cook, who fought at

The Esplanade in the 1920s with the Imperial, a purpose-built hotel, in the middle distance.

Trafalgar). Thomas' ale-house is thought to have been called the **Ivy Bush**.

The Ivy Bush was closed long before the fashionable South Cliff estate was built in the 1860s and '70s and became Tenby's own little 'temperance town'. One property on the corner of South Cliff Street and Victoria Street is said to have been planned as a pub, with a canted corner designed to take the entrance door, but it never opened as such and became a boarding house instead. And when, in the early 1870s, Newman Glover attempted to open a new pub in respectable Culver Park the residents of the surrounding streets were so horrified at the thought of 'roughs' being drawn to the area that they signed a petition opposing the plan and it was duly thrown out. Although the **Builders Arms** is mentioned in 1880 in connection with a court case involving a drunken fisherman, this was presumably a short-lived beer house, opened to cater for

IMPERIAL HOTEL,
TENBY, WALES.

THE LEADING HOTEL IN SOUTH WALES
Fully Licensed.
ROOMS WITH PRIVATE BATH AND TELEPHONE.
—— GARAGE ——

Brochure from Managing Director : G. PERL.
Tels. : 28 and 246.   'Grams : Imperial, Tenby.

The cliff-top position of the Imperial Hotel is well shown in this 1947 advert.

234

the men building the new houses, and the area soon reverted to its 'dry' status. And there are still no pubs in the area, although plenty of the hotels and guest houses are now licensed.

On the outskirts of Tenby, the **Victoria** on the Marsh Road was recorded in 1841 when Thomas Williams from Begelly and his wife Mary were in charge. It was run by William and Rebecca Skyrme between 1867 and 1890, initially as a beer house and later as a fully-fledged pub. Being on the road between the town and the artillery range at Penally it was a popular port of call for soldiers, whose 'disgraceful conduct' prompted a letter to the *Tenby Observer* in 1885.

> The Marsh Road seems to be the general resort of a great number of soldiers who go there no doubt to obtain a little "refreshment" at the road-side inn. It is very hard if they cannot keep their insinuating remarks to themselves.

The pub seems to have closed in the 1890s and is now a private house.

Just outside the town, the **Three Bells** was an old farm-house, possibly medieval, which began selling ale and offering lodgings when the 'new' coach-road between Tenby and New Hedges was opened in the 1830s. This road replaced the previous stiff climb over the Windmill Hill which was unpopular with coach drivers and their horses. Thomas Morris was

Victoria Cottage — formerly the Victoria Inn.

the innkeeper in 1839 when two of his lodgers were arrested for forgery and passing counterfeit coins. A haulier and road repairman, Morris was still there in 1848.

Benjamin Davies was licensee from 1854 until 1862, in which year he seems to have been declared insolvent. George Thomas, who was landlord from 1867 to 1891, made ends meet by also running a small dairy herd; he was lucky to survive an encounter with the Rowson prize bull in 1869. Thomas Davies held the licence from 1895 to 1900, during which time the pub was put up for auction. It failed to reach its reserve, although the local press reported that it had been sold afterwards 'for a good price'.

A 1950s view of the Three Bells.

In 1900 the local magistrates granted a transfer of the licence from Thomas Davies to Harry Watkins who ran the Bells for some years with his wife Lizzie. However the pub had closed by 1910, in somewhat unusual circumstances. It is said that the purchaser of the property in 1898 was a lady from Saundersfoot who was in the habit of travelling to church in Tenby every Sunday in a carriage and pair. Naturally this would take her past the Three Bells which was invariably packed with supposedly *bona fide* travellers — usually mine-workers from the Kilgetty area. So upset did the lady become at this debauchery on the Sabbath that she gave the Watkins family notice to quit and installed new tenants who were under strict instructions never to run the place as a pub.

Now a private house, the Bells has been much altered — but happily the old pub is remembered in a stained-glass panel above the front door which shows three merrily chiming bells.

Bibliography

Much of the information in this book has been gleaned from old newspapers, notably the *Welshman*, the *Carmarthen Journal*, *Potter's Electric News*, the *West Wales Guardian*, the *Tenby Observer*, the *Pembrokeshire Herald*, the *Pembroke and Pembroke Dock Gazette* and the *Haverfordwest and Milford Haven Telegraph*.

The various trade directories have also proved very useful, particularly those published at various times between 1811 and 1925 by Slater, Kelly, Pigot, Holden and Hunt.

General

Ale and Hearty, Alan Wykes, 1979.
Drink and the Victorians, Brian Harrison, 1971.
Farmhouse Brewing, Elfyn Scourfield, 1974.
The English Pub, Peter Haydon, 1994.
The English Pub, Michael Jackson, 1976.
The Old Inns of England, A.E. Richardson, 1934.
Prince of Ales — The History of Brewing in Wales, Brian Glover, 1993.
The Pubs of Leominster, Kington and North-west Herefordshire,
    Ron Shoesmith & Roger Barrett, 2000.
Victuallers' Licences, Jeremy Gibson and Judith Hunter, 1997.
Welsh Pub Names, Myrddin ap Dafydd, 1991.
The Wordsworth Dictionary of Pub Names, Leslie Dunkling & Gordon Wright, 1994.

Pembrokeshire

A Calendar of the Public Records relating to Pembrokeshire,
    Cymmrodorion Record Series,1911.
The Cambrian Directory, 1800.
Best Pub Walks in Pembrokeshire, Laurence Main, 1994.
Descriptive Excursions through South Wales & Monmouthshire, E. Donovan, 1804.
The Description of Penbrokshire, George Owen, 1603; ed. Henry Owen 1906.

The English Theatre in Wales, Cecil Price, 1948.

A Guide to Pembrokeshire Inns and Pubs, Michael Fitzgerald.

Historical Sketches of Pembroke Dock, George Mason, 1906.

A Historical Tour Through Pembrokeshire. Richard Fenton, 1811.

The History of Little England Beyond Wales, Edward Laws, 1888.

The History of Pembroke Dock, Mrs. Stuart Peters, 1905.

The Inn Crowd, C. I. Thomas (publ.).

The 'Landsker Borderlands' series of publications, SPARC (publ.).

The Meyricks of Bush, Michael McGarvie, 1998.

A Murder of Crows - The Story of Penally, Margaret Davies, 2001.

Nicholson's Cambrian Travellers' Guide, 1840.

Old Inns, Taverns and Hotels of Tenby (unpublished manuscript). Arthur Stubbs.

Patriarchs and Parasites, David W. Howell, 1986.

Pembroke People, Richard Rose, 2000.

Pembrokeshire County History, Vol III. Brian Howells (editor).

Pembrokeshire in By-gone Days (West Wales Historical Records. Vol IX),
    Francis Green.

Pembrokeshire Sea-trading Before 1900, Barbara George, 1964.

Pembrokeshire Shipwrecks, Ted Goddard, 1983.

Pembrokeshire Under Fire, Bill Richards.

The Place-names of Pembrokeshire, B. G. Charles, 1992.

Princes, Pigs and People of Tenby, Wenby Osborne, 1974.

Reminiscences of Tenby 1854 - 1934, T.W. Hordley.

The Railways of Pembrokeshire, John Morris, 1981.

St. Florence Past and Present, edited by Zena Jarvis, 1996.

Some Old Inns and Reminiscences of Pembroke Dock. H.H.R. Reynolds, 1939.

Tales and Traditions of Old Tenby. Alison Bielski, 1979.

Tavern Tokens (Article in Seaby's Coin and Medal Bulletin No.849, April 1990).
    Simon Hancock.

Tour Through a Part of South Wales, William Matthews, 1786.

Tenby, Mr. and. Mrs. S.C. Hall, 1865.

*Tenby Guides and Tenby Visitors (Article in The Journal of the
Pembrokeshire Historical Society, 1987).* R.F. Walker.

The Towns of Medieval Wales, Ian Soulsby, 1983.

*A Tour of Pembrokeshire in 1823 (Article in The Journal of the Pembrokeshire
Historical Society, 1989).* Thomas Lloyd.

*Wales' Maritime Trade in Wine During the Later Middle Ages
    (Maritime Wales, 1992).* K. Lloyd Gruffydd.

*The Welsh Sunday Closing Act 1881 (Article in The Welsh History Review,
    December 1972),* W.R. Lambert.

Index

In the following index all pub names, old and new, are indexed — where there has been name changes they are cross-referenced and shown in brackets. 'Inn' is not normally used in the title (apart from 'New Inn'). To avoid confusion the parish or village is shown for country inns; in Pembroke, Pembroke Dock and Tenby the street name is included. Page numbers in bold type indicate the main entry for that inn.

Adelphi (Railway Hotel) Apley Terrace, Pembroke Dock — **154**
Albany Hotel (White Hart) Norton, Tenby — **230**, 231
Albert, Dimond St., Pembroke Dock — 12, 148, **157**
Albion (Globe) King St., Pembroke Dock — 83, **92**, 131
Albion, The Quay, Tenby — 12, 102, 192, **210**, 211
Alexandra Vaults (Pages Hotel) Laws St., Pembroke Dock — 85, 150, **151**, 159
Alhambra Tavern (Bird in Hand - Mariners) Lewis St., Pembroke Dock — **149**
Alma, North St., Bufferland — **132**, 133
Anchor (Blue Anchor) Angle — **16**
Anchor, The Quay, Pembroke — **78**
Anchor Tavern (Cobourg) High St., Tenby — 193, **196**, 197
Angel, Dark Lane, Pembroke — **72**
Angel, Meyrick St., Pembroke Dock — **147**
Apothecarys Hall, Dimond St., Pembroke Dock — **153**
Apple Tree, Monkton — **32**, 33
Armstrong Arms (Stackpole) Stackpole — **26**
Army and Navy (Royal Exchange) The Green, Pembroke — **80**
Army and Navy, Dimond St., Pembroke Dock — **157**

Ball, St. Florence — **182**, 184
Bank Tavern, The Green, Pembroke — **81**
Barley Sheaf, Charlton Place, Pembroke Dock — **144**
Bear, St. Marys St., Tenby — **228**
Bee Hive, Main St., Pembroke — **64**
Bee Hive, Commercial Row, Pembroke Dock — **107**, 141
Bee Hive, Frog St., Tenby — **224**
Bell and Lion, Commercial Row, Pembroke Dock — 13, **108**, 109
Bennetts Wine Cellar (Butchers Arms - Five Arches Tavern - George) St. Georges St., Tenby — **221**, 222, 224
Bird in Hand (Alhambra Tavern - Mariners) Lewis St., Pembroke Dock — 148, **149**
Black Angel, Bosherton, Angle — 27
Black Horse, Jameston — **179**
Black Horse, Lamphey — **174**

Black Horse, Main St., Pembroke	**48**, 49
Black Horse, King St., Pembroke Dock	**93**, 101
Black Horse (Coach and Horses) Frog St., Tenby	**215**
Black Rabbit (New Inn) Orange Gardens	37
Blacksmiths Arms, Main St., Pembroke	**50**
Blenheim (Cardiff Arms - Nash Brewery - Talbot) Meyrick St., Pembroke Dock	**147**
Blue Anchor (Anchor) Angle	**16**
Blue Ball, Frog St., Tenby	193, **219**
Blue Bell, Dimond St., Pembroke Dock	**158**
Bombay Hotel (Criterion) Water St., Pembroke Dock	**161**, 164
Boot and Shoe (Lion) Manorbier	**180**
Bottle, St. Julian St., Tenby	**208**
Bridgewater Arms, King St., Pembroke Dock	**93**
Brig, Cosheston	**171**
Brig, St. Julian St., Tenby	**208**, 210
Bristol Arms (South Wales) London Rd., Pembroke Dock	**164**
Bristol Arms, Castle Hill, Tenby	**210**
Britannia, Commercial Row, Pembroke Dock	**109**
Britannia Arms, High St., Pennar	**134**
British Workman, Cresswell St., Tenby	**228**
Brooksies (George and Dragon - Three Crowns) Dimond St., Pembroke Dock	**154**
Brown Cow, Monkton	**34**, 68
Brown Cow, Front St., Pembroke Dock	**90**
Brown Cow, Milton Terrace, Pennar	**135**
Brown Cow, Norton, Tenby	**231**
Buccaneer, St. Julian St., Tenby	**208**
Builders Arms, Norton, Tenby	**234**
Bull, High St., Tenby	**205**
Bunch of Grapes (Kings Arms - Old Kings Arms) Main St., Pembroke	**66**, 67
Bunch of Grapes (Prince Albert Spirit Vaults) Market St., Pembroke Dock	**122**
Burton Brewery, Dimond St., Pembroke Dock	**156**
Bush, Main St., Pembroke	**54**, 55
Bush, Princes St., Pembroke Dock	**124**
Bush (Hole in the Wall) Frog St., Tenby	13, 192, 220, **221**
Bush Hotel, Laws St., Pembroke Dock	86, 118, **143**, 144
Bush Tavern, Bush St., Pembroke Dock	**142**, 154
Bushes, Hundleton	**25**
Bushes, Monkton	**35**
Butchers Arms (Pig and Whistle) East Back, Pembroke	**51**
Butchers Arms, King St., Pembroke Dock	**96**
Butchers Arms (Bennetts Wine Cellar - Five Arches Tavern - George) St. Georges St., Tenby	**221**, 222
Buttiland, Manorbier	**179**
Caledonia (Ellards Hotel) Princes St., Pembroke Dock	**124**
Caledonia (New Caledonia) High St., Pennar	131, 132, 133, 136
Caledonia (Caledonian) Wesley Row, Pennar	**131**
Caledonian, Pembroke Dock	**130**
Caledonian (Caledonia) Wesley Row, Pennar	**131**
Cambrian, Prospect Place, Pennar	131, **136**
Cambrian, Wesley Row, Pennar	**131**, 136
Cardiff Arms (Blenheim - Nash Brewery - Talbot) Meyrick St., Pembroke Dock	**147**
Cardigan, West Williamston	**129**
Carpenters Arms, Cosheston	**171**, 173
Carpenters Arms, Monkton	**31**
Carpenters Arms, Main St., Pembroke	**48**
Castle, Angle	**16**
Castle, Llandovery	**70**
Castle, Manorbier	**180**, 181
Castle (Hawthorn) Clarence St., Pembroke Dock	83, **109**, 110

Castle, London Rd., Pembroke Dock   **163**
Castle [1] Main St., Pembroke   **61**
Castle [2] Main St., Pembroke   **64**
Castle [3] (Golden Lion - Lion Hotel - New Inn) Main St., Pembroke   7, **69**
Castle and Dragon, Main St., Pembroke   **63**
Cavalier, Main St., Pembroke   **57**
Celts (Prince of Wales - Prince Regent) Laws St., Pembroke Dock   **150**
Chain and Anchor (Shamrock and Harp) Front St., Pembroke Dock   **90**
Charlton, Bush St., Pembroke Dock   14, 85, **139**, 140
Clarence, Main St., Pembroke   **64**, 139
Clarence, Pembroke St., Pembroke Dock   115, **116**, 117, 118, 148, 163
Clarence, High St., Pennar   132
Coach and Horses, Monkton   **34**
Coach and Horses, London Rd., Pembroke Dock   **164**
Coach and Horses (Black Horse) Frog St., Tenby   192, **215**, 216
Coach House, Main St., Pembroke   **49**
Cobourg (Anchor Tavern) High St., Tenby   192-3, **196**, 197-200, 203, 219, 224, 230
Coburg, Meyrick St., Pembroke Dock   **147**
Commercial, Main St., Pembroke   42, **45**
Commercial, Commercial Row, Pembroke Dock   **108**
Commercial, Pembroke St., Pembroke Dock   **120**
Commercial (Flying Boat) Queen St., Pembroke Dock   85, **98**, 99, 100, 149
Commercial (First and Last - Greenland - Last Step - Waterloo) Waterloo, Pembroke Dock   **165**, 166
Commercial, Military Rd., Pennar   **128**, 129
Commercial (Normandie Hotel) Frog St., Tenby   192, 216, **217**, 218
Cosheston Brewery, Cosheston   **171**, 172
Cresselly Arms, Cresselly   13
Criterion (Bombay Hotel) Water St., Pembroke Dock   85, 104, **160**, 161
Cromwells, Dark Lane, Pembroke   **72**
Cross, Penally   **187**, 188
Cross Keys, Market St., Pembroke Dock   **121**
Crown (Crown and Cushion - Crown Stores) Princes St., Pembroke Dock   **123**, 124
Crown, Penally   **188**, 189
Crown, Lower Frog St., Tenby   192, **226**, 227
Crown and Anchor (Hudmans) Front St., Pembroke Dock   13, **90**
Crown and Cushion (Crown - Crown Stores) Princes St., Pembroke Dock   **123**
Crown Stores (Crown - Crown and Cushion) Princes St., Pembroke Dock   85, **123**, 124
Crowther, Rhoscrowther   **22**
Crystal Palace, Market St., Pembroke Dock   **121**

Devonport, Queen St., Pembroke Dock   **101**
Dial, Lamphey   14, **174**, 175
Dock, Cosheston   **171**
Dock Gate, Princes St., Pembroke Dock   **124**
Dolphin, Angle   **17**
Dolphin, Beach Rd., Llanreath   **137**
Dolphin, King St., Pembroke Dock   **93**
Dolphin (South Wales Hotel) St. Georges St., Tenby   **224**, 225
Dragon, Monkton   **31**
Duke of Wellington, Commercial Row, Pembroke Dock   **107**, 108
Duke of York, Pembroke St., Pembroke Dock   12, **119**, 120
Duke of York, Princes St., Pembroke Dock   119, **124**
Dumfries, Water St., Pembroke Dock   76, **159**, 160

East Gate (Rose and Crown) East End Square, Pembroke   **43**, 44, 76
Edinburgh, Pembroke Dock   148
Ellards Hotel (Caledonia) Princes St., Pembroke Dock   **124**
Elm, Main St., Pembroke   **52**
Elms, Hundleton   24, **25**
Evergreen, Norton, Tenby   192, **231**, 232

Farmers Arms, Monkton 31
Farmers Arms (Vine) Market St., Pembroke Dock **120**, 121, 125, 149
Farmers Arms, New Rd., Pembroke Dock **157**
Faulkners Hotel, High St., Tenby **195**
Ferry House, Bulwell, Angle **21**
Ferry House (Ferry Side) Monkton 30
Ferry House (Watermans Arms) Pembroke Ferry, Pembroke Dock 152, 161, **167**, 168, 169
Ferry Side (Ferry House) Monkton **30**
Ferryboat, Monkton **35**
First and Last (Commercial - Last Step - Waterloo) Waterloo, Pembroke Dock 165, **166**
Fishermans Arms, The Quay, Tenby **212**
Five Arches Tavern (Bennetts Wine Cellar - Butchers Arms - George)
    St. Georges St., Tenby 192, 220, **221**, 222, 223, 224
Flag (Old Flag) Monkton 35
Flying Boat (Commercial) Queen St., Pembroke Dock 85, **98**
Foresters (New Foresters) King St., Pembroke Dock 85, 95, **96**
Foresters Arms (Old Foresters) King St., Pembroke Dock 12, 95, **96**
Fountain, Cresswell St., Tenby **228**
Four Horseshoes, King St., Pembroke Dock **95**
Fox, Main St., Pembroke **71**
Freemasons Arms, Main St., Pembroke **64**
Freshwater (Grotto) Freshwater East **176**

George, Dark Lane, Pembroke **72**, 74
George, Lower Commercial Row, Pembroke Dock **109**
George (Bennetts Wine Cellar - Butchers Arms - Five Arches Tavern)
    St. Georges St., Tenby 192, **221**, 222, 223, 224
George and Dragon (Brooksies - Three Crowns) Dimond St., Pembroke Dock **153**
Georges Hall (Spirit Vaults [2]) Main St., Pembroke **58**
Gilbeys Stores, High St., Tenby 192, **202**
Globe, Angle **17**
Globe, Pembroke **71**
Globe, Main St., Pembroke **74**, 75
Globe (Milford Haven) Commercial Row, Pembroke Dock 86, **107**
Globe (Albion) King St., Pembroke Dock 83, **92**, 93
Globe, Queen St., Pembroke Dock **98**
Globe, Frog St., Tenby **219**
Globe, Market St., Tenby 193, **205**
Gloucester, Military Rd., Pennar **130**
Glyders, Manorbier **182**
Golden, Golden Hill, Pembroke **81**
Golden Cross, Main St., Pembroke **72**
Golden Lion (Castle [3] - Lion Hotel - New Inn) Main St., Pembroke 6, 55, 60, **69**, 70, 195
Golden Lion (Lion) Queen St., Pembroke Dock **98**
Golden Plover, Castlemartin **23**
Grapes, Monkton **32**
Grapes, High St., Pennar **134**
Green Dragon, Main St., Pembroke 6, 44, 55, **58**, 59, 60, 65, 67, 68, 69
Green Dragon, Market St., Tenby **205**
Green Mead (Oriels - Union) Main St., Pembroke 55, 56
Greenland (Commercial - First and Last - Last Step - Waterloo) Waterloo, Pembroke Dock 165
Grey Horse, High St., Tenby 124, **203**, 204
Grey Horse, St. Georges St., Tenby **225**
Greyhound, Monkton **31**
Greyhound, Meyrick St., Pembroke Dock **141**, 142
Griffiths Brewery, Main St., Pembroke **61**
Grotto (Freshwater) Freshwater East 173, **175**, 176
Guard Room, Llanion, Pembroke Dock **163**
Gun Tavern, Queen St., Pembroke Dock 12, 85, **102**, 103, 148

Hand and Heart, Park St., Pembroke Dock   **145**
Hat and Oyster Barrel (Oyster Barrel) Market St., Tenby   **206**
Hawthorn (Castle) Clarence St., Pembroke Dock   **110**
Hearts of Oak, Front St., Pembroke Dock   **89**
Hibernia, Angle   **19**
Hibernia, Front St., Pembroke Dock   **91**
Highgate, Hundleton   **25**
Hill House, Cosheston   **173**
Hilton, Norton, Tenby   192, 200, **232**, 233
Hole in the Wall (Bush) Frog St., Tenby   **221**
Holly Bush, Pwllcrochan, Angle   **21**
Hope, East End Square, Pembroke   **41**, 42, 43
Hope, Meyrick St., Pembroke Dock   **146**
Hope and Anchor, St. Julian St., Tenby   192, **209**, 210
Horse and Groom, Cresswell St., Tenby   **228**
Horseshoes, Main St., Pembroke   **52**
Hotel Bristol (Pembroke Dock Brewery) Meyrick St., Pembroke Dock   **146**
Hudmans (Crown and Anchor) Front St., Pembroke Dock   90

I.B.D., Norton, Tenby   **231**
Imperial (Pestle and Mortar) Meyrick St., Pembroke Dock   **148**
Imperial, Norton, Tenby   192, **234**
Ivy Bush, Market St., Pembroke Dock   **121**, 122, 123
Ivy Bush, Norton, Tenby   **234**
Ivy Green, Hundleton   **26**

Jasperley, High St., Tenby   192, **202**, 205
Jenny Kibbles, Ridgeway   **187**
Jolly Sailor, Burton Ferry   87
Jolly Sailor, The Quay, Pembroke   **78**
Jolly Sailor, Lexden Terrace, Tenby   **209**

Kerry (Railway - Welshmans Arms) London Rd., Pembroke Dock   **165**
Kilwendeg (Sherlock Holmes) Military Rd., Pennar   **129**, 130
Kimberley, Milford Haven   172
Kings Arms, Angle   **16**
Kings Arms (Bunch of Grapes - Old Kings Arms) Main St., Pembroke   5, **65**, 66, 67, 69
Kings Arms (Shipwright) Front St., Pembroke Dock   **86**, 88, 100
Kings Arms, St. Georges St., Tenby   5, 193, **221**
Kings Head, Pembroke   **72**
Kings Head (Shipwright) Front St., Pembroke Dock   86
Kings Head, Crackwell St., Tenby   **214**

Lamb, Main St., Pembroke   **55**, 62
Lamb, Queen St., Pembroke Dock   **100**
Lamb, High St., Tenby   192, 200, **201**, 202, 230
Lamb and Flag, Meyrick St., Pembroke Dock   **147**
Landshipping (Narberth Arms) Queen St., Pembroke Dock   85, **98**
Last Step (Commercial - First and Last - Greenland - Waterloo) Waterloo, Pembroke Dock   165
Launch, King St., Pembroke Dock   **95**
Lawrenny, King St., Pembroke Dock   **95**
Lifeboat Tavern (Wheatensheaf - Wheatsheaf) Tudor Square, Tenby   **206**, 207
Lion (Boot and Shoe) Manorbier   **180**
Lion (Castle [3] - Golden Lion - New Inn) Pembroke   10, 67, **69**, 70
Lion (Golden Lion) Queen St., Pembroke Dock   98
London House, Pembroke St., Pembroke Dock   **120**
London Tavern, Clarence St., Pembroke Dock   **99**
Lord Raglan, Cresswell St., Tenby   **228**
Lydstep Tavern, Lydstep   **186**

Malsters Arms, Gooses Lane, Pembroke 44
Mariners, Haverford West 163
Mariners, Front St., Pembroke Dock 90
Mariners (Alhambra Tavern - Bird in Hand) Lewis St., Pembroke Dock 149
Mariners Arms, Angle 16
Mariners Arms (Three Mariners) Dark Lane, Pembroke 74
Market Tavern (Prices Brewery) Pembroke St., Pembroke Dock 113, **114**, 115
Masonic (Paterchurch) Front St., Pembroke Dock 91
Masons Arms, Monkton 34
Masons Arms, The Green, Pembroke 81
Masons Arms, Market St., Pembroke Dock 121
Masons Arms, Norton, Tenby 231
Melville, King St., Pembroke Dock 94
Mermaid, High St., Tenby 205
Mermaid, Lexden Terrace, Tenby 210
Milford Arms, Main St., Pembroke **49**, 50
Milford Arms (Sloop) Front St., Pembroke Dock 90
Milford Arms, Queen St., Pembroke Dock 85, **97**, 98
Milford Haven (Globe) Commercial Row, Pembroke Dock 107
Milford Haven (Watermans Arms) Front St., Pembroke Dock 89
Milford Tavern, Pembroke 49
Miracle, Freshwater East 14, 176
Montague, Dimond St., Pembroke Dock 158
Myrtle Tree, High St., Pennar 134

Narberth Arms (Landshipping) Queen St., Pembroke Dock 98
Nash Brewery (Blenheim - Cardiff Arms - Talbot) Meyrick St., Pembroke Dock 146
Nash Rectory, Cosheston 173
Navy, Melville St., Pembroke Dock 125
Navy Tavern (Tommy Tuckers) Pembroke St., Pembroke Dock 86, **113**, 114, 122, 135, 147
Nelson, Pembroke Dock 146
Nelson (Triumph) Park St., Pembroke Dock 145
Nelson, Tenby **210**, 213
Nelson Tavern, Tenby 210
New Caledonia, Wesley Row, Pembroke Dock 92
New Caledonia (Caledonia) High St., Pennar **131**, 132
New Foresters (Foresters) King St., Pembroke Dock 96
New Inn, Bentlass 26
New Inn, Jameston 177
New Inn, Lamphey 174
New Inn, Minerton 182
New Inn, Monkton 34
New Inn (Black Rabbit) Orange Gardens **36**, 37
New Inn (Castle [3] - Golden Lion - Lion Hotel) Pembroke 69
New Inn (Sailors Return) Front St., Pembroke Dock 88
New Inn, St. Florence **184**, 185
New Inn, Norton, Tenby 231
New Swan, Ferry Rd., Pennar 100, **130**
No Name Bar (Sun) High St., Tenby 201
Normandie Hotel (Commercial) Frog St., Tenby 218
North Wales Tavern, Princes St., Pembroke Dock 124

Odd Fellows Arms, Main St., Pembroke 48, **64**
Odd Fellows Arms, Queen St., Pembroke Dock 102
Old Castle, Manorbier 181
Old Cross Saws, Main St., Pembroke **50**, 51
Old Flag (Flag) Monkton 35
Old Foresters (Foresters Arms) King St., Pembroke Dock 96
Old Kings Arms (Bunch of Grapes - Kings Arms) Main St., Pembroke **67**, 218, 221
Old Lion, King St., Pembroke Dock **93**, 94

244

Old Point House, Angle 14, **20**
Old Red Lion (Red Lion) Commercial Row, Pembroke Dock 109
Old Ship, King St., Pembroke Dock **93**
Old Swan, Queen St., Pembroke Dock 130
Old White Hart, Main St., Pembroke **57**
Olive Bar (Spirit Vaults) Pembroke St., Pembroke Dock **115**
Oriels (Green Mead, Union) Main St., Pembroke 55
Oyster Barrel (Hat and Oyster Barrel) Market St., Tenby **206**

Packet, Front St., Pembroke Dock **91**
Paddock, Penally **189**
Pages Hotel (Alexandra Vaults) Laws St., Pembroke Dock 151
Parsonage, St. Florence **185**
Paterchurch (Masonic) Front St., Pembroke Dock **90**, 91
Pelican, Main St., Pembroke **50**
Pembroke Dock, The Green, Pembroke **80**
Pembroke Dock Brewery (Hotel Bristol) Meyrick St., Pembroke Dock **146**
Pembrokeshire Arms, Bush St., Pembroke Dock **140**, 147, 148
Pestle and Mortar (Imperial) Meyrick St., Pembroke Dock **148**
Phoenix, Meyrick St., Pembroke Dock **141**, 147
Picton, Main St., Pembroke **63**
Picton Castle, Market St., Pembroke Dock **121**
Pier Hotel (Three Lamps) London Rd., Pembroke Dock **161**, 165, 169
Pig and Whistle (Butchers Arms) East Back, Pembroke **51**
Pilot, Pembroke Ferry **167**, 169
Pilot Boat, Front St., Pembroke Dock **91**
Pirates Lantern, Manorbier **182**
Plough, Jameston **178**
Plough, Lamphey **174**
Plough, Pembroke **68**
Plough, Main St., Pembroke **64**
Plough, Brewery St., Pembroke Dock **110**
Plough, Pembroke Ferry **169**
Plough and Harrow, Queen St., Pembroke Dock **98**
Plough and Harrow, Military Rd., Pennar **129**, 130
Porter Brewery, Bellevue Terrace, Pennar **132**
Porter House, Water St., Pembroke Dock **159**
Porter Stores (Royal Exchange) Commercial Row, Pembroke Dock **109**
Porter Stores, High St., Pennar **132**
Prices Brewery (Market Tavern) Pembroke St., Pembroke Dock **114**
Prince Albert, Main St., Pembroke **52**
Prince Albert (Sun) Front St., Pembroke Dock 85, **89**, 156
Prince Albert Spirit Vaults (Bunch of Grapes) Market St., Pembroke Dock **122**, 123
Prince of Wales, Bush St., Pembroke Dock **139**, 147
Prince of Wales (Celts - Prince Regent) Laws St., Pembroke Dock 108, 139, 147, **150**, 153
Prince of Wales, Meyrick St., Pembroke Dock **147**
Prince of Wales, Frog St., Tenby 192, **216**
Prince of Wales (Railway Tavern) Frog St., Tenby **217**, 221
Prince of Wales, St. Julian St., Tenby **208**
Prince of Wales [1] Main St., Pembroke **62**
Prince of Wales [2] Main St., Pembroke **62**
Prince Regent (Celts - Prince of Wales) Laws St., Pembroke Dock **150**
Princes Head, Bridge St., Tenby 192, **213**
Priory, Monkton **30**
Prospect Tavern, Prospect Place, Pembroke Dock 86, **136**, 137

Quarry, Lydstep **185**, 185, 186
Quay Head, Water St., Pembroke Dock **159**
Queens, Queen St., Pembroke Dock **104**, 148, 154, 161

Railway (Ship - Swan Lake) Jameston   **177**
Railway, Lamphey   **174**
Railway, Lamphey Rd., Pembroke   **40**, 41, 47, 173
Railway (Adelphi) Apley Terrace, Pembroke Dock   154, **155**
Railway (Kerry - Welshmans Arms) London Rd., Pembroke Dock   164, **165**
Railway, Penally   **188**
Railway Tavern (Prince of Wales) Frog St., Tenby   **217**
Railway View, Prospect Place, Pennar   **135**
Red Cow, Monkton   **34**
Red Lion, Main St., Pembroke   47, 48, 49, 64
Red Lion (Old Red Lion) Commercial Row, Pembroke Dock   **109**
Red Rose, High St., Pembroke Dock   113, **135**
Red, White and Blue, Dark Lane, Pembroke   **77**, 78
Rifle Corps Arms, East End Square, Pembroke   **44**
Ring of Bells, Church St., Tenby   **225**
Rising Sun, Lamphey Rd., Pembroke   **41**
Rising Sun, Queen St., Pembroke Dock   79, **100**, 101
Rising Sun, Ridgeway   **186**
Roebuck, Monkton   **32**
Rope and Anchor, Monkton   **31**
Rose and Crown (East Gate) Main St., Pembroke   **43**, 48, 49, 88
Rose and Crown, Queen St., Pembroke Dock   **101**, 102
Rose and Crown, High St., Tenby   **205**
Royal, Hobbs Point, Pembroke Dock   105, **163**
Royal (Royal Edinburgh) Queen St., Pembroke Dock   **104**, 105, 106, 163
Royal Edinburgh (Royal) Queen St., Pembroke Dock   **105**, 106, 163
Royal Exchange (Army and Navy) The Green, Pembroke   **80**
Royal Exchange (Porter Stores) Queen St., Pembroke Dock   98, **109**
Royal Gatehouse, High St., Tenby   192, **196**, 197
Royal George, Dark Lane, Pembroke   43, 74, **75**, 76, 77, 78
Royal George, Queen St., Pembroke Dock   **101**
Royal Lion (White Lion) High St., Tenby   192, **194**, 196, 197
Royal Marines, Upper Park St., Pembroke Dock   **144**, 145
Royal Oak, Main St., Pembroke   41, 45, **47**
Royal Oak, Commercial Row, Pembroke Dock   14, 86, 106, **107**
Royal Oak, Military Rd., Pennar   **130**
Royal Oak, Stackpole   **26**
Royal Oak, High St., Tenby   **202**
Royal Standard, Llanreath   **138**
Royal William, Jameston   **179**
Royal William, The Green, Pembroke   **80**
Royal William (White Hart) Pembroke St., Pembroke Dock   **111**, 112

Sailors Return (New Inn) Front St., Pembroke Dock   **88**
Sailors Return (Shipwrights Arms) King St., Pembroke Dock   **93**
Salutation, Monkton   **29**
Salutation, Lewis St., Pembroke Dock   **148**, 149
Setting Sun, Bachelors Row, Pembroke Dock   **162**
Shamrock and Harp (Chain and Anchor) Front St., Pembroke Dock   **90**
Sherlock Holmes (Kilwendeg) Military Rd., Pennar   **129**
Ship, Cosheston   **171**
Ship (Railway - Swan Lake) Jameston   **178**
Ship, The Quay, Pembroke   **78**
Ship (Shipwrights Arms) Pembroke Dock   **161**
Ship Aground, Norton, Tenby   **231**
Ship and Castle, High St., Tenby   **202**, 203
Ship on Launch, King St., Pembroke Dock   **95**
Ship under Weigh, Cresswell St., Tenby   **228**
Shipwright (Kings Arms) Front St., Pembroke Dock   **86**, 87, 88
Shipwrights Arms (Ship) Pembroke Dock   **161**

246

Shipwrights Arms, Front St., Pembroke Dock 89
Shipwrights Arms (Sailors Return) King St., Pembroke Dock 93
Shipwrights Arms, St. Marys St., Tenby 192, **227**, 228
Shoe and Boot, Upper Frog St., Tenby **220**
Shoulder of Mutton, The Green, Pembroke **81**
Sloop, Bentlass, Angle **26**
Sloop, Main St., Pembroke **62**
Sloop (Milford Arms) Front St., Pembroke Dock **90**
Sloop, Quay Hill, Tenby **214**
Soldiers Return, Meyrick St., Pembroke Dock **146**
South Wales (Bristol Arms) London Rd., Pembroke Dock **164**
South Wales Hotel (Dolphin) St. Georges St., Tenby 222, **224**
Speculation, Orielton **23**, 24, 25
Spirit Vaults (Olive Bar) Pembroke St., Pembroke Dock **115**
Spirit Vaults [1] Main St., Pembroke **57**
Spirit Vaults [2] (Georges Hall) Main St., Pembroke **58**
Spirit Vaults [3] Main St., Pembroke **61**
Square and Compass, Norton, Tenby **231**
St. Govans, Bosherton, Angle **27**
Stackpole (Armstrong Arms) Stackpole, Angle **27**
Stag (Stags Head) Main St., Pembroke **62**, 63, 68, 77
Stag, King St., Pembroke Dock **96**
Stage Door, Frog St., Tenby **196**
Stags Head (Stag) Main St., Pembroke 62
Star, Apley Terrace, Pembroke Dock **152**, 169
Star, Lower Frog St., Tenby **226**
Station, Dimond St., Pembroke Dock **156**
Steam Hammer, Charlton Place, Pembroke Dock **144**
Steam Packet, Pembroke St., Pembroke Dock **115**, 124
Sun, Maidenwells **28**
Sun, East End, Pembroke 51
Sun (Prince Albert) Front St., Pembroke Dock **89**
Sun, Queen St., Pembroke Dock 12, 85, 100, **101**
Sun, St. Florence **183**
Sun (No Name Bar) High St., Tenby 192, **199**, 200, 201, 202, 225, 232
Swan, Pembroke **47**
Swan, Queen St., Pembroke Dock 98, 99, **100**
Swan, High St., Tenby **205**
Swan Lake (Railway - Ship) Jameston **178**

Talbot (Blenheim - Cardiff Arms - Nash Brewery) Meyrick St., Pembroke Dock **147**
Talbot, St. Marys St., Tenby **228**
Temple Bar, Prospect Place, Pennar **137**
Tenby House Hotel, Market St., Tenby 206
The Grapes, High St., Tenby **205**
The Wells, Maidenwells, Angle **28**
Three Bells, Norton, Tenby **235**, 236
Three Crowns (Brooksies - George and Dragon) Dimond St., Pembroke Dock **153**, 154
Three Crowns, Laws St., Pembroke Dock **86**
Three Cups, East End, Pembroke **46**
Three Cups, Norton, Tenby **229**
Three Horseshoes, Gravel Lane, Pembroke Dock **91**
Three Horseshoes, St. Florence **183**
Three Horseshoes, Frog St., Tenby **220**
Three Lamps (Pier Hotel) Tremeyrick St., Pembroke Dock **162**
Three Mariners (Mariners Arms) Dark Lane, Pembroke **74**
Three Mariners, St. Georges St., Tenby 192, **224**, 225
Three Tuns, Dimond St., Pembroke Dock 122, **156**
Tommy Tuckers (Navy Tavern) Pembroke St., Pembroke Dock 113

Travellers Rest, Ridgeway   **187**
Triumph (Nelson) Lower Park St., Pembroke Dock   **146**

Unicorn, The Green, Pembroke   **81**
Union (Green Mead - Oriels) Main St., Pembroke   **55**, 56, 161
Union, Frog St., Tenby   **218**, 219

Venison, Lamphey   **173**
Victoria, Monkton   **35**, 36, 48
Victoria, Pembroke   10, **143**
Victoria, Norton, Tenby   **235**
Victoria Hotel, Victoria Terrace, Pembroke Dock   113, 115, 116, **117**, 118
Vine (Farmers Arms) Market St., Pembroke Dock   **121**
Vine, High St., Tenby   **204**, 205

Wallaston Arms, Wallaston   **22**
Waterloo (Commercial - First and Last - Greenland) Waterloo, Pembroke Dock   **166**
Waterloo Arms, Milton Terrace, Pennar   **135**
Watermans, The Green, Pembroke   **78**, 79, 169
Watermans Arms (Milford Haven) Front St., Pembroke Dock   **89**
Watermans Arms (Ferry House) Pembroke Ferry, Pembroke Dock   **168**
Waverly, Water St., Pembroke Dock   **159**
Weary Traveller, Chapel Row, Llanreath   **138**
Weighbridge, Commercial Row, Pembroke Dock   **109**
Welcome, Castlemartin   **23**, 176
Welshmans Arms (Kerry - Railway) London Rd., Pembroke Dock   164, **165**
West End, Dark Lane, Pembroke   **74**
Westgate, Pembroke   **71**
Wheatensheaf (Lifeboat Tavern - Wheatsheaf) Tudor Square, Tenby   **206**
Wheatsheaf, High St., Pennar   **133**
Wheatsheaf (Lifeboat Tavern - Wheatensheaf) Tudor Square, Tenby   192, **206**, 207
Wheelabout, Ridgeway   **187**
White Hart, Main St., Pembroke   62, **68**, 69
White Hart (Royal William) Pembroke St., Pembroke Dock   **111**, 112, 113, 125, 218
White Hart (Albany Hotel) Norton, Tenby   192, 193, 202, **229**, 230, 231
White Lion, Main St., Pembroke   **44**, 45, 47
White Lion (Royal Lion) High St., Tenby   6, 70, 193, **194**, 195, 196, 199, 219, 230
Windsor Castle, Cross Park, Pennar   **131**

York Tavern, Main St., Pembroke   14, **53**, 54, 63